THE POOR ARE MANY

This publication is no. 15 in the series KTC (KERK EN THEOLOGIE IN CONTEXT - CHURCH AND THEOLOGY IN CONTEXT) of the Faculty of Theology of the Catholic University of Nijmegen, The Netherlands.
Editorial staff of the series:
prof. dr. P.H.J.M. Camps
drs. Kristin De Troyer
dr. H.S.M. Groenen
prof. dr. H. Häring
prof. dr. J. van Nieuwenhove

THE POOR ARE MANY

POLITICAL ETHICS IN THE SOCIAL ENCYCLICALS, CHRISTIAN DEMOCRACY, AND LIBERATION THEOLOGY IN LATIN AMERICA

Frank Sawyer

UITGEVERSMAATSCHAPPIJ J.H. KOK – KAMPEN 1992

This is the commercial edition of the thesis, defended under the same title, on which occasion professor G. Manenschijn acted as supervisor.

CIP-GEGEVENS KONINKLIJKE BIBLIOTHEEK, DEN HAAG

Sawyer, Frank

The poor are many : political ethics in the social encyclicals, Christian Democracy, and liberation theology in Latin America / Frank Sawyer. – Kampen : Kok. – (Kerk en theologie in context, ISSN 0922-9086 ; 15)
Ook verschenen als proefschrift Nijmegen. – Met bibliogr., lit. opg., reg.
ISBN 90-242-7371-4
NUGI 639
Trefw.: bevrijdingstheologie ; Latijns-Amerika / christelijke politiek ; Latijns-Amerika

© Copyright 1992 by Frank Sawyer, Kampen, the Netherlands
Licensed edition, published by Uitgeversmaatschappij J.H. Kok b.v.,
P.O. Box 130, 8260 AC Kampen, the Netherlands
Cover design: Dik Hendriks
ISBN 90 242 7371 4 / NUGI 639

For our Latin American friends

Acknowledgments

At the completion of this study my thoughts go back to the memory of Prof.dr.G.Th.Rothuizen under whom I began research on the roots of Christian Democracy in. Europe. That was in 1980. At that time I did not know that I would soon be living and working in Latin America. The result is seen in the change of topic this project underwent.

I am grateful to my promoter, Prof.dr.G.Manenschijn of the ethics department of the *Theologische Universiteit*, Kampen, for allowing me to continue along the path already begun by the time I came under his tutelage, and for steering it further. He has encouraged me through his astute analytical eye for detail, and by prompt and decisive judgments all along the way. It has been a joy to work under his guidance. I thank him for the freedom he gave me in research and his knack for bringing matters to focus.

I was also privileged to have the guidance of Prof.dr.J.Van Nieuwenhove of the missiology department of the *Katholieke Universiteit*, Nijmegen, as copromoter. Prof.Van Nieuwenhove's knowledge of Latin America and of Gustavo Gutiérrez' thought proved invaluable for a balancing of issues with which I struggled. Without a Latin American specialist this study could not have been properly carried out. I am grateful for his careful challenges.

Further, I am indebted to Prof.dr.J.Carrière of CEDLA (Center for Latin American Research and Documentation), Amsterdam, who kindly read the manuscript when it was in a rough shape and commented on several issues which helped me strengthen the line of thought. I thank him for the friendly interest he showed.

I must add, that inspite of such excellent help by all of these, any unfounded interpretations are entirely mine.

The *Johannes Calvijn Academie* provided a research grant during the last two years, for which I am very grateful. Without adequate libraries it is impossible to track down the necessary resources. A thank you is due to the personnel of the library at the *Theologische Universiteit* for often sending away for books. It was also a privilege to use the resources of the CEDLA library.

From students in Honduras, Nicaragua, and El Salvador I learned much about Latin American realities. My friend, Rev.Jan Bouma, provided a listening ear and questions on many occasions as we jogged around the Zwarte Dyk. A further thanks goes to the personnel of the *Johannes Calvijn Lyceum* who facilitated the bridging of cultural changes for our children. A special thanks goes to Erik, Aria, Krista and Ineka for living in three cultures and enjoying it. I thank my wife, Aria, for her supportive interest which helped bring the book to completion, for reading and rereading during many years, and for the long discussions which enhanced the research immensely.

During this study, which consists of a symposium of perspectives, I have felt the pull of contending spiritualities involved, and have become more convinced with the Psalmist (36) who says of the God of life: "In your light we see light."

THE POOR ARE MANY

Political Ethics in the Social Encyclicals, Christian Democracy, and Liberation Theology in Latin America

Table of Contents

CHAPTER ONE

Posing the Problem

CHAPTER TWO

Latin America: Political Ethics in a Changing Context

Table of Contents

CHAPTER THREE

A Hopeful Option?

CHAPTER FOUR

Option for the Poor?

Table of Contents

CHAPTER FIVE

Central America: Transformation in Freedom?

CHAPTER SIX

Conclusions: *Veritas Omnia Vincit*

CHAPTER ONE

POSING THE PROBLEM

Los pobres son muchos
y por eso
es imposible olvidarlos.[1]

The poor are many
and that's why
it's impossible to forget them.

*

¡Señor! clamo de nuevo,
en tus catedrales se ora...¡Señor!
por esta tu América: desnuda, hambrienta, descalza.
¿Qué se opone para que podamos bastarnos
por nosotros mismos, en esta Hispanoamérica?[2]

Lord, I call anew,
in your cathedrals they are praying...Lord!
for this your America: naked, hungry, shoeless.
What prevents us from being able
to provide for ourselves, in this Hispanicamerica?

Introduction

While today all can see that the impoverished countries are "struggling for survival in a world dominated by economic Leviathans"[3], interpretations of causes and cures vary greatly. The fact that the poor are many leads to a questioning of why this is so. *Our purpose in this study* is to investigate how expressions of ethical theory by Christian Democracy (especially Eduardo Frei) and by Liberation Theology (especially Gustavo Gutiérrez) relate to social transformation in Latin America, with our primary attention on the development/liberation (or underdevelopment/dependency) debate[4] concerning the origins of, and solutions for, poverty.

---

[1]Roberto Sosa, *Los Pobres* (Tegucigalpa: Guaymuras, 1983). [*Footnote policy*: the first time a work is cited in any chapter we shall include the full details of where the work is published. When cited again we shall either say *op.cit.* or give a shortened title when there is some distance from the previous time cited. When referred to consecutively we shall use *ibid.*]

[2]Eva Thais, *Catedrales y Espejos* (Tegucigalpa: Guaymuras, 1985), poem 25.

[3]Virginia Held, *Rights and Goods: Justifying Social Action* (New York: Free Press, Macmillan, 1984), p.178.

[4]While the 'development' position says the main problem in the poor countries is underdevelopment, the 'liberation' position says that the main problem has now become dependency. While both sides may recognize other factors, these tend to be interpreted within the perspective given by the dominant idea (of either development or liberation). The 'development' position is also often referred to as the 'modernization' position, meaning that the key to transformation is

Our study also includes an overview of the Vatican Social Encyclicals because of their influence upon Latin American Christian social thought. An historical-political analysis of Central America will function as a case study for concretization of the problematics.

Chapter one

This first chapter is meant to introduce the parameters and texture of the field of inquiry. We shall,
i)   mention what we may expect from an ethical study;
ii)   introduce our ground for comparing the political ethics of Christian Democracy and Liberation Theology;
iii) present an overview of development debate around the 'modernization' and 'liberation' perspectives;
iv)   provide an introduction to political-economic ideologies in relation to Latin America and clarify some of the terminology;
v)   give an outline on the chapters that compose the rest of the book

I. A STUDY IN ETHICS

1. Ethics

This is a study in applied ethics about the problem of transformation in Latin America. By *ethics* we mean a study of morality,[5] or principles of conduct, which includes a descriptive and a normative (or valuative) task. Moral discourse is done in relation to facts and principles, and in relation to interpretations of the state of affairs amid contending interests and rights. The ethical perspectives we are tracing are entwined with politico-economic ideologies, understood as idea-systems (which have their vested interests) and which include a "complex weaving together of values and beliefs",[6] as for example in capitalism, socialism, democracy, authoritarianism, and the like. Given this complexity, ethics needs to strive for conceptual clarity.

2. Political ethics

By political ethics we are thinking in this study of especially two concepts:

i)   The search for the "common good" (*el bien común*) for the *polis*, that is, for society in its several aspects. The expression "common good" is rather problematic, first because there is no single definition, and secondly, because it has often been used as an excuse to quickly "reconcile" conflict situations while actually leaving the weak and exploited to their lot. However, because the term is widely used in Latin America, it will provide a good point of

---

the move from an agrarian to an industrial society.
[5]William K.Frankena, *Ethics* (Englewood Cliffs, N.J.: Prentice-Hall, 1963), p.4.
[6]cf.J.Philip Wogaman, *Christians and the Great Economic Debate* (London: SCM Press, 1977), p.10 and ch.2.

reference as we examine views on the organization and balancing of power.
ii)   We also keep in mind what has come to be called a "preferential option for the poor" (*una opción preferencial por los pobres*). This, likewise, is problematic, because it has no single definition. Even though the general idea is that we must pay attention to where the need is greatest, the term has connotations (such as 'class struggle' and the poor as the true subjects of history) which are accepted by some, but not by all who use it. However, the wide use of this concept likewise provides a good point of reference.

Development and liberation are more than economic or technical problems; they are also moral-political ones.[7] It is of the nature of communities that they need decision-making procedures. Such housekeeping rules may function to maintain or to transform the status quo. In order to indicate our multidimensional approach, we shall not merely speak of 'political', but often speak of transformation in 'social--economic-political' terms.

3. Approach to Christian social ethics

Our study of the political ethics of Christian currents ties into theology. However, the point of our research is not to build a system of theological ethics,[8] but to listen to and evaluate applied ethics. Thus our study is not about biblical hermeneutics, nor exegesis, important as those are; rather, our focus is on empirical states of affairs and ethical concepts. The theological aspect brings a discourse on faith into the picture. We cannot ultimately separate *cogito* (I think) from *credo* (I believe). These in turn cannot be separated from *volo* (I will). Part of the theological contribution is that we shall want to keep a wary eye on the dangers of the pseudosacred,[9] whereby we must remember that religion can also function as a negative ideology when it uncritically legitimizes political positions. There is the all too frequent problem that: "Persons adopt moral and social causes, whether from the extremes of right and left, or in the middle, and develop from the theological tradition those principles which provide religious authorization for their moral preferences."[10] The search for social justice must take into account the ideological faith commitments of an age or culture.[11] It has often been observed that human rights in western civilization cannot be understood apart from their biblical Christian roots.[12] At the same time we must be careful not to assume that we can

---

[7]cf.Piero Gheddo, *Why is the third World Poor?* (Maryknoll: Orbis Books), p.139.

[8]cf.G.Manenschijn, *Mogelijkheid en Noodzakelijkheid van een Christelijke Ethiek* (Kampen: Kok, 1989). Also, Marciano Vidal, "The confused epistemological status of theological ethics", p.83f. in *Concilium: The Ethics of Liberation - The Liberation of Ethics* (April 1984).

[9]As John Kenneth Galbraith writes in *The New Industrial State* (New York: New American Library, 1968), p.174: "That social progress is identical with a rising standard of living has the aspect of a faith."

[10]James M.Gustafson, *Theology and Ethics* (Oxford: Blackwell, 1981), p.188.

[11]Reinhold Niebuhr, *Nature and Destiny of Man, vol.II* (New York: Scribner's, 1964), p.256.

[12]Arnold Toynbee writes in *Christianity Among the Religions of the World* (New York: Scribner's, 1957), p.52: "This belief in the rights of individuals is, I believe, of Christian and Jewish origin." Also Max L.Stackhouse, *Creeds, Society, and Human Rights: A Study in Three Cultures* (Grand Rapids: Eerdmans, 1984).

deduce a political programme or specific political ethics from the Bible. The following is important:

> "If the major premise of my argument is drawn from Scripture (e.g., God hates injustice), but the minor premise is based on empirical analysis (e.g., capitalism is unjust), I cannot assert that the conclusion (e.g., God hates capitalism) is simply the teaching of the Word of God. I can say that God hates injustice and that, in my judgment, capitalism is unjust. But the truth of the minor premise is not determined either by the truth of the major premise or by the validity of the argument. Continually repeating the major premise with prophetic fervor will not demonstrate the truth of the minor premise. Only sustained examination of the facts and argumentation from them can do that."[13]

Development and liberation have been called the "focus of redemptive hopes and expectations".[14] One cannot ignore the tendency today to call the extremes of consumerism and poverty in our world a confessional issue for the churches.[15] We even hear that "economics" itself has become the modern religion.[16] Amid that challenge, we hope to allow a fruitful discussion to arise out of elements from possible paradigms.[17]

II. CHRISTIAN DEMOCRACY AND LIBERATION THEOLOGY

1. Two movements

During the last decades Christian Democracy and Liberation Theology have been of strong influence in Latin America as ways through which Christians - often consciously as Christians - have expressed their hope for political (social-economic) transformation. When we say 'as Christians', we mean that these movements, the one with a political party focus and the other with a theological contribution, each lean on the idea of a communal Christian contribution to change. They form possible strategies for what is sometimes called public discipleship in the polis. Even when we speak of two movements, we do so for convenience. It is not our intention to evaluate all aspects of these movements. Rather, we shall look at one important representative of each movement, especially from the point of view of the development/liberation debate. This will allow us to see how a major contributor from each current has addressed the problem of transformation in Latin America. It also shows us important moments in the formation of each current.

---

[13]cf.Kenneth A.Myers, "Biblical Obedience and Political Thought: Some Reflections on Theological Method", in Richard John Neuhaus, *ed.*, *The Bible, Politics and Democracy* (Grand Rapids: Eerdmans, 1987), p.23.

[14]Peter L.Berger, *Pyramids of Sacrifice: Political Ethics and Social Change* (New York: Basic Books, 1974), p.18.

[15]Ulrich Duchrow, *Weltwirtschaft Heute: Eine Welt für bekennende Kirche?* (Munich: Kaiser Verlag, 1986).

[16]cf.Hans Achterhuis, *Het rijk van de schaarste: van Thomas Hobbes tot Michel Foucault* (Baarn: Ambo, 1988), p.52ff.

[17]The interrelating of theology and economics can be done in numerous ways. cf.Th.Salemink, "Economische theologie: object en methode", *Tijdschrift voor Theologie* 29 (1989) p.344-364.

2. Ground for comparison

An initial question to consider, is: how are we to compare Frei, a representative of a political party movement, with Gutiérrez, a representative of a theological movement? The answer is given by the focus of our comparison. Our posing of the problem stems from an inquiry in ethical theory. Since both Christian Democracy and Liberation Theology speak of transforming Latin America for the good of all, we will be inquiring into what that transformation means. It would self--evidently be unfair and also misguided to ask for a full theology from Christian Democracy or a full political party programme from Liberation Theology. At the same time we may surmise that Christian Democracy has an implicit theological direction (since it bears the name 'Christian'), and that Liberation Theology has an implicit political tendency (since it goes by the title of 'liberation' - which, as we shall see, is certainly political, even though not exclusively political). We come then to the conclusion that while we may not compare these two movements on the unequal footing of their different purposes, we may compare them on the common ground where their intentions overlap. Examples of common ground, are, that both Christian Democracy and Liberation Theology in Latin America intend to: (1) relate their Christian faith integrally to a political praxis; (2) make an analysis of the root problems of Latin American societies in turmoil; (3) find a perspective of transformation which gives a hopeful option to the poor. Our approach to such factors is by way of a comparison of their ethics of transformation.

3. Genre and specifications

Another factor to be taken into account, is that there is an on-going reorientation in the Social Encyclicals, just as there are various expressions of Christian Democracy and of Liberation Theology. Yet we shall maintain the collective names, not in order to deny the variety of specifications, but rather to indicate the genre, or identifiable root. We do not wish to suggest that one can extrapolate from an exemplary inquiry within one framework to a definitive view on all expressions of these movements. We make no pretense on that matter. However, we shall point out *tendencies* which we find along the way. Another limitation to our scope, besides the focus on a particular issue, namely political ethics of transformation, is our choice of the authors to be examined. We have selected two thinkers, namely, Eduardo Frei of Chile and Gustavo Gutiérrez of Peru, as each representing the beginning of one of these movements in Latin America. Both are already 'classical' representatives, given the short history of Christian Democracy and the even shorter history of Liberation Theology on that continent. We hope, by beginning at what seems to be two starting junctures, to arrive at a better understanding of where each movement is coming from. Often warned by Latin American thinkers of the need for contextualization and a critical praxis, we turn, in what may be called our 'case study', to Central America. The reasons for this choice are personal experience in the region, as well as the fact that Central America displays so many of the features for which Christian Democrats, Liberation Theologians and others in Latin America are seeking transformation. A description of two views on that kind of situation is our next consideration.

III. TRANSFORMATION IN LATIN AMERICA: THE DEVELOPMENT/LIBERATION DEBATE

Transformation ethics in Christian Democracy and in Liberation Theology must be recognized as pertaining for a considerable part to the development/liberation debate which has arisen during the last twenty years of struggles and failures to gain what Third World countries are demanding: the initiation of a *New International Economic Order* (NIEO). In this regard, the *United Nations Conferences on Trade and Development* (UNCTAD) give us an orientation to a global view.[18] A review of the search for a New International Economic Order shows that the 1973 increase in petroleum prices led to profound problems in much of the Third World. The *Group of 77* (later 119) countries from the Third World, which was formed in 1962 and called forth the first UNCTAD conference in 1964, obtained approval in 1974 for an action programme for the establishment of a New International Economic Order. The kind of agenda items for this new order have been, for example, control of natural resources, fair prices for raw materials, regulation of the activities of the transnational corporations, solution to the external debt problem of the Third World, technological assistance, and a following through on justice rather than charity: "not aid but trade".[19] These 'global negotiations' are an important step in the right direction, without as yet yielding the hoped for results. A consideration of these issues brings to light what for some decades has been announced in Latin America: the problem of dependency. Whereas during the 1950s and early 1960s the approach to development was the *modernization* theory, or "stages of economic growth" theory, the emphasis turned in the late 1960s and during the 1970s to the *dependency* theory, or "international - structuralist" model.[20] We shall briefly review these.

1. Modernization theory

The roots of the modernization approach to development theory are often attributed especially to Max Weber (1864-1920) who sought to explain the uniqueness of western society along lines of a modern rationalization process. Weber's stress on the importance of values and ideas (so that economic development is more than an economic problem) has remained as a key to at least some approaches to 'modernization'. Those who accept something of Weber's orientation will often tend to see ethical-cultural values or "spirit" (attitudes) as a prior key to development.[21] Many expressions of modernization theory also rely on Adam Smith and

---

[18]cf.*Third World Guide* (Editoro Terceiro Mundo: Rio de Janeiro, 1986), p.541ff: "New International Economic Order: Twenty Years of Frustration". Also: P.van de Meerssche, *De Noord-Zuid Confrontatie en de Nieuwe Internationale Economische Orde* (The Hague: Martinus Nijhoff, 1981). *Informe de la Comisión Brandt: Diálogo Norte-Sur* (Mexico: Editorial Nueva Imagen, 1981).

[19]Similar ideas were already discussed at the World Council of Churches meeting in Geneva, 1966: *World Conference on Church and Society: Christians in the Technical and Social Revolutions of our Time* (Geneva: WCC, 1967).

[20]cf.Michael P. Todaro, *Economic Development in the Third World: An introduction to the problems and policies in a global perspective* (New York: Longman, 1977), p.51ff.

[21]cf.Max Weber, *The Protestant Ethic and the Spirit of Capitalism* (New York: Scribner's,

the "invisible hand" philosophy (namely, that the free market is self-regulating). Modernization approaches have further been influenced by Talcott Parsons[22] and others on the process of institutional differentiation and more efficient functioning that replaces the personal ties of clientelism which typifies closed societies.[23] The general framework for the modernization perspective suggests that societies move from tradition to modernity. Elements of modernity include: functional rationality, plurality of institutions and ideas, urbanization, and progress-orientation (especially through scientific and technological revolutions), whereby goals of individual freedom and personal development are of high importance. Modernization theory would tend to see economic problems in Latin America as tied into the colonial-feudal structures, into oligarchic domination, and factors such as lack of education and technical training. There is, it is suggested, a failure to find the secret of how to create wealth through inventive use of land, work and capital (and a high regard for the profit motive). The *modernization* idea of stages of economic growth often seems to equate development with economic growth. If the right amount of the GNP can be saved and invested, a country should reach the 'take-off' stage of accelerated development.[24] Development is then usually defined along lines of industrialization and democratization, or progress as defined by western civilization, which, it is assumed, is farther down the historical road and can be followed by other world regions. What modernization theory often does not take into account is that Third World countries have more obstacles to remove than their low level of capital formation, since they are situated in a *world system* of economic and political structures, whereby interdependency also means dependency because of the powerful effects of international trade, the role of the multinationals and even military intervention. It has also become better known that when economic growth does occur in the Third World, it goes largely to the benefit of the elite and not to the poorer - and larger - segment of the population.[25] Without democratization of the world economy, it is then said, there can be no true transformation of the present situation.[26] The problem then is called 'dependency' rather than 'under-development'.

2. Dependency theory

The dependency perspective concentrates on the long history of colonialism and

---

1958). Also, Ernst Troeltsche, *The Social Teaching of the Christian Churches* (New York: Harper, 1931). R.H.Tawney, *Religion and the Rise of Capitalism* (New York: Harcourt & Brace, 1926).

[22]cf.Roland Robertson & Bryan S.Turner, *Talcott Parsons: Theorist of Modernity* (London: Sage, 1991).

[23]cf.Peter F. Klarén and Thomas J. Bossert, *Promise of Development: Theories of Change in Latin America* (Boulder, Colorado: Westview Press, 1986), p.3ff: Introduction.

[24]cf.W.W.Rostow, *The Stages of Economic Growth* (Cambridge: Cambridge University Press, 1960).

[25]cf.Gunnar Myrdal, *The Challenge of World Poverty* (New York: Random House, 1970). G.J.Kruijer, *Bevrijdingswetenschap: Een partijdige visie op de Derde Wereld* (Meppel: Boom, 1983).

[26]Anthony Carty, "Liberal Economic Rhetoric as an Obstacle to the Democratization of the World Economy", *Ethics*, vol.98, July, 1988 (University of Chicago Press).

imperialism, or the external factors and the internal result, from a political viewpoint of intervention and domination. The dependency perspective believes that the mode of insertion into the worldwide political-economic system, through colonialism, and neocolonialism, explains the on-going poverty. The beginnings of the dependency theory are traceable especially to Raúl Prebisch (1901-1968), Argentine economist and director of the Economic Commission for Latin America (ECLA) of the United Nations during the 1950s.[27] ECLA studies showed that conventional development ideas were not working since Latin America relied on export of coffee, bananas, sugar cane and other primary goods in exchange for imported industrial goods whose rising costs were far outracing the value of primary goods. While a tractor in 1960 was worth three tons of bananas, in 1970 it would cost ten tons. The answer of ECLA was that Latin America must follow a policy of import-substitution industrialization. Other emphases, such as land reform, were slow in taking hold, when at all. The ECLA emphasis on centre and periphery was accepted by numerous investigators, some of whom thought it could best be understood within a more Marxist-Leninist orientation.[28]

The *dependencia* theory, as it arose in Latin America, views the 'neocolonial' countries of the Third World as the *economías periféricas* (peripheral economies) and the industrialized, developed nations as the *economías centrales* (central economies).[29] The coexistence of the rich and the poor nations is a double-sided factor of the one international system, whereby - intentionally or unintentionally - it becomes more and more difficult, if not impossible, for the Third World (periphery) to achieve self-reliance because of the domination of the developed nations over trade prices and international finances, even to the point of influencing internal political-economic factors of the Third World, encouraging them to apply nonendogenous development models. In André Gunder Frank's often quoted phrase, this contributes to the "development of underdevelopment".[30] The dependency theory, in its stronger form, holds that international capitalism both produces and maintains underdevelopment in the poor nations. This is facilitated through cooperation between Latin America's internal elites and the banks and corporations from the First World. The Third World economy is tied into export of low priced agrarian products and import of high priced consumer goods. This is complicated by such factors as brain drain, capital flight (acquisition of foreign assets without

---

[27]cf.David Lehmann, *Democracy and Development in Latin America: Economics, Politics and Religion in the Postwar Period* (Cambridge: Polity Press, 1990), ch.1.

[28]Klarén and Bossert, *op. cit.*, p.16ff.

[29]cf.F.H.Cardoso & Enzo Faletto, *Dependencia y Desarrollo en América Latina* (Mexico: Siglo Veintiuno, 1969), p.24. Theotonio Dos Santos, Imperialismo y Dependencia (Mexico: Ediciones Era, 1978). Eduardo P.Archetti, Paul Cammack & Bryan Roberts, *Latin America: Sociology of 'Developing Societies'* (London: Macmillan, 1987), part 1: "The 'Dependency' Perspective". Joseph L.Love, "The Origins of Dependency Analysis", *Journal of Latin America Studies*, vol.22, part 1, February 1990. Herald Muñoz, *From Dependency to Development: Strategies to Overcome Underdevelopment and Inequality* (Boulder, Colorado: Westview Press, 1981). Magnus Blomström & Björn Hettne, *Development Theory in Transition: The Dependency Debate and Beyond: Third World Responses* (London: Zed Books, 1984).

[30]André Gunder Frank, *Latin America: Underdevelopment or Revolution: Essays on the Development of Underdevelopment and the Immediate Enemy* (New York: Monthly Review Press, 1969). Also, *idem, Sobre el Subdesarrollo Capitalista* (Barcelona: Anagrama, 1977).

repatriating the profits), cheap labour, foreign debts and even external support for the local military, justified by the 'national security doctrine', which places emphasis on maintaining the status quo. The combination of these factors leads, at best, to "growth without development", since mainly the elite benefit from economic growth, while the masses continue in misery. The results in Latin America are said to be stagnation, marginality, and denationalization. Almost like planets locked by gravity into orbit, so the periphery revolves around the economic and military centres, becoming more dependent and poorer all the time. In a sense, the dependency theory attempts to turn the tables on the modernization theory by including all the internal reasons for underdevelopment within the factor of dependency on foreign domination, starting from the colonial period onward. Of course, the modernization theory may be expected to reply that the continued dependency is a result of internal problems. The dependency position has been especially characterized by its attempt to interpret underdevelopment in Latin America as something *more* than merely a problem of *historical lag* in stages of economic growth (due to lack of capital and technology), while going beyond the theory of a *dualist society* (i.e., which has a traditional peasant sector and a modernized sector).[31] Dependency theory suggests that the structural poverty is due to more than these two factors; and that 'more' includes dependency upon the capitalist centres which help hold the lag (underdevelopment) and the dualist contrasts (rich and poor) in place. This *more* is thus interpreted to be a political will to economic (and military) dominance.

In any case, according to these insights of the dependency theory, development is not just a matter of improving[32] the GNP, but first of all a question of liberation from dominance and oppression.[33] For our present investigation it is important to note that the *dependencia* approach has entered into the social perspectives of the Latin American bishops,[34] and may also be called a constitutive element in the epoch-making *Teología de la Liberación* by Gustavo Gutiérrez.[35] The dependency approach can also be said to be at the heart of what some Latin Americans see as a Latin American philosophy.[36] The centre-periphery model is also an important

---

[31]cf.Gonzalo Arroyo, "Afhankelijkheidstheorie, een geldige bemiddeling voor de Bevrijdingstheologie?", in Jacques Van Nieuwenhove, *Bevrijding en Christelijk Geloof in Latijns-Amerika en Nederland* (Baarn: Ambo, 1980), p.55ff.

[32]As Immanuel Wallerstein states it in "The Present State of the Debate on World Inequality", in Wallerstein, *ed.*, *World Inequality* (Montreal: Black Rose, 1975), p.23: "The key factor to note is that within a capitalist world-economy, all states cannot 'develop' simultaneously *by definition*, since the system functions by virtue of having unequal and peripheral regions."

[33]For a schematic comparison of the development model and the structural liberation model, see John Lucal, "Het pragmatisme van de kerkelijke ontwikkelingsorganisaties" in *Concilium: Christelijke ethiek en economie: het Noord-Zuid-conflict*, 1980 - 10, p.96f. Also, Georges Enderle & Ambros Luthi, "Economische afhankelijkheid en dissociatie", in *Concilium*, 1980 - 10, p.56ff. Also Klaus Nurnberger, "Dependenztheorien in der Entwicklungsdebatte als Thema der theologischen Ethik", in *Zeitschrift für Evangelische Ethik*, 1985;4, p.438ff.

[34]*Documentos de Medellín*, Vol.II, ch.x.2: the bishops say that underdevelopment (*subdesarrollo*) in Latin America relates to the structures of economic, political and cultural *dependencia* on the industrialized metropolies. Similarly, *Puebla: III Conferencia General del Episcopado Latinoamericano*, par.66.

[35]Gustavo Gutiérrez, *Teología de la Liberación, Perspectivas* (Lima: CEP, 1971).

[36]cf.Leopoldo Zea, *Filosofía latinoamericana* (Mexico: Trillas, 1987). Enrique Dussel, *Filosofía Ética de la Liberación (Buenos Aires: Aurora, 1987)*. This has been applied by Paulo

element in publications of the World Council of Churches and the conciliar process toward *Justice, Peace and the Integrity of Creation.*[37] Dependency theory, as spoken of in our present study, rejects the modernizationist view that it is sufficient to say that Latin American culture and institutional structures largely account for underdevelopment. Those who present the dependency problem often speak of three colonial pacts: i) direct colonial conquest and political-economic domination; ii) the neocolonial system, based on the exchange of raw materials for manufactured goods; iii) the 'development model' imposed externally whereby the oligarchy recaptures "power within its own nations with the help of the multinational corporations. The agreement between oligarchy and international corporations promoted and continues to maintain military dictatorships all over Latin America."[38] It is thus argued that the neocolonial pact of 'developmentalism' (*desarrollismo*), whereby the oligarchy ties into export markets and leaves the internal market undeveloped, leads to impoverishment and in the face of rising popular demands (emancipation of the marginalized masses) sets the stage for the national security state (military authoritarianism).[39] The result is that the marginalized become even more oppressed.

3. Transition theories in relation to our field of inquiry

The development/liberation, or as we saw above, the modernization/dependency debate, has entered into analyses of the roots of poverty and strategies for change in Latin America as well as the Third World in general, also within a Christian approach to social-political ethics. We may indicate this very briefly here as follows:

i) Development is a theme that arose in the 1950s and '60s, entering into the Vatican social teaching, especially with John XXIII, as well as leading to other expressions of hope in modernization and democracy.

ii) The crisis in development in Latin America, especially since the much referred to failure of the *Alliance for Progress* (begun in 1961 by John F.Kennedy as a response to the 'Cuba crisis'), has been complicated by the 'oil crisis', increased 'debt peonage', population growth, and other factors so that development has become increasingly questioned in Latin America.[40] This is brought out strongly in John Paul II's encyclical *Sollicitudo Rei Socialis.*

iii) Liberation as a theme in theology and other studies - in contrast to older development models - has more and more dominated the dialogue in Latin

---

Freire, *Pedagogía del Oprimido* (Mexico: Siglo Veintiuno, 1970).

[37]cf.Ulrich Duchrow & Gerhard Liedke, *Shalom: Biblical Perspectives on Creation, Justice and Peace* (Geneva: WCC, 1989); part I relies on the dependency model.

[38]José Comblin, *The Church and the National Security State* (Maryknoll: Orbis, 1979), p.57.

[39]cf.José Míguez Bonino, *Toward a Christian Political Ethics* (London: SCM, 1983), ch.5: "Latin America: From Democracy to the National Security State".

[40]For an analysis of the failure of the *Alliance for Progress*, see Richard L.McCall, "La Alianza Para el Progreso: Una Evaluación", ch.12 in William Ascher & Ann Hubbard, *eds.*, *Recuperación y Desarrollo de Centroamérica* (San José: Tomás Saraví, 1989).

America during the last two decades, especially since the Medellín (1968) Conference of Latin American Bishops (CELAM: *Consejo Episcopal Latino-americano*).

iv) The present status of the debate has not been wholly resolved: we are confronted with a problem in analysis often in combination with ideological differences that have entered into the political ethics of development and liberation. We presently see a struggle of paradigms.[41]

4. Theory and complex reality

Development and liberation are not just a matter of the shortest route from point 'a' to point 'b', since there are many obstacles (often unacknowledged, inadequately analyzed and changing) between the point of departure and the point of arrival.[42] Further, it is not a matter of progressing within one aspect (such as the economic) from point 'a' to point 'b', for development and liberation require a progressing within several aspects (for example, the political, the educational and the technical) and the cultural conjunction of these. For that reason we cannot ultimately view economic values apart from values of justice.

Now, we have seen that many in Latin America include the 'centre-periphery' concept in their understanding of underdevelopment.[43] It is thus worth noting some evaluation on both the modernization and the dependency perspectives. The following points apply to tendencies and not to all expressions of each position.

M o d e r n i z a t i o n

Strengths

i) a taking into account of various dimensions;
ii) an emphasis on cultural traditions and change;
iii) an understanding of scientific, innovative and entrepreneurial progress;
iv) the presence of historical models in the 'advanced' countries.

Weaknesses

i) a cultural bias in favour of industrial capitalistic culture;
ii) an assumption that poor countries can follow in the steps of the rich countries;
iii) a tendency to think that development = economic growth;
iv) a technocratic rather than human ecological approach;
v) analysis of local economies and cultures without taking into account world systems;
vi) sometimes more emphasis on values than on structures (a microethical approach rather than a macrostructural approach to justice).

---

[41]cf.Th.Salemink, "Economische theologie: object en methode", in *Tijdschrift voor Theologie* 29 (1989), p.347f.

[42]cf. Steven Vago, *Social Change* (London: Prentice Hall, 1989), p.75ff.

[43]cf.also Ricardo Antoncich, *Christians in the Face of Injustice: A Latin American reading of Catholic Social Teaching* (Maryknoll: Orbis, 1987), p.69.

D e p e n d e n c y

Strengths
 i)   taking into account colonial history and neocolonial systems;
 ii) an emphasis on actual relationships of domination and exploitation;
 iii) insight into the reality of underdevelopment as more than mere lag in development, since global patterns prevent equal modernization;
 iv) historical models of domination in the Third World.

Weaknesses
 i)   a cultural bias against rationalization of material progress;
 ii) an assumption that the wealth of the rich countries comes mainly through exploitation;
 iii) insufficient concentration on how peripheries can become new centres;
 iv) sometimes a disregard of the prerequisite values that enter into development.[44]

We shall approach further inquiry open to the double assumption that dependency causes underdevelopment and that underdevelopment causes dependency. This vicious circle no doubt calls for liberation, which then must always be defined in regard to development (and vice-versa). The challenge is not so much to "solve" the modernization/liberation (underdevelopment/dependency) debate as to include both perspectives in an open analysis, for both have observed data which should not be ignored. For that reason we shall be listening to a symposium of opinions from various viewpoints. Any perspective pushed too far without inductive analysis of historical situations becomes inadequate. While it is sometimes thought that the two positions have nothing in common but their field of analysis, that is not so. They do agree considerably on the negative role of oligarchic leadership holding back democratic progress. While the modernization position has usually been content to say that this leadership was more feudal than entrepreneurial, the dependency position has seen that there arose a cooperation between the elite and external forces (governments, aid programmes, multinational corporations and armies), leading to enclave development that does not tie into national development. Analysis of underdevelopment and dependency is thus complex, as also are strategies for improvement.[45]

History's advancements and regressions continue. If there is no short-cut to deal with the fact that "the poor are many" (and are increasing), to ignore this is one of

---

[44]An interesting comparison was made in the now classical work of Uruguayan philosopher José Enrique Rodó, entitled *Ariel*, published in 1900, in which he sees a need for Latin America to maintain its own identity and ideals over against North American aggrandizement of material welfare.

[45]Wayne G. Bragg, "From Development to Transformation", in Vinay Samuel & Chris Sugden, *eds.*, *The Church in Response to Human Need* (Grand Rapids: Eerdmans, 1987), p.20ff. speaks of four approaches to development, explaining and evaluating theories on 1) modernization, 2) dependency, 3) Global reformism through a New International Economic Order, and 4) Alternative endogenous and self-reliant development. He then posits a separate Christian perspective on transformation which however tends to flounder because it appears too immune to the very problems in question.

the worst of options. Suitable approaches need to be based both on specific elimination of abuses and on long-term changes. At every turn we must be wary of ideological self-justification. For that reason our investigation must be willing to expose the shadow side of any myths, be they developmentalist or liberationist, which do not adequately account for poverty nor sufficiently contribute to transformation.[46]

IV. POLITICAL-ECONOMIC IDEOLOGIES AND LATIN AMERICA

In this section we review some of the terminology which is unavoidably connected with political ethics in Latin America. Drawn into the emerging capitalist economies via colonial mercantilism (sometimes called the "milkcow" system of draining the raw resources from the colonies) Latin America has traditionally been agrarian, with a late arrival of industrialization. Especially during the last several decades, the spiraling difference between earnings on raw materials (coffee, bananas, sugar, wood) and the cost of importing manufactured goods has helped create a debt crisis. The traditional political values have roots in medieval feudalism. After three hundred years of such values combined with the colonial conquest, liberal democratic values began to arrive and then added to this in the twentieth century came socialism. Today there are currents of feudalism, liberalism, and socialism, all struggling for recognition in Latin America. Each have their virtues and vices, rotating around the poles of stable harmony, creative production, and social justice. Naturally, there is a great variety of situations in the different countries. Further, political values are mixed in different ways with other values, such as old and new views on the Christian faith, as well as the voicing of indigenous rights by the Indian peasantry, 500 years after Columbus. We shall now consider some of the terminology more closely.[47] However, the following overview of concepts is not intended to provide ready-made definitions. We shall always have to ask how particular thinkers use such concepts.

1. Corporative Society, Feudal Latifundismo, Colonial Mercantilism
The *corporative*[48] view of society places high value on an organic-state idea (whereby state and society are little differentiated), using the paradigm of a body

---

[46]cf.Arthur F. McGovern, *Marxism: An American Christian Perspective* (Maryknoll: Orbis, 1981), p.141f.: "In 1900 the gap between the per capita incomes of the more affluent nations and the poorer ones was two to one. Today the gap is nearly twenty to one. ...Whether justly or not [voices within the Third World] often blame their situation on their economic 'dependence' upon the United States and other western European countries. ... If Marxists and other critics sometimes create new myths about underdevelopment, the more prevalent capitalist myths about it should also be challenged. For the impact of foreign influence on Third World conditions has been great."

[47]cf.Walter Montenegro, *Introducción a las Doctrinas Político-económicas* (Mexico: Fondo de Cultura Económica, 1986). N.Poelman, *Panorama der Ideologieën* (Baarn: Nelissen, 1982). Jan van Putten, *Politieke Stromingen* (Utrecht: Aula, 1985). J.Philip Wogaman, *Economics and Ethics: A Christian Enquiry* (London: SCM, 1985).

[48]cf.Howard J.Wiarda, *Corporatism and National Development in Latin America* (Boulder, Colorado: Westview Press, 1981).

(*corpus*) wherein the various (corporate) parts function for the good of the whole. Latin American Iberian culture has strong roots in such a corporative perspective, traced to Aristotelian and Thomist[49] influences. The idea of the "state as perfect community" (perfect in the sense of complete and sufficient)[50] became a corporative ideology in support of very imperfect practices in Latin America. While this position aims to offer a way of avoiding extremes of individualism and collectivism, providing representation by "corporate" entities (of which the dominant during colonial times in Latin America were the Spanish crown, the church, the military and the elites),[51] the shadow side shows up in the fact that the old estates and distinction between classes were viewed as fixed complementary parts of a community, often said to be ordained by God. *Corporativism* thinks more in terms of social groupings than in terms of the individual and his political rights (as in liberal politics). Yet at the same time there is a deficiency of social actors, for in the corporative system governments make decisions for vertical units of society. Thus "corporate units", as the elites, the army, the church, the university, labour organizations and peasant organizations, are viewed as subsidiary parts of the same whole, leading to what has been called a lack of "sphere sovereignty"[52] (normative differentiation and relative independence of societal spheres). The result is a "predominance of the state over social actors"[53] and an incorporation of such social actors into a 'harmony' model whereby the idea of the 'common good' is somtimes appealed to in a retrogressive way, not in the interest of the populous.

Often the word *feudalism* is used in connection with Latin America, to refer to the structural relationships of the landed classes to day-labourers, whereby the concepts *encomienda*, *hacienda*, and *latifundismo* are historically dominant in this system of landocracy. In 1503 a legal arrangement was begun by the Spanish Crown to "entrust" (*encomendar*) rights over the indigenous Amerindians to Spanish military leaders and others. The *encomienda* was also supposed to protect the indigenous people but in practice it was usually a forced labour system which, when finally cancelled in the 18th century, was replaced by continued debt peonage. *Latifundismo* refers to the large estate (*latifundio*) system which formed the main economic and social unit in many parts of rural Latin America, often with absentee owners living in the capital city. A manager (*majordomo*) was then left in charge over the peasant labour force. The centre of the large estate was the

---

[49]cf.Thomas Aquinas, *Summa Theologica*, Josepho Pecci, *ed.*, (Lethielleux, 1925), part II, Q.XC, art.II:"...omnis pars ordinetur ad totum, sicut imperfectum ad perfectum...omnis lex ad bonum commune ordinatur."

[50]cf.Frederick Copleston, *A History of Philosophy*, vol.2, partII (New York: Garden City, 1962), ch.40: "St.Thomas Aquinas: Political Theory", p.135: "The State is a 'perfect society' (*communitas perfecta*), that is, it has at its disposal all the means necessary for the attainment of its end, the *bonum commune* or common good of the citizens." This includes: i) peace within society; ii) the unified direction of activities; iii) adequate provison of basic needs; iv) protection from crime and foreign enemies.

[51]cf.Howard J.Wiarda & Harvey F.Kline, *Latin American Politics and Development* (Boulder, Colorado: Westview Press, 1990), p.24ff: "Colonial Society: Principles and Institutions".

[52]Herman Dooyeweerd, *Roots of Western Culture* (Toronto: Wedge Publishing, 1979), ch.2.

[53]Alain Touraine, "Power and Protest in Latin America", in Fernando Enrique Cardoso, *et al.*, *The Crisis of Development in Latin America* (Amsterdam: CEDLA, 1991), p.121.

hacienda, or manor, which was usually a self-sufficient and self-governing unit with a store, a chapel, and its own guards. Often the wealthy landlords whose main attention was elsewhere did not worry about improving production on their estates.[54] Through a system of *mayorazgo* (primogeniture inheritance) estates were inalienable. One of the results of this system was that "no large middle class, no backbone of the small farmer, no development of industry or industrial workers would for centuries be able to challenge the absolute power of landownership".[55] The manorial system declines when industrialization arrives.

In relation to the colonial feudal set up, relationships of *clientelismo* developed, meaning the social and economic support system whereby jobs, positions and various favours as signs of loyalty toward family, friends, and associates are distributed according to personal relationships rather than according to more objective measures of functional merit. While attitudes of *clientelismo* are socially supportive, many see these as economically deleterious (placing loyalty above achievement) and the root of a personalist bending of public law.[56]

Another feature which typified Latin America was the system of *colonial mercantilism*. Dominant from the 1500s into the late 1700s, mercantilist economics concentrated on balancing a nation's wealth, especially in terms of its stock of gold and silver, mainly through terms of trade rather than by concentrating on production and technical advancement; since setting the right prices was considered important, it did not favour free trade. To keep the trade favourable, high tariffs on imports became common. In the colonial system this included monopolization by "chartered" trading companies and exclusive trade with Spain. Since no trade was allowed between colonies, transport and commercial centres were externally orientated.

2. Liberalism, Democracy, Capitalism

There have been major liberal reforms in Latin America which have at the same time been thwarted by other tendencies. *Liberalism* developed in reaction to authoritarian regimes, hoping to install governments based on the rule of public law and on the consent of the governed, to be held in check by open elections, with voting rights granted to all, rather than restricted to the property owning class or the educated as in oligarchic systems. This presumes safeguard from state terror at the hands of the police or armed forces. Political liberalism is pluralistic, placing high value on individual civil liberties, encouraging freedom of conscience, of the press, of political parties and of religion. Modern liberalism includes room for government programmes of economic security, minimum wages, health care measures, old-age pensions, and so forth, though this has not been accomplished in much of Latin America. *Economic liberalism* refers to the idea of the free market whereby entrepreneurial competition is more important than state regulation. The

---

[54]cf.Ernst E.Rossi & Jack C.Plano, *The Latin American Political Dictionary* (Oxford: Clio Press, 1980).

[55]John A. Crow, *The Epic of Latin America* (Berkley: University of California Press, 1980), p.xxv.

[56]Eugene Nida, *Understanding Latin Americans* (Pasadena: William Carey Library, 1974), p.47.

word *democracy* also has a variety of meanings, such as *formal democracy* as a means of procedure and a strategy for renewal, and *social-economic democracy*, whereby the 'common good' is sought through social legislation towards a welfare society.

Capitalism can be defined according to a variety of characteristics, as, for example, the distinction between owners and nonowners of the production process whereby ownership gives control of decision-making. The capitalist system is based on an economy of profit and free market competition. The question of how to spend the profit remains a decision of the owners (who run the risk of loss). Nonowners receive a salary which normally is only indirectly related to profits and loss. The debate on capitalistic values is complex. We shall list typical characteristics commonly held against, and others in favour of, modern capitalism.[57] It will become apparent (cf.ch.3.1.b and ch.4.II.2) that the term 'capitalism' is highly in debate in Latin America.

The critics say:
i)   capitalism as a system produces unjust relationships between the rich and the poor;
ii)   private interest influences many decisions above public interest or the common good;
iii) capital benefits disproportionately from the profits created by the work force;
iv)   capitalism is seen by critics as interrelated with the weapon industry and neocolonial expansion;
v)   the system is said to lead to overproduction and a circle of economic crises, recessions and inflations;
vi)   some see capitalism as a major source of egoistic (systematically selfish) competitive relationships and the commercialization of all aspects of life;
vii) monopolies and multinationals cannot be controlled even by government legislation;
viii) it is further said that the system cannot continue expanding except with great detriment to the underdeveloped nations who form the new world proletariat and whose resources are already controlled by the wealthy nations.

The arguments for capitalism are somewhat as follows:
i)   capitalistic production processes have led to the highest standard of living;
ii)   many of the complaints about capitalism (or even worse ones) are found in socialist industrialized society as well;
iii) the market system has its own logic and allows for continued restoration: for example, when production and jobs close down in one sector they open in others;
iv)   the market system goes together with a wider sense of initiative, creativity, and democracy;
v)   utopian ideas of collective ownership do not function economically; in the

---

[57]cf.note 47; also, Peter L.Berger, *The Capitalist Revolution: Fifty Propositions about Prosperity, Equality, and Liberty* (New York: Basic Books, 1986).

noncapitalistic economies state bureaucrats control and often make unwise decisions;

vi)   noncapitalist societies create their own elites;

vii) capitalism can be accompanied by adequate social legislation and new models of cooperation between management and workers;

viii) the socialist superpower has been as ruthlessly imperialistic or more so than the capitalist one.

The expression *laissez faire, laissez passer* (let it be, let it pass) refers to the desire for more freedom in individual initiative and less taxation and time-consuming customs problems (let it pass through), and has come to generally mean that the state should not try to guide the economic realm.[58] But it has also been signalled that Third World nations which enter a phase of economic development often do that through a progressive programme involving a very active role of the state,[59] whereas the attempt at laissez faire in Latin America often throws oil on the burning fire of social instability of high unemployment, poverty and illiteracy. It is important to note that in Latin America capitalism often refers to 'foreign capitalism', or 'dependent capitalism' (of the periphery on the centre). Capitalism is then seen not only as an economic system, but as a political concept equated with imperialism. Since the more successful private enterprises in Latin America often tie into the 'domination by the dollar' and multinational activities, Latin Americans often associate "privatization" with "foreignization".[60] It is now commonly said that all the signs of the "social question" which earlier referred to the proletariat with their hard and underpaid work, poor housing, malnutrition and high deathrate of children, has today become the question of North-South relationships.

3. Socialism, Communism, Neomarxism

As for *socialism, communism* and *neomarxism*, scholars in Latin America are quite conscious of the different currents. In the rise of socialism there have been currents of 'utopian socialism', characterized by new ideas and experiments in social justice, whereby, in common with later *social democratic* ideas, new forms of social justice are thought possible through gradual reforms without using violent revolution. By way of contrast, *Marxist-Leninism*, usually understood as communism and sometimes called 'scientific' and 'revolutionary socialism', emphasized the dominant role of the party and the state to the exclusion of democracy. There are also currents of 'religious socialism' which includes variants on the 'social gospel' and contemporary 'liberation theology'. Some of these see an original 'communism' (shared wealth) in the Bible.[61] Neomarxism[62] refers especially to

---

[58]cf.Montenegro, *op.cit.*, p.40.

[59]Torcuato S. Di Tella, *Latin American Politics: A Theoretical Framework* (Austin: University of Texas, 1990), ch.10: "Reform and the Politics of Social Democracy".

[60]cf. Samuel Blixen, "Latin America: Debt policies benefit creditors", in *Latinamerica Press* (Vol. 23, no.8: March 7, 1991).

[61]cf.José Miranda, *Communism in the Bible* (London: SCM, 1982). José Miranda, *Marx and the Bible: A Critique of the Philosophy of Oppression* (Maryknoll: Orbis, 1974).

[62]cf.Martin Jay, *The Dialectical Imagination* (Boston: Little, Brown & Co., 1973). Herbert

on-going criticism of capitalist but also of socialist industrial society using, but also renewing and changing, approaches begun by Marx and Engels. In regard to currents of Christian social ethics, the value of listening to neomarxist critique has been summarized as follows:[63]

i)   "Marxism may force Christians to create a more authentically Christian way of coming to grips with burning social problems.

ii) Marxism challenges us to cease advocating contentment and acceptance of those elements of our lives which can and ought to be changed.

iii) Marxism challenges us Christians not to forget the prophetic impulse of the Old and New Testaments but to nurture the prophetic elements of our spirituality.

iv) Marxism forcefully calls to our attention the human need to be equal, and the dignity of labour.

v)   Marxism challenges Christians to see the idolatry of money.

vi) Marxism challenges us to re-examine our notion of freedom as practiced in Western democracies.

vii) Christians are challenged not to brush away too quickly the Marxist critique of religion as an alienating factor in human lives."

It has been said that while Smith exposed the invisible *hand* which leads to economic development, Marx exposed the invisible *foot* which kicks others into structural poverty.[64] Be that as it may, there has been a problem in Latin America because the word 'Communist' (in the bipolar Cold War sense) has often been rapidly and profusely applied to anyone who has spoken of social justice. The silence on socialism, that is, on educating people to distinguish between currents of reformist socialism, social democracy, and totalizing communism, has been faulty, with authoritarian regimes often oppressing proponents of basic human rights because they were 'Communists'.

4. Repressive military regimes

There are numerous ways of speaking of the repressive regimes in Latin America: one finds such terms as oligarchic militarism, authoritarianism, autocratic dictatorships, Latin American fascism, etc. The term 'fascism', in a contemporary sense, has become rather common to describe these repressive regimes, whereby the following characteristics play a role: authoritarian rule (backed) by the military; high disregard for democratic (egalitarian) values; marginalization and repression (sometimes with genocidal features) of the indigenous peoples; a leadership style of *caudillismo* (romantic personality-ideal of the strongman leader as head and saviour) which ties into fascist philosophies of the strong and the weak; national unity and group unity are placed above individual rights. This easily blends with a corporative approach to society which promotes stability to the exclusion of not

---

Marcuse, *One Dimensional Man* (London: Abacus, 1972).

[63]Douglas J.Elwood, *Faith Encounters Ideology: Christian Discernment and Social Change* (Quezon City: New Day, 1985), p.81.

[64]Achterhuis, *Het Rijk van de Schaarste*, p.218.

only class consciousness but even of the social question. Obedience is given more priority than creativity and initiative.[65] The excuse of preventing the rise of 'Communism' led to the rise of what is further commonly called the 'national security doctrine' in Latin America, whose characteristics can be summarized as follows:[66]

i)   juridical mechanisms of repression, ("emergency" legislation) to suspend constitutional rights;
ii) suspension of the electoral process; rule by military juntas;
iii) limitations of the right of association and labour organizations;
iv) control of the press and other communications;
v)   ideological censorship of culture (books, art, etc.);
vi) the suppression of *habeas corpus*.[67]

Thus regimes which use these measures are antipopular. We shall use the term *popular* in this study to refer to movements which desire structural changes which favour the need of the poor who are marginalized and oppressed.

5. Ideologies and conceptual clarity

If we now ask how the above ideological tendencies view the two concepts (cf.I.2) we posited as central for our approach to political ethics in this study, then the pattern runs as follows:

i)   The *corporative* view seeks the common good through an organic harmony of various sectors and classes, but is not overly disturbed by poverty. The idea of a preferential option for the poor sounds threatening to this view since a new economic balance would disturb the present 'harmony'.

ii) Economic *liberalism* in Latin America believes that the common good is reached via the individual good of private initiative and the conditions which allow and encourage this. Economic liberalism tends to think that poverty is basically the fault of the poor and does not deal thoroughly with the structures of poverty. However, it believes it offers an option for the poor by means of stressing production and economic growth.

iii) Various currents of *socialism*, though differing as to strategies, hold that the common good must be achieved via attention to the social indicators and through better distribution. An option for the poor means supporting *popular* parties and organizations which favour structural changes, and continuing *concientización*.

iv) *Repressive authoritarian* regimes think that only military control can keep the common good in place in the face of rising revolutions. An option for the poor, which also implies reducing the power and profits of those who gain

---

[65]cf.Theo G.Donner, *Formación del Pensamiento Moderno: Un Bosquejo* (Medellín: Seminario Bíblico de Colombia, 1984), p.81f.

[66]cf.José Míguez Bonino, *Toward a Christian Political Ethics*, p.71.

[67]The suspension of *habeas corpus* ("you may have the body", a writ to bring a prisoner before a court) means that many linger in prison without an inquiry into the lawfulness of their detainment.

from the poverty of the poor, has been suspected to be a slogan that opens the door to communism.

We shall keep this variety of approaches and understandings in mind during the next chapters.

V. DIVISIONS AND STRUCTURES OF THE CHAPTERS

In what follows our *methodology* tends to include four ways of aiming at an immanent critique: description, analysis, questions and evaluation.

i)   description (summary) is used to listen to the authors we study;
ii)   analysis involves pulling at the logical threading of concepts and systems of thought in order to reveal the coherence, tensions and (in)completeness of viewpoints;
iii) we question what is being said in order to keep the dialogue open;
iv)   we evaluate in order to draw some guidelines and possible conclusions.

It is, by the very nature of the theme, rather difficult to walk the fine line between clear opinion and opinionated judgments. Nor would we pretend that there can be a strict compartmentalization of description and evaluation, since the two will always be intertwined. But we have tried to be fair without becoming floppy. To do that we have striven to show more than one side of the various questions and have listened to analysts from a variety of perspectives.

In Chapter Two, *Latin America: Political Ethics in a Changing Context*, we examine the historical context of Latin America. Our purpose in Chapter Two is not to focus on ecclesiology, but rather on the context in which the church, theology and ethics find themselves in Latin America. This historical overview provides a fundamental backdrop to the modernization/liberation debate, which can only be understood when correctly contextualized. The structure of this second chapter is historical, proceeding from the colonial background to the present situation. We interweave this history with the main motifs of the Social Encyclicals, along with the rise of Christian Democracy and Liberation Theology. Our goal is to show some important junctures and streams of thought that have helped form the present situation in Latin America, politically and theologically, with the underlying social ethic involved.

Next we turn in Chapter Three, *A Hopeful Option?*, to a detailed analysis of Eduardo Frei's book, *América Latina: Opción y Esperanza*, as representative for Christian Democratic perspectives on politics and society. It is not our concern here to trace the party history, but to examine the political ethics (theory) of this movement. The choice of Frei rests on his wide influence on Latin American Christian Democratic thought. The choice of his major work for a chapter analysis on our part likewise is unavoidable, since in it he draws together a life-time of political-ethical reflection. It was, indeed, largely written as a response to the widely acclaimed failure of development and democracy. Section I of this third chapter summarizes and comments on Frei's book itself. We have chosen this method of expository description and discourse in order to allow the original source to show through more fully. Section II provides a perspectival overview on Frei, and then in section III we consider a critical appraisal of Christian Democratic political ethics in Latin America, including critique from the side of Liberation Theology.

In Chapter Four, *Option for the Poor?*, we pursue the same method with Gustavo Gutiérrez' *Teología de la Liberación*. As with Frei, Gutiérrez is chosen as a main source for a Latin American position relating to our field of inquiry. Again in section I we provide a summary and discourse of an important work, though other writings by Gutiérrez are included in our evaluation. Here, too, we do not claim to be making a complete investigation of Gutiérrez, let alone of Liberation Theology. Far from it. Our purpose remains the examination of the socio-politico current intertwined by Gutiérrez and others into the ethics of Liberation Theology, especially as to the relationship between development and liberation. After an expository description of his main thoughts, we give our interpretive comments and questions in the discourse sections. As in Chapter Three with Frei, so in Chapter Four with Gutiérrez, we attempt to draw out the typical features and relate them to our focus. We include a critical appraisal from the outspoken analyst, Michael Novak, which certainly livens the symposium.

In Chapter Five, *Central America: Transformation in Freedom?*, we turn to a historical-political overview of the situation in Central America. The title alludes partly to Frei's slogan: *Revolución en libertad*, which expects much from democracy and development strategies, and partly to Gutiérrez' and the liberationist questioning of such a possibility, especially through a critique of the dependency problem and 'national security' political doctrine. We must, however, be clear in that the relationship between the first four chapters and our fifth chapter is exemplary, rather than prescriptive. Having listened to Frei and Gutiérrez speak about the need for transformation in Latin America we thus look at the historical reality in one region from the viewpoints of development and liberation. We pay particular attention to the internal problems, the considerable differences between the countries, as well as the influence of the United States of America in the area. We try to assess the various factors in the crisis and ask how Central America contributes to the development/liberation debate.

Then in the sixth and final chapter, *Conclusions: Veritas Omnia Vincit*, we provide some final remarks which summarize and suggest our views.

Transition to chapter two

In this first chapter we introduced the debate around development and dependency. Our purpose in reviewing these two perspectives is a preparation for listening to how Christian Democracy and Liberation Theology, as represented by Frei and by Gutiérrez, have entered the debate. We further inquired into some political-economic concepts. It is now advisable from a bird's-eye view to look at Latin America in relation to colonialism, the Vatican social teaching, and the rise of Christian Democracy and Liberation Theology, as they have faced ethical dilemmas and new challenges in the contemporary crisis of transformation. That is what the next chapter is about.

CHAPTER TWO

POLITICAL ETHICS IN A CHANGING CONTEXT

[Oct.12-13, 1492]: "It seemed to me that they were a people very poor in everything. All of them go around as naked as their mothers bore them...they do not carry arms nor are they acquainted with them, because I showed them swords and they took them by the edge and through ignorance cut themselves. They have no iron. ...They should be good and intelligent servants...and I believe that they would become Christians very easily...I was attentive and laboured to find out if there was any gold...."
Diary of Christopher Columbus[1]

*

"The news coming out of Latin America the last few years - news of social unrest, guerrilla activity escalating in some cases to civil war, military coups, repressive governments, systematic violations of human rights, economic crises - cannot but prompt the question: whatever happened to the project for democratic modernization?"
José Míguez Bonino[2]

Introduction

Our purpose in this second chapter is to provide an introduction to the historical shifting in Latin America during the past five hundred years since Columbus sailed. Into this we weave a consideration of the Vatican Encyclicals and other documents which have been highly influential on, and interrelated with, Christian Democratic thought and Liberation Theology, since these last two movements quite naturally have kept an open ear to what the Church has been saying from Rome. However, the reverse is also true. Rome has been listening - if with measures of consternation - to Latin America as well. There are three elements which combine in Latin America and provide a high dynamic for our study, namely, the region: 1) shows marked poverty; 2) it is Christian (in an historical-colonial sense); and 3) it is rightly called a revolutionary situation (of pressures for change). While drawing together some dominant tendencies, we must keep in mind that Latin America is large, diversified and cannot be fully described through any generalizations. However, the following considerations are helpful to understand the region and, as it were, to sketch a grid for the ethical map we are drawing.

I. COLONIALISM AND NEOCOLONIALISM

1. Conquest: Cross and Sword

The church, theology, and other expressions of the Christian faith are always situated or contextualized, and must be so if they are to relate to issues of their

---

[1]Oliver Dunn & James E.Kelley, *The* Diario *of Christopher Columbus's First Voyage to America 1492-1493, Abstracted by Fray Bartolomé De Las Casas* (London: University of Oklahoma Press, 1989), p.65ff.

[2]José Míguez Bonino, *Toward a Christian Political Ethics* (London: SCM, 1983), p.65.

time. Sometimes forms of Christian expression are nearly indistinguishable from the dominant ideologies among which they may even build an all too comfortable niche; at other times we see a prophetic reaction to these ideologies. When Christopher Columbus[3] sailed in 1492, Christianity - and that was one kind of Christianity of a certain era - came to what has become known as Latin America through a crusade war (*guerra de crusada*) in which Spain, who had then just conquered the Turks and Islam, now felt challenged to continue a kind of holy war in the New World, for the glory of God - and Spain. When Columbus and the conquistadores arrived in the new world, glory, gold, and gospel became obnoxiously intertwined.[4] At the time of Columbus' arrival the indigenous cultures did not have iron nor need any use of the wheel, nor had they seen soldiers on horseback with guns. The great potential of this New World, upon looking back, has been "*muy bien explotada, aunque muy mal desarrollada*" (very well exploited, but very badly developed).[5] The church arrived in conjunction with the *conquistadores*.

The conquest of the indigenous peoples began against the Aztecs in Mexico, Hernando Cortés conquering the capital city Tenochtitlán in 1521. In the following years the conquest continued on down through the Maya territory of Central America. By 1531 Francisco Pizarro sailed to Peru and during three years his army marched some 4800 kilometres through the Andes mountains, conquering the Inca empire, and founding Lima in 1535. Whole populations of the indigenous peoples who were not killed in the wars of conquest were to die of diseases that arrived with the European settlers, and through the enforced labour in the fields and the mines. The Aztec, the Maya, and the Inca were pushed back into marginalization in the mountains and jungles. The *conquistadores* divided up the best land in a quasifeudal *encomienda* (large land holdings) system that required serf labour and tributes from the indigenous population in exchange for conversion to the Christian faith and a system of *patronato*[6] offering certain protections, arranged and legitimized by King and Church, in a kind of corporatist ontology and hierarchy of God, Saints, Pope, King, *Gobernadores*, Landowners, Criollos,[7] Mestizos,[8] and Indigenous serfs. Without an inside feeling for this heritage, much of traditional Latin America is not understandable.[9] The system of conquest, of *encomienda* and

---

[3]cf.Dunn & Kelley, *op.cit.*

[4]John A.Crow, *The Epic of Latin America* (Berkeley: University of California Press, 1980), p.70. Eduardo Galeano, *Las Venas Abiertas de América Latina* (Mexico: Siglo Veintiuno Editores, 1971), p.17f. *Concilium* 1990, nr.6: "1492-1992: The Voice of the Victims".

[5]Jacques Lambert, *América Latina: Estructuras sociales e instituciones políticas* (Mexico: Editorial Ariel, 1978), p.34. Cf.Giulio Girardi, *La Conquista de América: con qué derecho?* (San José: DEI, 1988).

[6]In the original *Patronato* system the Spanish king and the *Consejo de Indias* (Council for the Indies) had full authority in colonial matters, including religious as well as economic, administrative and political affairs. Cf.Enrique D.Dussel, *Historia de la Iglesia en América Latina: Coloniaje y Liberación 1492/1983* (Madrid: Mundo Negro-Esquila Misional, 1983), p.80ff: "El sistema de Patronato como institución de la cristiandad."

[7]*Criollos* were those of Spanish ancestry born in Latin America.

[8]*Mestizos* formed the new race created by the intermingling of the Latin American Indian and European.

[9]cf.Frank Tannenbaum, *Ten Keys to Latin America* (New York: Vintage, 1962). Also, Eugene

hacienda has been analyzed as a strong root of inertia in Latin America. The conquest and Christianization, or the conquering of territories and souls, went together, and so the church was often to be associated and implicated with authoritarian rule for some four hundred years. The church, as a situated element and even as prophetic voice in Latin America, must be understood in its social setting in order to grasp its older and newer social role.

2. Colonial Christianity as the expression of a cultural era

Colonial Christianity, which was an expression of a cultural era, can be understood in philosophical terms as characterized by 'ontological' rather than 'functional' attitudes. C.A. van Peursen, who distinguishes between 'magical', 'ontological' and 'functional' stages of culture, attributes the following kinds of characteristics to the 'ontological' approach:[10]

i)   While reason begins to triumph over ritual magic, it remains deductively abstract rather than empirical.

ii) A hierarchical teaching on being (ontology) draws clear distinctions in an attempt to fit the smaller pieces into a larger pattern (cf.ch.1:IV.1: "corporative society").

iii) Substantialism, as a way of interpreting things, leads to an isolated understanding of theology (abstract system) and church (institute of objective grace) and has a rigidifying influence on social teaching.[11]

iv) In the cultural pattern resulting from the 'ontological approach', a person's position is more important than functional effectiveness.

We would suggest that an understanding of this kind of 'ontological' approach, especially as it was combined with what has been called Latin American 'paternalism',[12] helps explain various characteristics of Latin American political ethics and the penchant for feudal (señorial) values, as also the often referred to abstract idealism (in contrast, for example, to North American pragmatism). The 'ontological' approach was an all too useful thought pattern when it came to avoiding a close scrutiny of what is now recognized to be a system of social immobility and of great contrasts between those who gain from the system and those who are marginalized.[13] It is now said that there is a crisis of rationality, also for the theologian, in the sense that the "acid test" of any thought pattern is whether it transforms history or merely abides by "the application of abstract truths and idealist interpretations".[14]

A.Nida, *Understanding Latin Americans: With special reference to Religious values and movements* (Pasadena, California: William Carey Library, 1981).

[10]cf.C.A.van Peursen, *Cultuur in Stroomversnelling* (Amsterdam: Elsevier, 1975), ch.III: "Het Ontologische Denken".

[11]cf.the quotation of Roger E.Vekemans, Chapter Four, note 104, on the *espiritualidad eticoreligiosa latinoamericana*.

[12]cf.Chapter Three, note 57.

[13]Eduardo Frei, *América Latina: Opción y Esperanza* (Barcelona: Pomaire, 1977), p.148: "No hubo, pues, en América Latina verdadera movilidad sino rigideces y contrastes sociales."

[14]Gustavo Gutiérrez, "Praxis de Liberación y Fe Cristiana", in *La Fuerza Histórica de los*

3. Bartolomé de Las Casas

There were exceptional voices raised. Such was the case with Bartolomé de Las Casas (1474-1566).[15] Born in Seville, Spain, he arrived on the island of Hispaniola in 1502. Later, as bishop and historian he came to struggle all his life in order to change the inhumane treatment of the Indians, writing treaties on such topics as *The Indians Are Free Men and Must Be Treated As Such*, and on *The Only Method of Attracting All People to the True Faith*. This method was to be non-exploitive. Las Casas "pointed out that the Spaniards were placing their own salvation in jeopardy by their behaviour toward the Indians."[16] In 1546, at the first synod of bishops in Latin America, a *Declaration of the Rights of the Indians* was approved at the instigation of Las Casas. All this was, however, too little come too late. Present day Liberation Theology has gone back to Las Casas for reflection on a theology of oppression and liberation.[17] The old colonial system was that of the "Royal Patronage of the Indies", whereby Madrid even more than Rome dominated the church in Latin America. There was little room for theological reflection about any new role for the church in the New World. The unquestioned unity between throne and altar led the church to resist political and social change. In other words, the church was caught in a kind of sociological captivity, whereby reform - let alone liberation - was often almost unimaginable. However, this does not mean that no good word may be said about the role of the missions. These have been described as showing economic and developmental stewardship, with concern for the education of the indigenous people, as well as attempting to protect the Amerindian from slavery.[18] But the forthright protest of Bartolomé de Las Casas and others was often but a voice in the wilderness where an expansionist and racist ethic so easily justified serf labour to the mind of many colonists.

4. Colonial-mercantilist underdevelopment

While England and her colonies in North America went on to a liberal-capitalist revolution, which was for a great part based on the values of work by the colonists in homesteading their own land (not, however, to forget the slavery in the southern U.S.A.) and technical improvement, Spain remained behind with her system of "fictitious economics" of mercantilism based on gold and silver drawn from the colonies rather than on industrialization and rationalization of the economic process which was more characteristic of the northern approach. This short-cut to riches in the long run hurt both Spain and her colonies.[19] Latin America, so rich in resources, did not reach her potential.[20] Along with this we may mention the *cor-*

Pobres (Salamanca: Sígueme, 1982), *La crisis de racionalidad*, p.76ff.

[15]cf.Juan Friede & Benjamin Keen, *Bartolomé de Las Casas in History: Toward an Understanding of the Man and His Work* (Northern Illinois University Press, 1971).

[16]Gutiérrez, "Teología desde el reverso de la historia", *op.cit.*, p.250ff.

[17]cf.Gustavo Gutiérrez, *Freedom and Salvation: A political problem*, ch.III.A: "Gospel Preaching and the Indian", in Gutiérrez and Shaull, *Liberation and Change* (Atlanta: John Knox Press, 1977).

[18]Crow, *The Epic*, ch.15: "Flowering of the Missions".

[19]Dussel, *op. cit.*, p.136ff.

[20]Crow, *op.cit.*, p.163 and 348 where he speaks of the 'absurd policy' of much of colonial

poratist arrangement of society, by which we understand a society which seeks to avoid the class struggle by giving every part of the body (*corpus*) its place under an authoritarian and statist politics dominated by elites. It is thus predemocratic and pejorative toward popular (emancipatory) movements.

5. Wars of Independence

As things changed in Europe, from the Protestant Reformation (1517) on to the Peace of Westphalia (1648) and to the French Revolution (1779), ideas and movements reached across to Latin America. However, the difference between drawing up "perfect legalisms" on paper and the actual facts of malpractice is said to typify Latin America both before but just as assuredly after the independence from direct Iberian control.[21] The colonial patronage system in Latin America led its own life. However, in the first decades of the 1800s revolutionary independence movements agitated for changes, influenced by the American (1775) and French Revolution, and new opportunities when Napoleon drove Ferdinand VII from the Spanish throne in 1808. There was discontent on the part of the *criollos* who saw the best government positions go to those born in Spain (*peninsulares*, those from the Iberian peninsula who formed the dominant social class in the new world), and much more reason for discontent on the part of the *mestizos* and indigenous who had no social or political standing. The region's resources were shipped off to Europe and no trade was allowed between the colonies themselves. The bureaucracy lacked an adequate vision of economic-social progress. The Wars of Independence swept through the continent. The Mexican Revolution began in 1810, winning independence from Spain in 1821. Central America broke with Mexico in 1823 to form five United Provinces (under Francisco Morazan), but this began collapsing in 1838, leading to divisions and problems right up until the present time. In South America, Simón Bolívar and San Martín led the independence revolutions. Brazil won freedom from Portugal without war: when the Portuguese ruler Prince Juan left his son Pedro to rule and Brazil demanded independence, Pedro declared the country an independent empire and became Pedro I of Brazil in 1822. After independence, Latin America remained very troubled for decades by inexperienced governments, dictatorships, and border disputes, which set a pattern only slowly overcome. The independence armies became the national guards[22] who kept the dictators in power while the wealthy elite (land owners and entrepreneurs in coffee, bananas, sugar cane and cattle ranches) could be very controlling, even of governments.

6. Neocolonialism

---

settlement patterns "based on the presumption then current throughout the world that gold and silver were of more value than a well-developed agrarian economy."

[21]Dussel, *op.cit.*, p.82: "La conquista tenía un sentido esencialmente misional, *en la intención de los monarcas y en las leyes y decretos emanados de la Corona o el Consejo de Indias, pero de hecho*, ese sentido misional fue muchas veces negado... América quedará marcada por este 'legalismo perfecto' *en teoría*, y la injusticia y la inadecuación a la ley en *los hechos*."

[22]cf.Abraham F.Lowenthal & J.Samuel Fitch, *eds.*, *Armies & Politics in Latin America* (New York: Holmes & Meier, 1986).

The Roman Catholic church in Latin America, bound as it was to Spain, often took a conservative role during the independence struggles and was antiliberal and antidemocratic. England, and then the United States of America, made in-roads into Latin America and a kind of neocolonialism began. New ideologies of Protestant-ism,[23] political Liberalism, financial investment, development, democracy, science and technology, began to appear. By the time of Pope Leo XIII (1879-1903) and the epoch-making encyclical *Rerum Novarum* (1891), Latin America was into a new phase in which neocolonialism became dominated by the United States of America. Already in 1823, in the much referred to *Monroe Doctrine*,[24] the U.S.A. had formulated its interests in Latin America, attempting to exclude Europe. 'America for the Americans' was soon to appear to mean 'America for the North Americans'.[25] Latin America has often suspected that the United States of America is overtly or covertly attempting to control the entire hemisphere, and it can hardly be said that there is lack of evidence. A glance back shows the annexing of Mexican territory (1846-48); Puerto Rico (1898); and Panama (1903). A permanent stationing of U.S.A. marines in Nicaragua (1912-33) (whereupon the Somoza regime was founded); Haiti (1915-34); Dominican Republic (1916-24). To this must be added a long list of marine invasions;[26] a C.I.A.-planned and execut-ed coup in Guatemala (1954);[27] the flawed Bay of Pigs attempted invasion of Cuba (1961); invasion of the Dominican Republic (1965); economic embargo against Allende in Chile (1970-73)[28] which helped lead to the Pinochet regime (1973-89); the support of the *contras* and economic policy to destabilize Nicaragua during the 1980s;[29] the 1989 invasion of Panama; and more than a decade of financial military prop-up of El Salvador. Just as important as the sending of U.S.A. troops has been the policy of training and maintaining the military of Latin America,[30] and especially the use of financial pressures, so that one would seem justified in saying that the old social role of the church[31] in blessing the military

---

[23]cf.Pablo Alberto Deiros, *Los Evangélicos y el Poder Político en América Latina* (Grand Rapids: Eerdmans, 1986). For an update, cf.Carmelo Alvarez, "Protestantism in Latin America: Coming of Age", *Latinamerica Press*, vol.23, no.43 (Nov. 21, 1991).

[24]cf.Richard McCall, "From Monroe to Reagan: An Overview of U.S.- Latin American Relations", ch.2 in Richard Newfarmer, *From Gunboats to Diplomacy: New U.S. Policies for Latin America* (Baltimore: John Hopkins Univ., 1984).

[25]Trevor Beeson & Jenny Pearce, *A Vision of Hope: The Churches and Change in Latin America* (London: Fount Paperbacks, 1984), p.15. Also, Thomas Draper, *ed.*, *Democracy and Dictatorship in Latin America* (New York: H.W.Wilson, 1981).

[26]cf."Latin America: U.S.Interventions 1800-1985", p.530ff. in *Third World Guide* (Editora Terceiro Mundo: Rio de Janeiro, 1986).

[27]Stephen Kinzer and Stephen Schlesinger, *Bitter Fruit* (New York: Double Day, 1981).

[28]Penny Lernoux, *Cry of the People: The Struggle for Human Rights in Latin America - The Catholic Church in Conflict with U.S.Policy* (New York: Penguin, 1982), p.297: "U.S. congressional investigations have established that the CIA spent $13 million to thwart Allende."

[29]For a detailed list of chronology 1979-86, Rosa María Torres & José Luis Coraggio, *Transición y Crisis en Nicaragua* (San José: DEI, 1987), p.135ff.

[30]This is especially true in Central America, cf.Raúl Vergara Menses, *et al.*, *Centroamérica: La Guerra de Baja Intensidad* (San José: DEI, 1988).

[31]For a critical review, Enrique Dussel, "La politique vaticane en Amérique Latine: essai d'in-terprétation historico-sociologique", *Social Compass*, 37(2), 1990, p.207-224.

regimes has now been taken over by the U.S.A.[32]

Meanwhile, the church has found its prophetic voice again in regard to the severe misery and repression. This has led to what has been perceived as "the Catholic Church in conflict with U.S. policy".[33] There is the evident problem, as Chomsky and Herman state it, that "U.S.-controlled aid has been positively related to investment climate and inversely related to the maintenance of a democratic order and human rights."[34] A reading of Latin American history after it entered the neocolonial era is at the same time a reading of U.S.A. foreign policy in the region.[35] While Latin American problems are by no means all born in Washington, the external influence has been great, indeed, and the controlling factors which the U.S.A. has, for good or bad, exerted in Latin America are part of the hemispheric pattern of the Americas. This has led to awakening and concern among the U.S.A. churches for the "ideological struggle for Latin America".[36] While earlier colonial projects aimed "to milk the continent of its mineral wealth"[37], the neocolonial arrangement was facilitated by Latin America's introduction into the world economy as a supplier of raw materials and an importer of manufactured goods. At the same time large sectors of the population live on the margin of the money economy while the "export-oriented enclosures" assure themselves of the use of the best land and other resources. An industrial base came late and is in much of the region still behind the need of the hour. Meanwhile the masses have become aware of the possibility of change and the demands are time and again more urgent. Neocolonialism thus refers to economic trade arrangements whereby Latin America is perceived as caught in a web[38] of external debts, inflation, production of food for export, and a myth about *desarrollismo* (developmentalism), or development which is seemingly always off-set by other factors, including population growth. It must be kept in mind that those who use the term 'developmentalism' refer to what they see as the misled notion that the necessary economic take-off will come through *foreign* investment and integration into the world economy along the *present* patterns.

It comes, after this short sketch, as no surprise that the situation in Latin America goes by many epithets, such as "revolutionary situation" or "circle of violence and repression", which point to the great longing for change amid many hindering factors. Church, theology, and a Christian approach to political ethics, it is now more starkly apparent than in the days of unquestioned "Christendom", are called to be more than legitimizations of their social-economic-political context.

---

[32]Third World Guide, p.489ff.: "Intelligence and Intervention: CIA in the Third World".

[33]Penny Lernoux, *op.cit.*

[34]Noam Chomsky and Edward S.Herman, *The Washington Connection and Third World Fascism* (Montreal: Black Rose, 1979), p.44.

[35]For an overview, cf.Jan van der Putten, *Latijns-Amerika, politiek: Ontwikkelingen en gebeurtenissen in 25 landen* (Amsterdam: Van Gennep, 1981).

[36]Ana Maria Ezcurra, *The Neoconservative Offensive: U.S. Churches and the Ideological Struggle for Latin America* (New York: Circus Publications, 1983).

[37]Beeson and Pearce, *A Vision of Hope*, p.14.

[38]For an overview, cf.*Third World Guide* (Rio de Janeiro: Terceiro Mundo, 1986). Also: *Concilium*: "Christelijke ethiek en economie: het Noord-Zuid conflict", 1980.

We shall now begin an unfolding of ethical theory which has been promoted in Latin America, beginning first with the social teaching of the Vatican, and later moving on to the Christian Democrats and Liberation Theology.

II. FROM *RERUM NOVARUM* TO VATICAN II[39]

1. Changing orientation

The foregoing review of Latin American social-political history certainly indicates a problematic but also changing situation. We shall now review the social teaching of the Roman Catholic church, illustrating something of its influence from the Vatican reaching out to Latin America, and also after Medellín (1968) how Latin American political ethics - by setting the agenda - reaches back to the Vatican. The general movement has clearly been away from the theocratic idea (understood as church and state in unity) to Christian organizational action (the 'new Christianity' idea of Christian political and union movements) and then on to the prophetic model (whereby the role of the church and of Christians is seen as an 'option for the poor').[40] The pattern of Roman Catholic social teaching (now often called social thought) over the past one hundred years reflects a revision of attitudes according to new awareness, such as the on-going pluralization of society, the globalization of economics and politics, and the continued contrasts between extreme poverty and increasing riches. If the traditional groundmotives and thought patterns[41] of Roman Catholic philosophy and theology are correctly typified by such

---

[39]An overview of important social encyclicals and other documents is as follows:

    1891 - Rerum Novarum (Leo XIII)
    1931 - Quadragesimo Anno (Pius XI)
    1961 - Mater et Magistra (John XXIII)
    1963 - Pacem in Terris (John XXIII)
    1964 - Ecclesiam Suam (Paul VI)
    1965 - Gaudium et Spes (Vatican II)
    1965 - Dignitatis Humanae (Vatican II)
    1967 - Populorum Progressio (Paul VI)
    1968 - Documents of Medellin (CELAM II)
    1971 - Octogesima Adveniens (Paul VI)
    1975 - Evangelii Nuntiandi (Paul VI)
    1979 - Discourses of John Paul II in Mexico.
    1979 - Documents of Puebla (CELAM III)
    1980 - Dives in Misericordia (John Paul II)
    1981 - Laborem Exercens (John Paul II)
    1987 - Sollicitudo Rei Socialis (John Paul II)
    1991 - Centesimus Annus (John Paul II)

[40]cf.Daniel H.Levine, "From Church and State to Religion and Politics and Back Again", *Social Compass: Journal of the International Federation of Institutes for Social and Socio-Religious Research*, vol.37(3), 1990.

[41]Herman Dooyeweerd, *Roots of Western Culture: Pagan, Secular, and Christian Options* (Toronto: Wedge, 1979), ch.5. Alfredo Fierro, *El Evangelio Beligerante* (Estella: Verbo Divino, 1974), ch.2: "La renuncia a la cristiandad." Roger E.Vekemans, "Desarrollo económico", in William V.D'Antonio and Fredrick B.Pike, *Religión, Revolución y Reforma* (Barcelona: Herder, 1967), ch.viii. Peter De Vos, *et al.*, *Earthkeeping: Christian Stewardship of Natural Resources* (Grand Rapids: Eerdmans, 1980), ch.7: "The Medieval View of Nature". Compare James M.Gustafson, *Protestant and Roman Catholic Ethics: Prospects for Rapprochement* (Chicago: University of Chicago Press, 1978).

factors as a dualism between nature and grace, the vision of a corporative (organic) society, a natural ethic ideal, a hierarchical church and social structure, there are amid what has often been seen as all-too conservative attitudes also strands of thought that work out more progressively, such as the emphasis on integral humanism, on the democratization process, and during the last decades on development, solidarity and liberation. As in all expressions of faith and social attitudes, concepts may be interpreted and applied in either a progressive or a retrogressive fashion, as, for example, is the case with the traditional idea of natural law, given the ambiguity of the term "natural".[42] Obviously, that is also true of concepts such as development and liberation, as well. As we trace the history of the Social Encyclicals something of the struggle to renew reflection on socio-political ethics shall become apparent. Rather than offer models whereby societal arrangements are conceived as if they are part of a natural order that can be argued deductively, the demand now is for inductive analysis and (self)critical dialogue.[43]

2. Leo XIII: *Rerum Novarum* (1891)

A hundred years ago Pope Leo XIII (1878-1903) more or less opened up Roman Catholic social teaching with his encyclical *Rerum Novarum* in which he criticized both capitalistic exploitation of workers as well as the dangers of socialism and the class-struggle theory. This dissatisfaction with both movements has remained characteristic of expressions of the church's social teaching and has also been a strong factor in the Christian Democratic movement. *Rerum Novarum* tries to protect the social and economic rights of the workers and the poor while at the same time saying that government must not overstep its role by dominating other areas. Government is seen as a facilitator more than as a manager, according to this view. While *Rerum Novarum* by no means places the church on the side of the poor against the rich, it does take a step toward placing the church on the side of the working class against exploitation.[44] Even when criticizing both capitalist and socialist excesses, Pope Leo XIII insists on the duty of the state to protect the poor.[45] While the ideal for the state in this encyclical seems one of little intervention, the practice called for is more social minded than mere *laissez faire*. The model is, as might be expected, not one of conflict but of cooperation. One of the solutions proposed for class conflict is the increase in property ownership by the working class, along with the role of trade unions.[46] It has been remarked that Leo's view includes a prophetic task for the church to speak out on justice, but the strategy envisioned for change is basically from the top down, rather than - as more recently - emphasizing change at the base (grassroots) level.[47] The general

---

[42]Ricardo Antoncich, *Christians in the Face of Injustice*, p.53ff.

[43]cf.G.Manenschijn, "Het Christelijke Sociale Denken en de Feitelijke Belangenbehartiging", in J.M.M.De Valk, *Vernieuwing van het Christelijk Sociaal Denken* (Baarn: Ambo, 1989).

[44]Donald Dorr, *Option For the Poor: A Hundred Years of Vatican Social Teaching* (Maryknoll: Orbis, 1985), p.15.

[45]*Rerum Novarum*, par.29. We are using the numbering given by the Vatican with the reissue of RN in 1931.

[46]*Rerum Novarum*, par.33; 40.

[47]Dorr, *op.cit.*, p.18.

direction of the encyclical *Rerum Novarum* is toward justice, but in the context of stability. Especially the expectation that the powerful and privileged will relinquish their disproportionate gains and advantages under moral pressure has been perceived as unrealistic.[48] However, "the insistence on a *just wage* made justice, and not simply charity, a focus of Church concern. Above all the encyclical brought to serious attention the condition of the working class and the weight of the Church's influence in its defense."[49] In response to those socialists who wanted to do away with private property, Leo's answer is: everyone has a right to private property. Thus the principle of private property is relativized by the principle that the needs of all must be met. It is not uncommon to find critique which sees *Rerum Novarum* as too much on the side of property and too accepting of a passiveness on the part of workers.[50] Later encyclicals would become more nuanced in regard to both socialism and private property.[51] At the time that Leo wrote, the church was rather fearful about new ideas on freedom and equality for the untutored multitude; liberalism was seen as a source of individualism and atheism.[52] There was insufficient distinction between the state and society, for the state was seen as organic and hierarchically ordered. The challenge is to assess the strengths and weaknesses of such social teaching in a renewing way for our time without falling into new lacunae.

3. Pius XI: *Quadragesimo Anno* (1931)

Pope Pius XI (1922-39) worked further in the line of *Rerum Novarum* with the publication forty years later of *Quadragesimo Anno*. He reminds us that private ownership should always have a *social* function. In fact, the usual title in English for this encyclical is 'The Social Order'. One finds here a search for some kind of middle way or alternative to economic liberalism and socialism. There is an attempt to envision new structures for society not via classes but rather through vocational groups.[53] While this corporatist line of thought has been found wanting, the contribution in this encyclical remains the wrestling with questions of justice, the common good, and the questioning of dominant ideologies, capitalist and socialist. The corporative society approach was actually intended to be progressive: the idea was to give workers more voice, job security and a share in the ownership.[54] But in practice it had the ambiguity of playing into the hands of conservative forces;

---

[48]*Ibid.*, p.50.

[49]Arthur F.McGovern, *Marxism: An American Christian Perspective* (Maryknoll: Orbis, 1981), p.99. cf.Paul Christophe, *La Historia de la Pobreza* (Estella: Verbo Divino, 1989), ch.16.

[50]cf.Lee Cormie, "Charting the Agenda of the Church: Vatican Social Teaching in a Changing Capitalist World System", *Social Compass* 37(2), 1990, p.225ff.

[51]cf.Edward L.Cleary, *Crisis and Change: The Church in Latin America Today* (Maryknoll: Orbis, 1985), p.55ff. Also, Kouwenhoven, *De Dynamiek van het Christelijk Sociaal Denken* (Nijkerk: Callenbach, 1989) p.67f.

[52]cf.Charles E.Curran, *Directions in Catholic Social Ethics* (Indiana: University of Notre Dame, 1985), p.7ff.

[53]*Quadragesimo Anno*, par.82.

[54]McGovern, *op. cit.*, p.104.

this was especially so with the Fascist build-up taking place.[55] While Leo XIII seems to have emphasized "reforms of conduct", Pius XI was looking for some kind of "structural as well as moral changes".[56] The answer envisioned was not the nationalization of ownership but the combined cooperation between capital and labour; the results of this cooperation do not belong wholly to either. It is clearly said that "the proper ordering of economic life cannot be left to free competition".[57] The subsidiarity principle, which holds that intermediary organizations must be given freedom and responsibility in their own areas of endeavour, within the wider framework of the common good, helps keep the social teaching alert towards the problem of totalizing systems. However, both those who favour the dynamic productive forces of capitalism and those who favour a stronger socialist turn toward the poor, find the approach too half-way. Though improvements had come since Leo XIII, Pius XI noted the concentration of wealth in the hands of few, as well as a concentration of power, widespread unemployment and poverty. At this stage in Vatican social thought there is still a propensity to think in terms of natural law, and to argue deductively from general principles, such as the right to private property and an organic society idea. But it should also be noted that such principles are balanced by other principles, such as the common good and the social use of property.

4. John XXIII and Vatican II (1962-65)

Pope John XXIII (1958-63) published *Mater et Magistra* in 1961. We see in the thought of Pope John a new optimism about the modern world and development. There had been rapid economic growth in the capitalist countries and the welfare state seemed to hold out a promise for other parts of the world. In this encyclical attention is brought to an already established principle, "that the right of every man to use [material goods] for his own sustenance is prior to all other rights in economic life, and hence is prior even to the right of private ownership".[58] Also spoken of is "a strict demand of social justice, which explicitly requires that, with the growth of the economy, there occur corresponding social development" and "distribution".[59] The idea of subsidiarity is emphasized more than once in the encyclical.[60] The use of the word 'socialization' in the Italian edition led to considerable debate, though the intention was, quite clearly, to take note of the increasing social interdependence and need for government responsibility.[61] Increased attention to developing countries was a step forward in *Mater et Magist-*

---

[55]cf.Ronald G.Musto, *The Catholic Peace Tradition* (Maryknoll: Orbis, 1986), ch.12.

[56]Dorr, *One Hundred Years of Vatican Social Teaching*, p.63.

[57]*Quadragesimo Anno*, par.89.

[58]*Mater et Magistra*, par.43. Our quotations are from the translation in Joseph Gremillion, *The Gospel of Peace and Justice: Catholic Social Teaching since Pope John* (Maryknoll: Orbis, 1976).

[59]*Ibid.*, par.73.

[60]*Ibid.*, par.53, 117, 152.

[61]*Ibid.*, par.59: the word 'socialization' was used in the Italian and early English translation, where the Latin text spoke of an increase in social relationships: 'socialium rationum incrementa'. Later texts followed the Latin.

ra, whereby it was said: "Economically developed countries should take particular care, lest in giving aid to poorer countries, they endeavor to turn the prevailing political situation to their own advantage, and seek to dominate them...this clearly would be but another form of colonialism...."[62]

Indeed, John XXIII was well known for a new open-mindedness and more optimistic approach. But in that last characteristic there could be a problem: will (rapid) economic growth conquer the roots of unequal distribution? The "trickle down" idea, which prefers to speak of growth rather than distribution, has come under increasing critique since the time of John XXIII, especially in the debates on the limits to economic growth. The cheap resources from the Third World are no longer so easily assumed to be fair, nor can we automatically justify the large use of resources by a small part of the world population. While Pope John XXIII brought the Roman Catholic church into better contact with modern society, this was at the same time to mean more acceptance of the Western model of economic growth, a general attitude of enlightenment, and not so much a coming down radically on the side of the poor as rather on the side of 'progress'. But 'progress' must also be questioned. It has been noted that there is sufficient shifting since *Mater et Magistra* to raise the question as to whether Christian social thought might be more congenial to the "left" rather than the "right". The alliance between Catholicism and socially conservative forces was beginning to change. This "opening to the left" in the Christian social view was to bring dramatic changes in the church and Christian action in Latin America in the next decades.[63]

In *Pacem in Terris* (1963) we find a listing of various human rights and words addressed to government responsibility, as well as to international relationships. There is an attempt to describe what is understood by the *common good* with steps toward giving *priority to the needy*. Since these concepts are important to our study, let us listen to the exact wording of the encyclical:

"The very nature of the common good requires that all members of the political community be entitled to share in it...every civil authority must take pains to promote the common good of all without preference for any single citizen or civic group. ...Considerations of justice and equity, however, can at times demand that those involved in civil government give more attention to the less fortunate members of the community, since they are less able to defend their rights and to assert their legitimate claims."[64]

It would soon be a small step from speaking of "more attention to the less fortunate" to the newer phrase "a preferential option for the poor". There is likewise considerable emphasis on the "formation of a world community, a community in which each member, while conscious of its own individual rights and duties, will

---

[62]*Ibid.*, par.171f.

[63]Dorr, *op.cit.*, p.111ff: "...right-wing authorities in Latin America seek in the Catholic faith an ideological support for their attitudes. They resist land reform and a more equal division of wealth, in the name of the sacrosanctness of private property. ...The 'option for the poor' which the church is making in many parts of Latin America could never have taken place unless the church had ceased to be an ally of the rich and powerful."

[64]*Pacem in Terris*, par.56.

work in a relationship of equality toward the attainment of the universal common good."[65] It is frankly said that "the present system of organization and the way its principle of authority operates on a world basis no longer corresponds to the objective requirements of the universal common good".[66]

John XXIII also initiated Vatican II, one of whose texts was the Pastoral Constitution, *Gaudium et Spes* (1965), which with "joy and hope" approaches the Christian contribution to today's world. Vatican II's opening of the windows turned the old view of grace "inside out": rather than "outside the church there is no salvation", the theme becomes oriented to "God's grace everywhere saving humankind".[67] The church was defined as the "Pilgrim People of God" at Vatican II, which led to a dislinking of the church with static, hierarchical authority and the status quo, so that new paradigms were potentially suggested along lines of solidarity and prophetic witness - routes which theologians and other church leaders in Latin America were quick to follow.[68] While there was a new openness at Vatican II to a positive approach to culture, to progress and economic-social development[69], in Latin America the suspicion was coming to light that this "human progress" affirmed at Vatican II was not so evident amid the utter poverty in Latin America. In fact, a new line of thought was emerging: that poverty and misery were not changing at all in Latin America through "development" models, and that "poverty was not so much the effect of 'backwardness' as of exploitation and dependence".[70]

Gaudium et Spes, the most influential document of the council, shows a new methodology. Rather than beginning with the Bible and theological or philosophical general truths and then deducing applications, the document describes the church in the world, making use of the social sciences and turning to theological reflection as the second step.[71] As to content, *Gaudium et Spes* notes that a certain economic mentality ignores social values, thus leading to a deteriorized situation for the poor. Economic development must help all parts of the world and combat present drastic inequalities. At the time of Vatican II, Third World problems were still viewed largely from a First World perspective; this was soon to change considerably. We read in *Gaudium et Spes* of growing interdependence of the whole world and all groups toward each other.[72] Indeed, "profound and rapid changes make it particularly urgent that no one, ignoring the trend of events or drugged by laziness,

---

[65]*Ibid.*, par.125.

[66]*Ibid.*, par.135.

[67]Concilio Vaticano II: documentos completos (México: Libería Parroquial, 1986).

[68]Daniel H.Levine, *Religion and Politics in Latin America: the Catholic Church in Venezuela and Colombia* (Princeton: Univ.Press, 1981), p.35f.

[69]Vatican II documentos, p.135ff.

[70]Philip Berryman, *The Religious Roots of Rebellion: Christians in the Central American Revolutions* (London: SCM, 1984), p.27.

[71]Curran, *op.cit.*, p.14ff notes: "In earlier documents there was a great insistence on the moral law as the antidote to any tendency to license. Now the emphasis is on conscience.... The historically conscious approach emphasizes the particular, the individual, the contingent, and the historical, and often employs a more inductive methodology. ...The earlier teachings were deductive, stressing immutable eternal principles of natural law."

[72]*Gaudium et Spes*, par.26.

content himself with a merely individualistic morality".[73] It is recognized that the church "in virtue of her mission and nature, is bound to no particular form of human culture, nor to any political, economic, or social system."[74]

As for socio-economic factors, it is noted that "many people, especially in economically advanced areas, seem to be hypnotized, as it were, by economics, so that almost their entire personal and social life is permeated with a certain economic outlook."[75] In our world, where "luxury and misery rub shoulders...technical progress must be fostered, along with a spirit of initiative....[so that] at every level the largest possible number of people have an active share in directing that development".[76] Without pretending to enter into the exact methods necessary, a pointed appeal is made toward helping and finding new structures to alleviate poverty. Thus we hear:

> "...the right to have a share of earthly goods sufficient for oneself and one's family belongs to everyone. ...remember the saying of the Fathers: 'Feed the man dying of hunger, because if you have not fed him you have killed him.' According to their ability, let all individuals and governments undertake a genuine sharing of their goods. Let them use these goods especially to provide individuals and nations with the means for helping and developing themselves."[77]

However one turns the question, it comes back to steps toward more economic equalization and a spreading of political power. A remark is made in *Gaudium et Spes* about landtenure reform in the underdeveloped nations: "In many underdeveloped areas there are large or even gigantic rural estates which are only moderately cultivated or lie completely idle.... At the same time the majority of the people are either without land or have only very small holdings...."[78] To the extent that this Vatican II document attempts to show the social obligation of private property, to that extent it also sounds 'subversive' to the minds of the landholding elite in Latin America, who defend the right to exorbitant private domination of most of the land by only a small percentage of the population (and by foreign domination).

In *Gaudium et Spes* there is emphasis on justice, which is seen to include the responsibility of a better sharing of the earth's resources, changes in international trade patterns, and the realization of a just economic order. While there is much that is praise worthy in this encyclical, it does not question the possibility of gradual development (for all areas of the world) but rather assumes this. The difficult question of distribution was thus more easily subsumed under a kind of faith in progress.[79]

---

[73]*Ibid.*, par.30.
[74]*Ibid.*, par.42.
[75]*Ibid.*, par.63.
[76]*Ibid.*, par.64.
[77]*Ibid.*, par.69.
[78]*Ibid.*, par.71.
[79]Dorr, *A Hundred Years*, p.93f.

III. CHRISTIAN DEMOCRACY: SKETCHING AN ORIENTATION

1. Introduction

Having reviewed Vatican social teaching up until Vatican II we shall now say something about Christian Democracy, which at that point had begun to flourish as a possible renewing element of political ethics. Starting in the 1930s, Catholic Action, or the encouragement of Catholic organizations in areas such as labour and student associations, laid the first steps toward a changing social consciousness among Roman Catholics in Latin America. Christian Democracy in Latin America relied upon European roots,[80] and was especially animated by drawing on the social teachings of the Papal Encyclicals and writings of the neothomist philosopher Jacques Maritain,[81] who had the long-lasting effect of contributing to the opening--up of the Roman Catholic ethos toward democracy. Maritain's approach advocated a pluralist society, and called for socio-economic-political reform. The framework he looked for was communitarian, or an attempt to avoid the individualism of the liberal *laissez-faire* attitude, as well as the collectivism of (Marxist-Leninist) communism. Maritain, it has been summed up, "felt capitalism was decadent, but he rejected Marxism as a pseudo-religion."[82] He was particularly concerned about a Christian idea of humanization which would detotalize philosophical and political absolutizations. His pluralist society vision desired to be founded on 'personalist' values, or the dignity of every person. Maritain is not to be identified with the Christian Democratic party movement as such,[83] but his terminology and critique toward the left and the right was widely spread throughout the Latin American Christian Democratic movement. Like the Social Encyclicals, the Christian Democratic movement has preferred to speak of "socialization",[84] rather than socialism. Let us now review some of the features of Christian Democratic political ethics.

2. Characteristic elements of Christian Democracy in Latin America:[85]

---

[80]For background studies, cf.Michael P.Fogarty, *Christian Democracy in Western Europe 1820-1953* (London: Routledge & Kegan Paul, 1957). R.E.M.Irving, *The Christian Democratic Parties of Western Europe* (Edinburgh: George Allen & Unwin, 1978).

[81]Maritain's most influential work is *Humanisme Intégral: Problèmes Temporales et Spirituels d'une Nouvelle Chrétienté* (1936), a series of lectures given at the University of Santander in 1934: "Problemas espirituales y temporales de una nueva cristiandad".

[82]McGovern, *Marxism*, p.106.

[83]Gregorio Peces-Barba Martínez, *Persona, Sociedad, Estado: Pensamiento Social y Político de Maritain* (Madrid: Edicusa, 1972), p.197ff.

[84]cf.Bestard Comas, *op.cit.*, p. 107: "El proceso de socialización." The concept 'socialization' has three meanings: 1) the economic-political meaning tends to be the nationalization or government control, as in the 'socialization' of medicine or the 'socialization' of the electrical industry; 2) the sociological meaning refers to progressive diversification of social relationships; 3) the psychopedagogical idea of 'socialization' means the integration of the person with others and with institutions in his environment. The use of the term in the encyclicals and in Christian Democratic writings is often to point out the need for social responsibility, especially the social-ethical aspect of economics, while avoiding the appearance of a socialism which it is feared errs on the side of collectivism and party dominance.

[85]cf.Rafael Caldera, *Especificidad de la Democracia Cristiana* (San José: Libro Libre, 1986). Pablo A.Deiros, "Ideologías y Movimientos Políticos en América Latina", p.275ff in Deiros,

i) *Christian*: the word 'Christian' in this movement refers to the attempt to draw social-economic-political values out of the Christian faith and tradition. As in Europe, Christian Democracy in Latin America began as a more denominational ('confessional') movement (Catholic Action) and widened into a more ecumenical and consciously non-ecclesiastical organization. 'Christian' mainly means that Christian Democrats in Latin America seek philosophical roots in a Christian humanism, that is, a Christian philosophical-ethical position which often goes by the name of integral humanism, as we shall see in the next chapter.

ii) *Democracy*: the second word in the movement's name refers not merely to electoral democracy, but also to social-economic ideals of more equality and to a *plural society*, in the sense of an alternative to individualist and collectivist social philosophies. This ties somewhat into the principle of *subsidiarity*, which Pius XI defines by saying:

"It is an injustice, a grave evil, and a disturbance of right order for a larger and higher organization to arrogate to itself functions which can be performed efficiently by smaller and lower bodies....Of its very nature the true aim of all social activity should be to help individual members of the social body, but never to destroy them."[86]

This means the promotion of "intermediary" organizations. A goal of the Christian Democrats in Latin America becomes the balancing out of the power of government, the armed forces, the multinationals and all such megapotencies, by means of intermediary organizations such as political parties, labour unions, and popular organization from the grassroots base. Democracy is linked to a *participatory society* by which is meant that there must be more spreading of power and opportunity among the popular sectors. Democracy is also understood to imply an ideologically plural society.[87]

iii) *El bien común* (common good): when Christian Democrats use this concept, they mean that they want to be known as 'social Christians' who wish to change the economic dualism of rich and poor, the situation of underdevelopment, and the abuse of human rights in Latin America. The Christian Democrats are usually classed as a middle party to the right of the Social Democrats.[88] The primacy of *el bien común* is also expressed with the concept 'solidarity'.[89] The intention is to help the marginalized sectors of the population, emphasizing the values of co-determination and cooperation. The state is seen as the guardian of the common good. Elements of this common good

---

op.cit. Walter Montenegro, *Introducción a las Doctrinas Político Económicas* (México: Fondo de Cultura Económica, 1986).

[86] *Quadragesimo Anno*, 1931, par.37.

[87] cf.Caldera, *Especificidad*, ch.II.

[88] Montenegro, *Doctrinas Político Económicas*.

[89] "Programa Basico de Gobierno: Partido Demócrata Cristiano de Honduras - período 1990-1994", *El Tiempo*, Tegucigalpa, Sept.9, 1989.

include:

a) the human person should have precedence over material interests;

b) work has high dignity and should be adequately remunerated;

c) property has a social function; public services need government regulation;

d) attention must especially be paid to the problem of poverty through social legislation and a process of development and integration of society;

e) regional as well as international justice are stressed.[90]

iv) *Third way*: The political philosophy of the Christian Democratic movement in Latin America has spoken of an alternative to the extremes of capitalism (which is understood to be unfair in its distribution) and socialism (which is understood to be short on individual freedom). There are continued references by critics to the Christian Democratic movement as a *tercerismo* (third-way-ism); when this term is used negatively it suggests that the movement is inept in reaching any lasting changes, just as the term *reformismo* (reformism) is used to mean ineffective reform attempts.

v) *Revolution through reform*: Social-economic-political transformation, according to Christian Democracy, is to be a "revolution in freedom", by means of a gradualist path to improvement.[91]

3. Present situation

The critique in recent years has been particularly sustained: the Christian Democratic movement is accused of cooperation with military juntas and of sliding off to the political right when choices have to be made.[92] The Christian Democrats have been criticized for their role in Chile, especially during the coup against Allende.[93] After having opened up steps toward more popular politics and land reform, they are said to have fallen prey to inherent ambivalence. They have also received much critique by the left during the years of Duarte in El Salvador[94] and under Cerezo in Guatemala.[95] The main thesis then is that they serve to mask the military regimes.[96] While they see the state as the guardian of the common good,

---

[90]Deiros, *op.cit.*, p.276-278.

[91]Writes Eduardo Frei Montalva, *The Hopeful Option* (Maryknoll: Orbis, 1978), p.178f: "The task of politics is to achieve a consensus, affirm a sense of solidarity, and try to involve all the members of the community in the quest for the common good. ...politics is a failure if it can triumph only through the use of force. It must create a consensus and a legitimacy that will make coercion and violence unnecessary."

[92]Franz J.Hinkelammert, "Socialdemocracia y Democracia Cristiana: Las Reformas y sus Limitaciones", in Hugo Assmann, *ed.*, *El Juego de los Reformismos frente a la Revolución en Centroamérica* (San José: DEI, 1981).

[93]Helio Gallardo, *Actores y Procesos Políticos Latinoamericanos* (San José: DEI, 1989), ch.2. Ronaldo Munck, *Latin America: The Transition to Democracy* (London: Zed Books, 1989), p.30.

[94]*El Salvador: Es La Democracia Cristiana Un Partido De Centro?* (CINAS - Centro de Investigación y Accion Social, Mexico, 1987).

[95]Edelberto Torres-Rivas, *Centroamérica: La Democracia Posible* (San José: EDUCA, 1987), p.174.

[96]Berryman, *The Religious Roots of Rebellion*, p.300: "The mere existence of electoral

the political practice has fallen short of the theory. The failure of the Christian Democrats has been said to be due to such factors, as:[97]

i) They look to the middle sectors in a polarized situation where there is no real centre.

ii) Their appeal to these weak middle sectors prevents them from truly acting as a popular party.

iii) While theorizing about justice, they do not in practice thoroughly challenge the results of oligarchic capitalism in Latin America.

iv) Their mobilization among the poor is mainly for partisan party politics, not for making the poor the subjects of their own history.

v) They lack a thorough analysis of contending political forces and a theory of how to effect the transformation toward the 'common good' of which they speak.

The idea of the Christian Democrats under Frei in Chile (1964-70) was that of 'revolution in freedom' (*revolución en libertad*) which was supposed to truly change injustices in the system in favour of the poor. But when the Chilean road to socialism did an about turn - Frei (1964) - Allende (1970) - Pinochet (1973) - there was open suggestion by the political left in Latin America that elected governments cannot change the social problems. More and more, church and theology were to find themselves in a revolutionary situation.[98] It became questionable if a revolution *for* freedom can also be a revolution *in* freedom.

IV. FROM VATICAN II TO CELAM II

Pope John XXIII and the Second Vatican Council, as we saw, were a turning point in the social awareness of the Roman Catholic church, the "final break with the Constantinian era"[99] and the beginning of new directions in which the social question could not longer be side-stepped.[100]

One of the signs of the radicalization of the social question was given by Camilo Torres. In the mid 1950s Torres went to the Louvain University, Belgium, to study

---

mechanisms, parties, and assemblies is regarded as positive even if they can be nullified at any moment with a coup. The task is seen as making them more functional - even minimal 'democracy' is considered preferable to none at all. Such an attitude has been characteristic of Christian Democratic parties, ever waiting in the wings as a 'third force' (between existing military/oligarchy combinations and Marxist revolutionaires), and of the United States government, ever willing to find signs of 'progress'. ...*Democratic forms are used to thwart democracy.*"

[97]Jean Carrière, CEDLA (Center for Latin American Research and Documentation), Amsterdam.

[98]cf.Jean Meyer, "Iglesia y Revolución", in Enrique Krauze, *América Latina: desventuras de la democracia* (Mexico: Editorial Planeta, 1984), p.43ff.

[99]Musto, *Catholic Peace Tradition*, p.187ff.

[100]For a schematic overview of church and political events in Latin America from the 1950s through the 1980s see Daniel H.Levine, "From Church and State to Religion and Politics and Back Again", in *Social Compass* 37 (3), 1990, p.331-351.

sociology and political science, at a time when the Christian Democratic thought was dominant. Back in Colombia, Torres became chaplain of the National University of Bogotá where he also taught sociology. He became more and more agitated by the need and the impossibility of reforming a system where the minority hold the power, and as he put it, "are incapable of working against their own interests". Increasingly in conflict with church authorities (his founding of a United Front - May 1965 - to give voice to the political left led to more conflict) Torres returned to lay status in order to devote his energy to politics. By October he had apparently joined a guerrilla front and was killed in a skirmish with the army, February 15, 1966, in the Colombian Andes. Torres represents a challenge especially because he argued his praxis of counterviolence as a "committed sociologist" and a "committed priest". Though not particularly successful in reaching his goal of transformation for the poor, in his death he became a mythic emblem for many.[101]

In 1967 Paul VI (1963-78) published *Populorum Progressio* in which he tries to understand the imbalance between rich and poor countries, noting that the social question had become worldwide. The encyclical draws attention to the problems of past colonialism, present neocolonialism, and unilateral power in trade relations. It suggests that "superfluous wealth of rich countries should be placed at the service of poor nations".[102] There is an awareness of domination by small privileged elites within poor countries as well as between countries, so that "poor nations remain ever poor while the rich ones become still richer".[103] Paul VI, more than John XXIII, goes beyond problems of attitude to problems of structure, noting injustices built into the present order of trade and domination. He calls for economic responsibility and proposes "solidarity", "dialogue" and "planning" on a global scale: "Development demands bold transformation, innovations that go deep". There are "situations whose injustice cries to heaven...whole populations destitute...." Amid such problems there is danger of revolutionary uprising which all too often "produces new injustices" - although the pope admits that in cases of "long-standing tyranny" revolution may become preferable to such a situation.[104] Though speaking forcefully, it appears that the encyclical still thinks the major agents of change to be the powerful rather than the poor themselves, and to that extent it is still "top down".[105] This was to shift considerably with the Medellín documents the following year. Meanwhile, the encyclical was drawing attention and served to keep the 'social question' urgent.[106]

V. CELAM II : MEDELLIN (1968)

---

[101]cf.François Houtart, *ed.*, *Camilo Torres, Revolutie: Christelijke Opdracht* (Utrecht: Bruna, 1969). François Houtart & André Rousseau, *The Church and Revolution* (Maryknoll: Orbis, 1971), p.188-202. Swomley, *Liberation Ethics*, p.136-43.

[102]*Populorum Progressio*, par.49.

[103]*Ibid.*, par.57.

[104]*Ibid.*, par.29-32.

[105]Dorr, p.162.

[106]Thirty-eight priests from some fourteen Latin American countries who met in Chile October-November 1967 signed a communiqué, "*Populorum Progressio* and Latin American realities" in which they encouraged leadership everywhere to listen to the encyclical. Cf.*Between Honesty and Hope*, (Maryknoll: Orbis, 1970), p.70ff.

Even though the outspoken meeting of CELAM (*Consejo Episcopal Latinoameri-cano: Conference of Latin American Bishops*) in Medellín surprised many, there were, on looking back, numerous factors and movements which had been gathering force in a new momentum.[107] To speak of CELAM II means we are no longer talking about the old pattern of Europe and North America explaining social issues to Latin America, but rather we must now listen to Latin America's response and contribution within the continued renewal of Roman Catholic social thought. In fact, with CELAM II we enter a new stage in the Latinamericanization of theologi-cal consciousness. It is evident that social analysis was adding a voice on the dependency idea, on the possibilities of import substitution, and on the role of the Inter-American Development Bank, the International Monetary Fund and the Transnational companies. Economic progress in Latin America was seen to primarily benefit a small local enclave plus the already developed world. So it was that Medellín, 1968, came to emphasize the theme of liberation in relation to dominance and dependence, and made a new turn toward becoming a church of the grassroots poor. Much preliminary study took place before the conference and part of the newness is in the very methodology (already exemplified in *Gaudium et Spes*) by proceeding according to 1) facts; 2) reflection; 3) recommendations.[108] It can thus be said that the Conference of Latin America Bishops in Medellín signalled a dramatic turning point for the Roman Catholic church in Latin America whereby the challenges could not go by unnoticed.[109] The significant contribution of the Medellín documents is that they sharpen the question of "social justice and an option for the poor and thereby pose a serious challenge to the whole church".[110] CELAM II was an unequivocable condemnation of the status quo situation in Latin America. There is since Medellín-1968:

i) A fuller awareness of *structural injustice* as "institutional violence".[111] While drawing attention to the institutionalized violence of the social struc-tures and referring to Paul VI's words in *Populorum Progressio*, no.31, on the legitimacy of revolutionary insurrection in the case of evident and pro-longed tyranny, the Medellín documents are also careful to state in par.19: "If we consider, then, the totality of the circumstances of our countries, and

---

[107]cf.Cleary, *Crisis and Change*, ch.1: "A New Leadership: From Inertia to Momentum", where he briefly discusses such factors as Catholic Action, the Cursillo Movement (conferences and short courses), missionary influx, the formation of CELAM, Vatican envoys, informal networks of new leadership groups, and Vatican II, as all combining in the new momentum.

[108]*Ibid.*, p.22.

[109]Thus Roberto Compton in *La Teología de la Liberación* (El Paso: Casa Bautista, 1984) says that Medellín was outspoken about:
  a) The condemnation of a colonialism that has kept Latin America underdeveloped.
  b) Opposition to liberal capitalism and its errors.
  c) Denunciation of authoritarian rule which favours the privileged and is contrary to the common good.
  d) Condemnation of international commerce with its monopolies and monetary imperialism.
  e) Condemnation of the violence in Latin America provoked by the privileged.

[110]Dorr, *op.cit.*, p.162.

[111]*Medellín Documents*, Section two: Peace, par.16. Cf.Gremillion, *The Gospel of Peace and Justice*, p.445ff.

41

if we take into account the Christian preference for peace, the enormous difficulty of a civil war, the logic of violence, the atrocities it engenders, the risk of provoking foreign intervention, illegitimate as it may be, the difficulty of building a regime of justice and freedom while participating in a process of violence, we earnestly desire that the dynamism of the awakened and organized community be put to the service of justice and peace."

ii) More attention to the *poverty of the church*.[112] A distinction is made between:

    a) *material poverty*, as a "lack of the goods of this world necessary to live worthily", and usually the result of injustice and sin;

    b) *spiritual poverty*, as "the attitude of opening up to God (*actitud de apertura a Dios)*, the ready disposition of one who hopes for everything from the Lord". While valuing the "goods of this world", we then yet recognize the "higher value of the riches of the Kingdom" of God;

    c) *poverty as a commitment (pobreza como compromiso)* by means of which one "assumes voluntarily and lovingly the conditions of the needy" as a witness to the evil of poverty, to spiritual liberation, and a way of following Christ. That the church and Christians should show solidarity with the poor is thus certain, but not reduced to one model, for there exist "diverse vocations" in relation to poverty: "All members of the Church are called to live in evangelical poverty, but not all in the same way."

iii) There is an emphasis on *concientización*. This means consciousness raising and the awakening of popular organizations seeking justice at the grassroots level, as agents of change and of their own development. This is a departure from the "top down" analysis and answers. However, it must also be noted that *concientización* refers to "all strata of society", and not just to the base: "We wish to affirm that it is indispensable to form a social conscience and a realistic perception of the problems of the community and of social structures. We must awaken the social conscience and communal customs in all strata of society... This task of *concientización* and social education ought to be integrated into joint Pastoral Action at various levels."[113]

iv) Awareness of the struggle for *liberation* is brought forward by the Medellín conference, which saw that along with development there is also anti-development. The bishops did not hide from the challenge of "tremendous social injustices existent in Latin America...dismal poverty...inhuman wretchedness" and the "deafening cry...from the throats of millions...asking their pastors for a liberation that reaches them from nowhere else".[114]

---

[112]*Ibid.*, Section four: "On the Poverty of the Church". The quotations are from Section four: II.4.a.ff.

[113]*Ibid.*, Section one: Justice, III.17.

[114]*Ibid.*, Section four, par.1 and 2.

A closer look at the economic analysis of the Medellín document shows a rejection of both "liberal capitalism" and "the Marxist system",[115] while the more detailed section on economics lists some basic problems of the present order,[116] namely: a) distortions of *international commerce* whereby countries exporting raw materials are losing economically; b) *capital-flight* and *brain-drain*; c) *Tax evasion* and *loss of gains* when foreign companies direct their profits back to the economic centres; d) *progressive debt* within the system of international credit without due attention to the true needs of the poorer nations; e) *international monopolies* and *imperialism*, whereby the "principal guilt for economic dependence of our countries rests with powers, inspired by uncontrolled desire for gain, which leads to economic dictatorship and the 'international imperialism of money'."[117] Thus the dependency theme is forthright in these documents. Yet while Liberation Theology, not without reason, makes much of Medellín, it may also be correctly said that the idea of liberation in the CELAM II document is not systematically defined. There are phrases that remind us of a combination of approaches, as when the document speaks of "integral human development and liberation". Similarly, the Medellín document does not shy away from using words like *reform.*[118] Yet it is clear that the steps in search of an adequate social ethos by the church in Latin America were passing from a status quo model to a catalyst model[119], whereby a critique of *desarrollismo* (developmentalism) and a concern for grassroots *concientización* and a prophetic critique of the dominant ideology of the oligarchies all began to mix and ferment the search for a theology of liberation amid oppression.

VI. LIBERATION THEOLOGY: SKETCHING AN ORIENTATION

1. Introduction

The revolutionary hope in Latin America, the rising waves of popular emancipation and opposition against the archaic socio-economic structures, took on a new urgency with Fidel Castro in Cuba (1959). Throughout the vast continent of Latin America new expectations were in the making. Soon the world was hearing of new ways of reaching the poor and challenging the system, whether it was Camilo Torres or Dom Hélder Câmara that caught the attention. Hélder Câmara, Brazil, was consecrated in 1952 as bishop. He became instrumental in the founding of CELAM, the Latin American Bishops' Conference. He was active in the 1950s and 1960s in a Movement for Basic Education which tried to spread literacy and training among the poor. In 1968 Dom Hélder formed an Action, Justice and Peace Movement to attempt nonviolent transformation in Brazil. He has been one of the outstanding voices for a praxis of "revolution through peace". One of his most

---

[115]*Ibid.*, Section two: Justice, par.10.

[116]*Ibid.*, Section three: Peace, par.9.

[117]This latter phrase was used by Paul VI in Populorum Progressio, par.26.

[118]For example, in Section two: Justice, par.16: "Faced with the need for a total change of Latin American structures, we believe that change has political reform as its prerequisite." Likewise, the phrase "developmental process" is used without qualms; Section two, par.22.

[119]*Ibid.*, Section two, par.22.

important contributions was the impulse for establishing *comunidades de base*, or grassroots Christian community movements which try to transform from the base, through *concientización* concerning alienation, marginalization and oppression, through vocational training, healthcare, and the like. Câmara believes in raising peoples' consciousness through creative nonviolence and showing love in the face of hatred. Yet he is clear that "Violence Number One" comes from the system. His work has been done amid threats, harassments, persecution, torture and death of some of his close associates and followers.[120]

Latin America - including the church - began to see that the choice was no longer simply between injustice and inertia, but might also be between injustice and transformation. It was also becoming clear that a theology dealing with issues of power, violence, oppression and liberation was necessary in order for the church to deal with the challenge of the social-economic realities. The church and theology were becoming consciously 'situated'. The move from a 'developmentalist' model to 'liberation' in some ways turns things up-side-down, making the poor the agents of change: "The present situation is created and sustained by the rich and the powerful. ...As they are part of the problem, they should not be expected to offer solutions. The poor who are victims of the present situation will be the ones to find the way out."[121]

2. Characteristics of Liberation Theology

It is not our intention to provide a full summary on Liberation Theology.[122] Keeping in mind our posing of the problem, the following points are useful for indicating relationships between Liberation Theology and the theme of transformation:

i)   Theology of Liberation finds that the traditional distinction between religion and politics, whereby the church, the gospel, theology, and God are considered above political identification actually leads in practice to the identification of the church, *et al.*, with the status quo.[123] An apolitical theology is still political, and therefore it seems better, say liberation theologians, to search out the true *praxis of faith*, according to an understanding of the God who liberates.[124]

---

[120]cf.Benedicto Tapia de Renedo, *Hélder Câmara: Proclamas a la Juventud* (Salamanca: Sígueme, 1976).

[121]Julio de Santa Ana, *ed.*, *Towards a church of the Poor: The Work of an Ecumenical Group* (Geneva: World Council of Churches, 1979), p.xix.

[122]cf. especially: Juan José Tamayo-Acosta, *Para Comprender la Teología de la Liberación* (Estella: Verbo Divino, 1989). Arthur F. McGovern, *Liberation Theology and its Critics* (Maryknoll: Orbis, 1989). Philip Berryman, *Liberation Theology: Essential Facts* (New York: Pantheon, 1987). Alfred T.Hennelly, *ed.*, *Liberation Theology: A Documentary History* (Maryknoll: Orbis, 1990).

[123]cf.Pablo Richard, "Iglesia, Estado Autoritario y Clases Sociales en América Latina", p.153ff in Elsa Tamez and Saúl Trinidad, *eds.*, *Capitalismo: Violencia y Anti-Vida, Tomo I* (San José: EDUCA 1978).

[124]An example of application to the pastoral situation is found in *Vamos Caminando: A Peruvian Catechism*, Pastoral Team of Bambamarca, *trans.*John Medcalf (London: SCM, 1985).

ii)   *Ideology-critique* of the church's teaching, preaching and other activities: traditional church and theological attitudes are seen as idealistic and quietist. Traditional theology started with Plato and Aristotle and ended with a spiritualistic ahistorical dualism.[125] The church often had nothing to say, or even the wrong things to say, in the face of the colonial-neocolonial and oligarchic suppression of liberty and justice.[126]

iii)   A basic starting point is the recognition of the *oppressive order* in Latin American authoritarian-military "national security" states.[127] The denunciation of this system by the church and theology is a prophetic witness that is part of liberative praxis.[128]

iv)   The revealing of oppressive structures is often aided by a referral to *neomarxist analysis*,[129] whereby Marxist sociology is said to be distinguished from Marxist ideology. The negative features of the capitalist-dependency system are exposed, whereby capitalism includes or is almost equated with imperialism toward Latin America.

v)   Liberation Theology includes the liberation of theology,[130] especially from ideological captivity to the sinful status quo in Latin America. There is a *new way of doing theology*, not just a new theme *for* theology.[131] Praxis is primary; theory is always theory-in-action. Theology is to be a critical, liberative reflection on historical praxis, becoming itself part of the struggle for a just society, "part of the process through which the world is transformed," says Gutiérrez.

vi)   Liberation Theology desires to make an *option for the poor*.[132] The church must become the voice of the voiceless.

---

[125]Gustavo Gutiérrez, *A Theology of Liberation* (Maryknoll: Orbis, 1973), p.166.

[126]Rubem Alves, *et al.*, *Religion, Instrumento de Liberación?* (Barcelona: Fontanella, 1973).

[127]José Comblin, *Doctrina de Seguridad Nacional* (San José: Nueva Década, 1988). José Antonio Viera-Gallo, "The Church and the Doctrine of National Security", p.30-42 in *The Church at the Crossroads: Christians in Latin America from Medellín to Puebla 1968-1978* (IDOC: Rome, 1978).

[128]cf. Cleary, *Crisis and Change*, ch.6: "A New Political Environment: The Church and the Military in Conflict".

[129]eg.José Miranda, *Marx and the Bible: A Critique of the Philosophy of Oppression*, trans.John Drury (Maryknoll: Orbis, 1974). Among the more adequate studies by liberation theologians on the strengths and ambiguities of ideologies, including both capitalism and Marxism, is Juan Luis Segundo's *Faith and Ideologies* (Maryknoll: Orbis, 1984). This builds on his critique of ideologies already begun in his *Liberación de la Teología* (Buenos Aires: Carlos Lohlé, 1975).

[130]Juan Luis Segundo, *op.cit.*

[131]Gutiérrez, *A Theology of Liberation*, p.15:"...theology of liberation offers us not so much a new theme for reflection as a *new way* to do theology."

[132]Gustavo Gutiérrez, *La Fuerza Histórica de los Pobres*, part II.4: "...the theology of liberation represents *the right of the poor to think*...and then insist upon that other right that an oppressive system denies them: the right to a human life."

vii) A basic feature is *concientización*, which is part of the strategy for facilitating the poor in becoming subjects of their own history. Liberation Theology wants to go the way of the poor, leaving behind the dominating centres,[133] in order to stand beside the 'nonperson', the marginalized of Latin America who are both "poor and believing".

viii) Sin includes *alienation*, which enters into social structures.

ix) It is not enough to think in terms of *development*; nothing less than *liberation* will do.

x) Liberation Theology's view of the church is *'popular'* rather than hierarchical. There is a focus on becoming a 'poor church', particularly through the *comunidades de base* movement.[134]

xi) The Bible functions through paradigms of liberation. What is needed, it is said, is a *re-lectura* (re-reading) of the Bible in the historical context of the Latin American situation of oppression.[135] This spirituality connects biblical text and social context; while that is not wholly new, the difference is that the suffering masses may now not only identify with the suffering Saviour, but also with the liberating function of the faith.[136] The rereading of the Bible and history now steer away from religion as inertia in order to understand it as prophetic critique.

xii) Ethics are situated and engaged, as mandated by an analysis of dependency, the class struggle and the *proyecto revolucionario*.[137]

3. Present situation

Just as we said a few words about the present situation of the Christian Democratic movement in Latin America, we may now do the same for Liberation Theology. It cannot be denied that during the last two decades Liberation Theology has been very influential. At the same time the resistance has been strong by those who fear ideologies of the political left (the repressions have been pronounced), as

---

[133]Gutiérrez, *op.cit.*: "Who would have thought that there could be theology outside the classic centres of theology, other than one merely parroting the theology of the dominators?"

[134]cf.Jon Sobrino, *Resurrección de la verdadera iglesia* (Santander, 1984). Leonardo Boff, *Ecclesiogenesis: The Base Communities Reinvent the Church* (Maryknoll: Orbis, 1986). Sergio Torres & John Eagleson, *eds.*, *The Challenge of Basic Christian Communities* (Maryknoll: Orbis, 1982). Casiano Floristán, *ed.*, *Comunidades de Base* (Madrid, Marova, 1971).

[135]Consider Bruce J.Malina, "The Social Sciences and Biblical Interpretation", p.11-25 and Sergio Rostagno, "The Bible: Is an Interclass Reading Legitimate? p.61-73 in Norman K.Gottwald, *ed.*, *The Bible and Liberation: Political and Social Hermeneutics* (Maryknoll: Orbis, 1984). Also, Mark Lau Branson & C.René Padilla, *Conflict and Context: Hermeneutics in the Americas* (Grand Rapids: Eerdmans, 1986).

[136]For example, Leonardo Boff, *Way of the Cross - Way of Justice* (Maryknoll: Orbis, 1982).

[137]cf.Berryman, *The Religious Roots of Rebellion*, ch. 9: "Ethics of the Revolutionary *Proyecto*". José Míguez Bonino, *Toward a Christian Political Ethics (London: SCM, 1983)*. Enrique Dussel, *Etica Comunitaria* (Madrid: Paulinas, 1986).

well as by those who fear a partisan mixing of theology and ideology (though they do not always hold the same critical eye towards status quo ideologies). It is sometimes suggested that Liberation Theology is already outdated because of the *perestroika* break-through in East Europe and the superior economic strength of market economies. Certainly Liberation Theology has had to reexamine some fundamental theses, also in its socio-economic "mediations". But those who suppose that Liberation Theology is about to disappear forget that such is unlikely: 1) as long as poverty and human rights issues are so shocking in Latin America; 2) as long as Liberation Theology seeks a popular connection to the masses; and 3) also because Liberation Theology may be quite capable of changing its social-analytical paradigms, all the while tying into new themes, for example, of a theology of life (in a situation of repression), a theology of the earth (in a situation of landless peasants), indigenous liberation, and so forth. Of course, as times and foci change, there are signs of both continuity and revision. The movement has been affected by questioning and condemnation within the ecclesial structures, but is not entirely determined by these.[138]

VII. FROM MEDELLIN (CELAM II, 1968) to PUEBLA (CELAM III, 1979)[139]

1. Paul VI: *Octogesima Adveniens* (1971)

Published on the eightieth anniversary of *Rerum Novarum*, this Apostolic Letter (of some twenty-five pages) forms yet another step in the search for Christian social thought. The document deals with 1) an analysis of world problems; 2) examines some basic ideological choices ("fundamental aspirations and currents of ideas"; 3) asks how Christians should face these problems and ideologies; and 4) calls for action. "Development" is less emphasized than in Paul VI's earlier encyclical *Populorum Progressio*. In fact, assumed progress is questioned in a search for what prevents development. Clearly stated is that progress is not just a matter of quantitative economic growth, for there is also the need for progress in moral growth, by acting on the demands for solidarity and justice. Thus we read: "Is not genuine progress to be found in the development of moral consciousness, which will lead man to exercise a wider solidarity and to open himself freely to others and to God?"[140] By this time it was acknowledged that while the Christian must be aware of the ideological dangers of both Liberalism and Marxism, these can be used as sociological tools provided that one does not fall into ideological closed-mindedness.[141] The word "liberation" appears, though reluctantly. Yet the shift is noticeable: development often focuses on economics, while liberation focuses on political action.[142] It begins to become clear that economic problems

---

[138]Peter Hebblethwaite, "The Vatican's Latin American Policy", ch.3 in Dermot Keogh, *ed.*, *Church and Politics in Latin America* (London: Macmillan, 1990).

[139]For Latin American documents of these years cf.*Los Obíspos Latinoamericanos entre Medellín y Puebla: Documentos Episcopales 1968-1978* (San Salvador: UCA, 1978).

[140]*Octogesima Adveniens*, par.41.

[141]Curran, *Catholic Social Ethics*, p.30.

[142]Dorr, *op.cit.*, p.163.

are related to political power and will need political solutions: "...in the social and economic field, both national and international, the ultimate decision rests with political power".[143] The model looked for is that of on-going economic democracy via political democracy. Yet some question the realism of this: as Dorr notes, there can be no reliance on dialogue if there is not a degree of equality between the partners.[144]

2. *Justice in the World* (Synod 1971)

This document was issued by the Synod of Bishops (Second General Assembly), with representatives present from all over the world. Similar to the Medellín documents, *Justice in the World* is concrete and realistic. It addresses the problem of structural injustice, colonial heritages and a "new form of colonialism in which the developing nations will be the victims of the interplay of international economic forces".[145] The document notes the "crisis of universal solidarity", the failure of economic growth to improve distribution, the ecological crisis arising from a circle of consumption and pollution, and the need for a new approach to global economics and justice.[146] An important contribution is that the bishops in this document, while still expecting progress through development, do not believe that the poverty in the world will be overcome solely through economic growth. Poverty is not just an economic problem; it involves political power to change the structures that lead to marginalization of many and megariches for the few. In a section on "Educating to justice" the document pays attention to a kind of education that will "awaken a critical sense, which will lead us to reflect on the society in which we live and on its values; it will make men ready to renounce these values when they cease to promote justice for all...".[147] We see here themes of conscientization and humanization which had already been formulated at Medellín. Indeed, *Justice in the World* speaks of justice as a "constitutive dimension of the Gospel" and the Church's "mission for the redemption of the human race and its liberation from every oppressive situation".[148] This acceptance of themes related to Liberation Theology raised questions about the nature of salvation, its relation to the economic-political, and the role of the Church. A new document on evangelization soon appeared in order to delineate this.

3. *Evangelii Nuntiandi* (1975)

Of relevance to our line of pursuit here is that *Evangelii Nuntiandi* sets out to explain what is to be understood by liberation. It soon becomes clear that Pope Paul is concerned about:[149]

---

[143]*Octogesima Adveniens*, par.46.

[144]Dorr, *op cit.*, p.174:"...genuine dialogue presupposes a degree of equality between the partners and this equality may be achievable only through a confrontation in which the rich and powerful are compelled to yield some of what they have to the poor."

[145]*Justice in the World*, par.16. Cf.Gremillion, *The Gospel of Peace and Justice*, p.513ff.

[146]*Ibid.*, par.7ff.

[147]*Ibid.*, par.51.

[148]*Ibid.*, par.6.

[149]For a discussion of these five points cf.Dorr, p.196-200.

i)   *Reductionism*: the evangelical idea of liberation "...cannot be limited to any restricted sphere whether it be economic, political, social, or cultural. It must rather take account of the totality of the human person...including the openness of the human person...to God".[150]

ii) The encyclical is concerned about *politicization*: the Church would lose its special meaning if it became purely political.[151]

iii) There are inherent *limitations* to political liberation, and for this reason the Church "relates, but never identifies, human liberation and salvation in Jesus Christ". This is because there are various perspectives on liberation, and also because the Kingdom of God is not arrived at solely through social development. The pope is well aware that various ideologies, from the right-wing idea of "national security" to the left-wing revolutionary ideologies, are capable of claiming religious blessing for political goals.

iv) There is concern about *violence*: the Christian idea of liberation excludes violence, since "violence generates new forms of oppression and servitude, sometimes worse than those from which they intend to liberate", says the pope. Violence is "contrary to the Christian spirit".[152]

v)   Another concern about the meaning of liberation Dorr calls *attitudinal change*. It is evident that the pope did not want liberation as a change of social structures to be thought sufficient to bring about *full* human liberation. Paul VI emphasizes human and just social structures as well as conversion of the heart.[153]

4. CELAM III - Puebla (1979) - John Paul II

The Puebla conference of Latin American bishops in Mexico was held among an atmosphere of tensions, particulary as to whether the perspectives of Medellín (1968) would be dismissed or continued. From Medellín to Puebla were years when the repression of the military regimes grew stronger in parts of Latin America while at the same time in parts of the church more conservative views gained in reaction to the Medellín documents. A struggle for direction took place before and during the Puebla conference. At Puebla the roots of an unjust situation were analyzed as follows:

i)   There is economic, technological, political and cultural dependence.

---

[150]*Evangelii Nuntiandi*, par.33.

[151]It must also be said that liberation theologians themselves have repeatedly agreed that the gospel is not to be reduced to a political ideology nor to a political movement, nor in any way to the political aspect. For example, Leonardo & Clodovis Boff, *Como Hacer Teología de la Liberación* (Bogotá: Paulinas, 1989), p.77f.: "Temptations for Liberation Theology", which we may summarize as follows: 1) *Ignoring of mystical roots* of communion with God; 2) *Maximalization of the political aspect* leading to a pejorative relationship to other aspects; 3) *Subordination of the dialogue on faith* to a dialogue on society; 4) *Absolutization* of Liberation Theology in relationship to other theologies; 5) *Excessive accentuation* of the break with the tradition of the church, leading to a detrimental relationship toward continuity; 6) *Negligence* in dialoguing with other churches, other contemporary theologies, or even with pontifical teaching; 7) *Inattention* to clear communication, resulting in a slowing down of the conversion of the church toward the poor and the question of human rights.

[152]*Evangelii Nuntiandi*, par.37.

[153]*Ibid.*, par.36.

ii) Latin America lacks integration and thus also lacks negotiating power.

iii) Low prices for raw materials, capital flight and brain drain, affect Latin America adversely.

iv) The arms race siphons off funding that could be used for development.

v) There is a lack of land reform and structural reforms in agriculture.

vi) There is a crisis in moral values leading to greed, exorbitant profits and an absence of social justice.

vii) There is a sinfulness combined with materialism that underlies such injustices.[154]

Puebla went on searching for a way of committing the church to the service of the poor and taking a stand for human rights, attempting also to understand and denounce the mechanisms that generate poverty. The Puebla document maintains the typical critique toward various ideologies: capitalist liberalism, Marxist collectivism, but also speaks directly about the "national security" doctrine which in Latin America leads to military control.[155]

One of the more notable sections is entitled: "A Preferential Option for the Poor".[156] For Puebla, the promotion of social justice in Latin America, where there is a "scandalous reality of economic imbalance", means the Church must seek "solidarity with the poor...a preferential option for the poor, an option aimed at their integral liberation".[157] Some feared that to speak of an option for the poor was to deny that the gospel is for all people, and that the church was accepting a Marxist 'class option', but that is hardly the case. The debate will, however, always be in how far concepts such as class struggle can be used as elements of analysis without entailing Marxist ideology.[158] Those who support the term "a preferential option for the poor" usually mean that "God has a preferential care for the poor and oppressed",[159] but not an exclusive one. It makes a difference if one were to suggest that the option for the poor is the primary theological hermeneutic

---

[154]*Puebla: III Conferencia General del Episcopado Latinoamericano: "La Evangelización en el Presente y en el Futuro de América Latina"* (Mexico: Libería Parroquial, 1979), par.64-70.

[155]*Ibid.*, par.542-550. For an overview cf.Enrique Dussel, "Puebla: Relaties tussen christelijke ethiek en economie", p.112-122 in *Concilium* 1980 - 10.

[156]*Ibid.*, part 4: par.1134ff.: "Opción preferencial por los pobres".

[157]*Ibid.*, par.1154. Cf.Tony Misfud, "The Development of a Liberation Ethic in the Documents of the Church since Vatican II", in *Concilium: The Ethics of Liberation*, 172-1984. Also, Antoncich, *Christians in the Face of Injustice - A Latin American Reading of Catholic Social Teaching*, ch.7. Franz J.Hinkelammert, *et.al.*, "La Opción por los Pobres como Criterio de Interpretación", *Revista de Interpretación Bíblica Latinoamericana* (San José: 1989, no.3). Dennis P. McCann, "Option for the Poor: Rethinking a Catholic Tradition", in Richard John Neuhaus, *ed.*, *Preferential Option for the Poor* (Grand Rapids: Eerdmans, 1988), p.35-52.

[158]cf.Pedro Arrupe, "Marxist Analysis by Christians", December, 1980, *Civiltà Catolica*, reprinted in Hennelly, *Liberation Theology: Documentary*, p.307-313. Of interest is the statement in the "Ratzinger report", "Instruction on Certain Aspects of the 'Theology of Liberation'" (Vatican: August, 1984), par.8: "...certain formulas are not neutral, but keep the meaning they had in the original Marxist doctrine. This is the case with 'class struggle.' This expression ...cannot be taken as the equivalent of 'severe social conflict'...." To this it is commonly replied, as we shall see by Gutiérrez, that to acknowledge the class struggle is not the same as to invent it nor necessarily to endorse it.

[159]Dorr, p.209.

through which all other aspects of praxis must be filtered and that this option demands one kind of social analysis, leading perhaps to only one kind of political option. There is often ambiguity on this. The ways will tend to part between those who see the poor as chosen by God to be the primary (or true) subject of history, and those who see the option for the poor to mean finding ways of ending poverty. Thus there is a difference between those who speak of a class option and those who speak of an option for the poor which is yet interclassist.

There has been much debate on how far Puebla accepts and builds on Medellín. Before the Puebla conference there was a build-up of more conservative forces who wanted to make sure that Medellín was not extended.[160] The final outcome, though not a direct disavowal of Medellín, nor of the basic Christian communities, nor of Liberation Theology, was a compromise.[161] With the changes[162] a few months after CELAM III toward a more cautious course when Archbishop Alfonso López Trujillo was elected as general secretary, the liberationist proponents came to rely more on the many groups and networks being formed on national and local levels.

VIII. LABOREM EXERCENS; SOLLICITUDO REI SOCIALIS; CENTESIMUS ANNUS

1. *Laborem Exercens* (1981)

We find by Pope John Paul II considerable awareness that "development" and the world economy are not solving the problem of starvation and malnutrition. In his speeches in Brazil in 1980, John Paul II expressed concern for the poor. He criticized the national security doctrine by saying that the right to peace and security in a country must come through the pursuit of the common good and respect for human rights. He told the Latin American bishops that they rightly want a preferential, though not exclusive, option for the poor. He is clear that it is not God who wills poverty. This is an important statement in the face of traditional Latin American spirituality of inertia and fatalism.

Laborem Exercens, published in 1981 as a celebration of the ninetieth anniversary of *Rerum Novarum,* offers a reflection on the human world and the economic order. Among the salient points is that this encyclical ties the value of work to the human person, the worker. Human labour cannot be reduced to an aspect of the

---

[160]Examples of suggestions and critique of the preparatory documents are found in *IDOC: The Church at The Crossroads: from Medellín to Puebla.* Cf.also John Eagleson & Philip Scharper, *Puebla and Beyond: Documentation and Commentary* (Maryknoll: Orbis, 1979).

[161]cf.Edward Schillebeeckx, "Bevrijdingstheologieën tussen Medellín en Puebla", in Jacques Van Nieuwenhove, *Bevrijding en Christelijk Geloof,* p.18-34. J.Van Nieuwenhove, "Puebla en de solidariteit met de armen", in *Wereld en Zending* 1979, p.343-352. Jon Sobrino, "The Significance of Puebla", p.289ff in Eagleson, *Puebla,* notes that the refusal to deal fully with the problem of martyrdom seems to indicate that the conference was shying away from confrontation with the real situation. He further sees a tension in the document between "liberation" and the theme of "communion and participation" (whereby the latter theme tends to take some of the progressive struggle out of the former theme). While the conference did not fully integrate the liberation theme, it also "could not turn back the tide", François Houtart, "CELAM: The Forgetting of Origins", ch.4 in Keogh, *Church and Politics.* However, it was ambiguous enough to help push the pendulum to the political right, Emile Poulat, "The Path of Latin American Catholicism", in Keogh, *op.cit.,* p.19.

[162]cf.Houtart, "CELAM: The Forgetting".

mechanism of production. Nor is there, in principle, an opposition between capital and labour, for capital is the accumulative result of labour.[163] It becomes clear that Pope John Paul distances his views from the idea that 'free enterprise' is only an ethically neutral mechanism. The purpose of *Laborem Exercens* is not to defend any present system, but to note the basic human principles that must be maintained in any system interested in justice. Without choosing sides in the modernization/liberation debate, the encyclical does affirm various contentions of the second perspective, when it notes, for example, that "the gap between most of the richest countries and the poorest ones...is increasing more and more, to the detriment, obviously, of the poor countries".[164] The encyclical connects poverty in the Third World to policies and trade practices of the highly industrialized countries, suggesting that we probably should have less economic growth in the more developed nations, and a change in life-style, if we are to resolve the economic gap. John Paul mentions that part of the fidelity to Christ is that the Church be the "Church of the poor".[165]

2. *Sollicitudo Rei Socialis* (1987)

In the next years there was strong critique coming from the *Vatican Congregation for the Doctrine of the Faith* in regard to Liberation theology.[166] This was especially as to its ideological identification, but not so much in regard to some of its themes, like the centre-periphery perspective which was showing up in the newer encyclicals themselves. In December, 1986, the papal commission *Iustitia Et Pax* published a document on *An Ethical Approach to the International Debt Question*, which calls for a better model of cooperation between highly industrialized and as yet developing countries, in order to solve the crisis of debt which is leading to antidevelopment in the Third World. A year later - the international year of housing for the homeless - the same commission published a document on *The Church and the Housing Problem*, noting for example, that some 20 million children live and sleep in the streets of Latin America.

John Paul's encyclical *On Social Concern* (*Sollicitudo Rei Socialis*), published in 1987, was received with considerable debate. Some even find a prejudice of "Third Worldism" - *tercermundismo* - behind the pope's vision. In this document there is critique of the East bloc (communism) and also of the West (capitalism); the latter critique can be partly attributed to Latin American influence and the persuasion that the U.S.A. has "failed to promote economic and political development in Latin America".[167] It is an eye-opener to read both North American and Latin American comments on the encyclical.[168] Phrases that stand out in *Sollicitudo Rei Socialis*

---

[163]*Laborem Exercens*, par.7-13.

[164]*Ibid.*, par.17.

[165]*Ibid.*, par.8.

[166]cf."Instruction on Certain Aspects of the 'Theology of Liberation'", reprinted in Hennelly: *Liberation Theology: Documentary*, p.293-413.

[167]Roberto Suro, "The Writing of an Encyclical", in Myers, *ed.*, *Aspiring to Freedom: Commentaries on John Paul II's Encyclical 'The Social Concerns of the Church'* (Grand Rapids: Eerdmans, 1988), p.168.

[168]A North American group, in Myers, *op.cit.*, writing from a free enterprise perspective,

refer, for example, to "the widening of the gap between the areas of the so-called developed North and the developing South".[169] John Paul sees that "modern underdevelopment is not only economic but also cultural, political, and simply human". He denounces the "economic, financial and social mechanisms" which "favour the interests of the people manipulating them", particulary in the more developed countries. These mechanisms become "perverse" when they leave aside ethical requirements and the need in the Third and Fourth World. The pope mentions that, in spite of development intentions, conditions have become "*notably worse*", as indicated, among other things, by "the question of the *international debt*". The mechanisms for 'progress' have "*aggravated underdevelopment*". This last sentence is clearly from the 'dependency' viewpoint rather than the 'modernization' viewpoint. Further, John Paul speaks of the Church's social doctrine as adopting "a critical attitude towards both liberal capitalism and Marxist collectivism".[170] The "existence of two opposing blocs" causes many problems, including imperialism, the arms race and arms trade, lack of cooperation, and forms of economic neocolonialism. John Paul says that "each of the two *blocs* harbors in its own way a tendency towards *imperialism*, as it is usually called, or towards forms of new-colonialism". The result is an "exaggerated concern *for security*, which deadens the impulse towards united cooperation by all for the common good of the human race".[171] He notes further that economic development is neither "automatic" nor "limitless". There is even the problem of "superdevelopment" which leads to "consumerism" and so much waste. He speaks forcefully about the "cult of 'having'" and the need to reflect more on the *"quality of life"*, especially in relation to natural resources, and the "pollution of the environment".[172] He then goes on to emphasize "social sin", and "structures of sin" which are rooted in "personal sin", the "*all-consuming desire for profit...the thirst for power...*'at any price'". The encyclical then explains that we need the courage to set out on a new path, which is called: *solidarity*.[173]

Noteworthy is that John Paul says that even though he is critical of liberal capitalism and Marxist collectivism, "the Church's social doctrine *is not* a 'third way' between" these.[174] He adds that the church's social doctrine constitutes a "category of its own". It is not a (political) ideology but a (moral) theology, he argues. Even when talking politics, the church does so as church, that is, he says:

---

finds John Paul out of line with the "empirical reality" of how economic development works. For example, Peter Berger, in *Aspiring*, p.112, says: "A good case can be made that this nonproductive ethic has been a factor in the poor economic performance of a number of Catholic countries, especially those coming out of the tradition of Iberian Catholicism." However, a Latin American group is disappointed that he was not more outspoken and concrete on the very topics of an option for the poor, Third World development and dependence, in such a way that it would be clearly seen that capitalism is the source of the problem; cf.Hinkelammert, *et al.*, *El Pensamiento Social de Juan Pablo II* (San José: DEI, 1988).

[169] *Sollicitudo Rei Socialis*, par.14ff. The italicized phrases are so found in the encyclical itself.

[170] *Ibid.*, par.21.

[171] *Ibid.*, par.22.

[172] *Ibid.*, part IV: "Authentic Human Development".

[173] *Ibid.*, part V: "A Theological Reading of Modern Problems".

[174] *Ibid.*, par.41.

to evangelize. We see here that the Vatican is careful to keep itself clear of over identification with, for example, Christian Democracy, often referred to as a 'third-way' in Latin America. Meanwhile, the encyclical continues to speak of the "church of the poor" and a preferential love for the poor.[175] While that may sound rather paternalistic, there is a strong line in this encyclical which demands a new world order, both politically and economically.

3. *Centesimus Annus* (1991)

The recent encyclical celebrating a hundred years of social teaching is divided into six sections: i) a looking back to the "Characteristics of *Rerum Novarum*" (par.4-11); ii) a focus on the world situation and "the 'New Things of Today'" (par.12-21); iii) reflections on "The Year 1989" (par.22-29); iv) a section on "Private Property and the Universal Destination of Material Goods" (par.30-43); v) attention to the relationship between "State and Culture" (par.44-52); and vi) final paragraphs on the importance of the actual person and the meeting of concrete needs, as the "Way of the Church" in fulfilling her calling.

John Paul, in publishing this social encyclical, has in mind the need to "look back" on the social teaching of the Church, to "look around" at the world situation, and to "look to the future" of "the third millennium of the Christian era." Looking back, he understands the relevance of *Rerum Novarum* to be that it not only spoke to a situation of increased "*conflict between capital and labour*", but was also aware that "*peace is built on the foundation of justice*".[176] John Paul underscores that Leo XIII affirmed the following rights of workers: "the *dignity of the worker*"; "the *dignity of work*"; "the 'social' dimension" of work; "the *right to private property*"; "the *universal destination of the earth's goods*"; the importance of freedom "to form private associations" (such as trade unions); "the limitation of working hours" and "Sunday rest"; and "the right to a just wage".

John Paul says that a rereading of *Rerum Novarum* shows "the continuity within the Church of the so-called 'preferential option for the poor'". This is soon followed by the reminder that "the State has the duty of watching over the common good". More is said about both these concepts in this encyclical. Since these are two concepts central to our inquiry we shall approach the encyclical from that angle.

The common good

The term "common good" appears numerous times throughout the encyclical, often without specific definition, but implies that all must be included in the available rights and goods. There is a close connection between the "common good...[and] a correct understanding of the dignity and the rights of the person". We also read that the common good entails "that every sector of social life, not excluding the economic one, contributes to achieving that good".[177] Or as also strongly stated, the market must be placed under juridical guidelines which serve the whole, and

---

[175]*Ibid.*, par.42.
[176]*Centesimus Annus*, par.5ff. Italicized quotations are so found in the encyclical.
[177]*Ibid.*, par.11.

thus also serve the poor and marginalized. The "market mechanism" is praised in the encyclical, but there is also warning of "'idolatry' of the market".[178] The common good is related to the concept of *subsidiarity*, explained to mean that proper economic freedom leads to increased wealth, while at the same this is balanced by the principle of *solidarity*, that is, of defending the weakest members of the community.[179] Much is made of the means for solving social problems through "dialogue and solidarity", through "peaceful protest, using only the weapons of truth and justice", "negotiation", the "power of grace", the "rule of law", and a number of such phrases which occur throughout, in contrast to what is called "force", "violence", "total war" and so forth. The hope is expressed that the largely peaceful changes within the Communist bloc may inspire further pursuit of justice using the above mentioned means.

An important passage in respect to the common good acknowledges that whereas ownership used to focus primarily on land, today of no less importance is "*the possession of know-how, technology and skill*". This leads to a discussion of the "source of wealth in modern society", which is attributed to factors of "organizing [production]...planning...initiative and entrepreneurial initiative ability...intelligence and training...disciplined work...collaboration with others... diligence, industriousness, prudence...reasonable risks... reliability and fidelity in interpersonal relationships."[180]

The preferential option for the poor

This concept is used various times, as are the terms marginalization, solidarity and liberation. John Paul suggests that *Rerum Novarum* "is an excellent testimony to the continuity within the Church of the so-called 'preferential option for the poor'". We hear more than once that a basic problem is that the marginalized have no way of entering the "net-work" of modern economics and jobskills. In fact, a "chief problem" for the poorer countries "is that of gaining fair access to the international market", as well as the "still largely unsolved problem of the foreign debt",[181] while in the wealthy nations there is a problem of *consumerism* which not only damages the environment but even the true understanding of the priority of values for human life. Thus it is said that "the poor - be they individuals or nations - need to be provided with realistic opportunities. Creating such conditions calls for a *concerted worldwide effort to promote development*, an effort which also involves sacrificing the positions of income and of power enjoyed by the more developed countries".[182]

The dependency theme is acknowledged by stating that where "decolonization" has occurred there is often little independence because "decisive sectors of the economy still remain *de facto* in the hands of large foreign companies which are unwilling to commit themselves to the long-term development of the host country.

---

[178]*Ibid.*, par.40.
[179]*Ibid.*, par.15.
[180]*Ibid.*, par.32.
[181]*Ibid.*, par.33 and 35.
[182]*Ibid.*, par.52.

Political life itself is controlled by foreign powers...."[183] There is repeated stress on international responsibility for more equal development around the globe.

Evaluative remarks

There are many admirable passages in this encyclical and the general tendency is to call the reader to worthy reflection about the social question in relation to the individual, to intermediary organizations, as well as in relation to regional and global dynamics. The position taken is sharp enough to touch the conscience, clear enough on economic responsibility and possibilities to remind us that better distributive justice is within reach if this were made a priority, and timely in its attempt to see the "new things" of the present situation.

But some matters could be taken in more than one way. For example, the use of the phrase "a preferential option for the poor" could be felt to provide new encouragement for the theme of liberation; however, the phrase appears to be couched in the rather all too soft bedding of what is called the "continuity" of the Church's social witness.[184] There are several idealistic references to the Church. We hear phrases like: "Faithful to the mission received from Christ her Founder, the Church has always been present and active among the needy...", and: "Over the past hundred years the Church has remained faithful to this duty...."[185] There is a silence on self-critique.

At times important issues touched on are not always sharpened the way they could be.[186] However, the theme of development is specifically connected to an international structural approach, also called in the encyclical "the globalization of the economy", and this can be appealed to by those who say that development of the poorer nations now presupposes liberation from oppression by the present world order.

Gustavo Gutiérrez, writing in the Lima weekly, *Signos*, said: "The Fathers of the Church were quite clear in expressing one central idea: The goods of the earth belong to everyone. ...The celebration of the 100th anniversary of *Rerum Novarum*...implies recognizing the causes of the terrible situation in which we find ourselves. A just society inspired by the great values present in Catholic social teaching is not possible if we continue to ignore the needs of the vast majority of our people."[187] Or, as the encyclical itself says, "the open search for truth...is renewed in every generation" and there must be a distinguishing between the "valid

---

[183]*Ibid.*, par.20.

[184]cf.Charles E.Curran, "A Century of Catholic Social Teaching", *Theology Today*, July 1991, vol.XLVIII, no.2.

[185]*Centesimus Annus*, par.40 and 62.

[186]By way of example: While it is rightly said that the foreign debts of the poorer nations are "unbearable sacrifices" (*Centesimus Annus*, par.35), the case could have been strengthened by mentioning the manner in which such high debts were contracted, namely through the high interest rates (reaching 16% in 1981), thus creating debt peonage in the south while at the same time financing the north. The World Bank (1991 Annual Report) collected more in capital repayments and interest from Latin America during 1987-91 than it actually disbursed to the region. Cf.Alex Brummer: "Third World Repays More than it Gets", *Guardian Weekly*, September 29, 1991, p.22.

[187]Gustavo Gutiérrez, quoted in *Latinamerica Press*, May 16, 1991, p.5 (vol.23, no.18).

elements" of a tradition and the "erroneous ones" as well as the "obsolete forms".[188] This encourages both a critical and a creative approach to Christian social ethics.

IX. THE CHALLENGE FOR CHRISTIAN SOCIAL ETHICS

The political options in Latin America have been summarized in various ways which tend to group around how serious one is about changing the present system, according to what kind of analysis and through what means. Of the two movements we are especially considering in this work, the Christian Democrats are usually considered to be part of the modernizer movement. Liberation Theology is of a popular persuasion, less class-reconciliary in tone, and more strident in its analysis of the need for a preferential option for the poor by means of empowering the poor.

The options circle around choices of supporting, correcting, transforming or overthrowing the *status quo*.[189] Pablo Richard provides five options,[190] whereby it must be said that for our purpose here we are thinking not only of the church, but also of Christian ethics:

i)   The church could cooperate with the military regimes and their doctrine of national security (cf.ch.1.IV.4). In this model the church separates its mission from politics and speaks in general terms of humanization.

ii) The church could turn inward, hoping for better times, and avoid any conflict with the military regimes. This model forgets that the Latin American dictatorships call themselves "Christian" (thus inviting a theological critique).

iii) The institutionalized church could try to save itself by pretending that the *iglesia popular* is but an overdone expression which unnecessarily confronts the military regimes.

iv) The church could witness to justice and to truth; history will do the rest.

v)   The church, as *iglesia popular*, weak before the dictatorial regimes, but

---

[188]*Centesimus Annus*, par.50.

[189]cf.J.Andrew Kirk, *Liberation Theology: An Evangelical View from the Third World* (Atlanta: John Knox Press, 1979), p.21f., who summarizes and comments on four positions. Cf.Houtart, *Camilo Torres, Revolutie: Christelijke opdracht*, where he summarizes four social patterns of Christians in Latin America:
   i) Those who see the system as basically good and themselves usually belong to the traditional oligarchy.
   ii) A second group which views the present social system as good but in need of improvement. This view doesn't get past the idea of charity and lacks any tendency to change at all.
   iii) A third position recognizes the inadequacies of the present system and demands quick action for change. The church's role is to inspire Christians in their political, social, cultural, and economic activities. This is characteristic of the Christian Democrat movement. The clergy within this third group are divided between those who believe in social action separated from the church, and those who believe in stimulating more social action through and by the church, as in the case of initiating labour unions and cooperatives among the peasants.
   iv) The fourth view sees the only path to be through (counter)violent revolution.

[190]Pablo Richard, "Iglesia Popular: A Church Born of the People's Struggles", p.111ff. in *The Church at the Crossroads*.

strong before the poor and God, can specifically confront the unjust system and side with those who are marginalized and with the mass movements rising up for change.[191]

Even when the direction of change desired is clear, the specific strategies for transformation will have to be evaluated.[192] As has been said: in the face of much *diversion* from the problems and *aversion* towards change, the church must examine its choice of *subversion* or *conversion* of the status quo.[193]

Summary and transition to chapter three

As we look back over one hundred years of Christian Social thought, we sometimes see an unfounded trust in the idea of social harmony, whereby it is expected that the privileged can be persuaded to give up their power and wealth in order to approach an ideal of the common good. However, the structural analysis gradually increases in the encyclicals and other documents. In later expressions we see much more attention to global relationships. While the 'common good' is one of the main pillars of Roman Catholic thought, this has historically been tied to a feudal-corporative approach within a colonial (señorial) setting in Latin America. The 'common good', meaning "in the public interest", can be used progressively or repressively. The variations on this theme will depend on whether one's idea of justice means, for example, to each according to their i) rank (feudalism); ii) initiative and work (liberalism); iii) need (socialism). It is the manner of mixing such factors that helps define ideas on the 'common good'. Such a norm also needs appropriate strategies in the historical situation.

At the same time we saw something of the rise of the theme of liberation, strongly in Latin America, more cautiously and suspiciously from the Vatican, as a way of approaching the failure of developmentalism. Given the failure of meaning which tends to accompany the expression, the 'common good', in Latin America, there has been a turn to emphasizing "the preferential option for the poor". This does not in itself clarify which strategy is to be preferred.[194] There is a struggle of paradigms taking place in Latin America. Our survey shows that the fact that religion shapes society and society shapes religion, now is taking on a whole new meaning in Latin America.

---

[191]cf.also "The Church of the Poor in the 1990s: Analysis from Pablo Richard", *Latinamerica Press*, 25 Oct., 1990, p.5.

[192]For the challenge to the church among repressions cf.Jon Sobrino, in Jacques Van Nieuwenhove & Georges Casalis, *eds.*, *Symposium: 'The Future of Europe: A Challenge to Theology - Towards a Dialogue with Third World Theologians/Pour un Dialogue avec des Theologiens du Tiers Monde* (Zeist: 'Woudschoten', 1981), p.34ff.

[193]CELAM, *Desafíos a la Doctrina Social de la Iglesia en América Latina: Cinco años después Puebla* (Mexico: IMDOSOC, 1984), p.339.

[194]Some critics think that the 'virtues of modernity' have not been fully appreciated in Roman Catholic social ethics. Cf.Dennis P.McCann, "Option for the Poor: Rethinking a Catholic Tradition", in Neuhaus, *The Preferential Option*. Reinhold Niebuhr wrote in 1961: "It has always been one of the virtues of Catholicism that it skipped the whole period of classical economy and never doubted that political authority should exercise dominance over the economic sphere in the interest of justice." Cf.Richard Harries, *ed.*, *Reinhold Niebuhr and the Issues of our Time* (Grand Rapids, Eerdmans, 1986), p.20.

In the next chapter we turn to Eduardo Frei's "hopeful option" for Latin America in order to see in some detail how this key representative of Christian Democracy has analyzed the situation and the strategy for transformation in Latin America.

CHAPTER THREE

A HOPEFUL OPTION?

La palabra democracia, hoy por hoy,
ha sido despojada de su significado.
...
En el mismo estado de descrédito, por razones idénticas,
ha caído en el vacío otra palabra mayor: Dios.

*

The word democracy nowadays
has been deprived of its significance.
...
In the same state of discredit and for the same reasons
another main word has fallen into emptiness: God.[1]

Introduction

In this chapter we are confronted with the basic question as to whether democracy, placed in relation to Christian values, has something hopeful to offer Latin America. We shall see that Eduardo Frei believes that it does, though he also affirms what Roberto Sosa has said so succinctly: both *God* and *democracy* have fallen into discredit in Latin America and for the same reasons, namely - as the poem later explains - because both these concepts have been abused by "hypocrites", "reactionaries", "assassins", and "land speculators".

Eduardo Frei Montalva, lawyer and editor, became a founder of a new party in Chile in 1938 which evolved into the Christian Democratic Party by 1957. Frei was president of Chile from 1964 to 1970. In 1977 he published *América Latina: Opción y Esperanza*, which is the major summary of his political ethics. He divides this work into three sections: 1) Humanism and democracy; 2) Latin America at the crossroads; 3) Democracy as an historical project. The first section deals with the crisis of democracy, which Frei wants to relate to a wider humanizing vision of politics and culture; the second section deals with the reality of Latin America, whereby Frei traces underdevelopment back to factors such as the lack of regional integration, a dualist society, and a cycle of violence and repression; the third section relates to the strengthening of democracy as the most important 'historical project' in Latin America.

In the sections I.1-3 we present a summary and discourse on Frei's political ethics. Section II provides an overview of Frei's ethics, also mentioning strengths and ambiguities. Sections III.1-5 take into consideration a variety of critique on the

---

[1]Roberto Sosa, "Caen en el vacío dos palabras mayores", *Secreto Militar* (Tegucigalpa: Editorial Guaymuras, 1985), p.27.

Christian Democratic position in Latin America, including by Liberation Theology.

I. SUMMARY AND DISCOURSE ON FREI'S: *THE HOPEFUL OPTION*

1. Humanism and democracy

a. Summary

Rapid change and progress: economic growth insufficient

Frei opens his book noting the rapid change taking place. Even the concept of *development* has changed: it can no longer be defined merely in terms of economic growth. The price of such 'growth' is the exploitation of the many.[2] Since the Club of Rome report on *Limits to Growth* we are more aware that the present problems are not purely technical.[3] In fact, says Frei, the policy in technology of *laissez innover* (unrestrained innovation) might be as undesirable as *laissez faire* (noninterference) in economics. True philosophers are needed who can offer us a "conception of the world" that goes deeper than data, in order to help us find criteria for a perspective on civilization, the limits to growth, consumption, and a view on what constitutes progress.

Marxism

Frei turns his attention to the expansion of *Marxism*, including its "inroads into the Christian churches", citing such examples as the *Cristianos por el Socialismo* in Chile[4] and liberation theologies. Marxism, Frei realizes, comes in many varieties. Born at the start of the modern industrial era, "Marxism has been fundamentally superseded" in several points, yet continues "to awaken faith and hope" just like religion.[5]

The *strengths* Frei sees in Marxism include:

i)   attention to social-economic analysis;
ii) a valuing of human work;
iii) a criticism of the inequality of the classes;
iv) attention to human alienation in industrial society;
v)   attention to the influence of material conditions on ideological superstruc-
      tures.

The *weaknesses* he mentions include:

i)   its criticism of capitalism has been superseded;

---

[2]Eduardo Frei, *América Latina: Opción y Esperanza* (Barcelona: Pomaire, 1977), p.22: "...es necesario poner adecuado equilibrio en los valores sociales y políticos del desarrollo frente a los del crecimiento puramente matemático-económico."

[3]Frei refers to Donella Meadows, *et al.*, *The Limits to Growth* (New York: Universe Books, 1972).

[4]cf.Pablo Richard, *Cristianos por el Socialismo: Historia y documentación* (Salamanca: Sígueme, 1976).

[5]*Opción y Esperanza*, p.30.

ii)   its labour theory of value is inadequate;[6]
iii)   its doctrine of ends and means;
iv)   its atheism;
v)   and especially its concept of mankind and liberty.

Economic liberalism

However, economic liberalism in turn, says Frei, is not an adequate response to Marxism. While political liberalism has contributed to democratic, parliamentary systems and human freedom, economic liberalism is not sufficient for answering "the demands now being voiced by the poor peoples of the earth". Unfortunately, "Money has become the driving force as never before. The yearning for profit and economic power knows no limits."[7] *Capitalism* is not a sufficient philosophy; it is inadequate for projecting "a plan for the elaboration of civilization" in the future. The 'free' world has arrived at an "ideological vacuum". Frei cites Jacques Maritain, who spoke of an "integral humanism" and "personalism";[8] so, today, we must continue to search out the social-political significance of *Christian humanism*, not to the exclusion of other views, but toward a civilization of freedom, justice and solidarity. While millions starve, the arms race goes on. Ironically, the "unwonted growth of the economies of the industrialized nations" is a "vulgar form of materialism", and no answer to the 'materialist' philosophy of Marxism. Frei suggests that dominance by "high-consumption society" has led to "exploitation of the underdeveloped countries".[9]

A choice between humanization and repression

What is true democracy, if not - in the words of Maritain - "a rational organization of freedoms that are grounded in law"? Christians can contribute to true liberation by emphasizing the common good (*el bien común*) above private egoism. Without inner strength, 'liberation' often becomes irresponsible and annihilates more than it liberates. Alluding to a warning by Maritain about a 'Machiavellian' style sophistry that justifies violence and political lies, Frei says:

> "This lie has found its principal supporters in the most 'conservative' sectors. In the past they supported the union of throne and altar. Then they joined with the most reactionary wing of the bourgeoisie to impede the democratic process. ...To achieve what they wanted they did not hesitate to use Christianity....Maritain could say: 'The working

---

[6]The common critique is that Marx's theory of value was too bound to a quantitative theory of labour value and did not sufficiently take into account qualitative utility value. Cf.F.Arnaudo, Las *Principales Tesis Marxistas (Buenos Aires: Editorial Pleamar, 1975), p.87ff. David Conway, A Farewell to Marx: An Outline and Appraisal of his Theories* (London: Penguin, 1987), ch.4.

[7]*Opción y Esperanza*, p.48.

[8]cf.Jacques Maritain, *Christianity and Democracy* (New York: Scribner's, 1947). Ricardo Herrero, *Mi Compromiso Cristiano* (Caracas: Colegial Bolivariana, 1977), ch.12: "Humanismo de inspiración cristiana". E.Mounier, *El Personalismo* (Buenos Aires: Editorial Universitaria, 1987).

[9]*Opción y Esperanza*, p.55: "La economía mercantil y la sociedad de consumo han conducido a una explotación de los países subdesarrollados a veces tan intensa como en la época colonial y tiende a agotar las reservaciones mismas de que éstos disponen para vivir o sobrevivir."

classes sought their salvation by rejecting Christianity while conservative Christian sectors sought their salvation by rejecting the temporal demands of justice and love.'"[10]

We need a new cooperation between the Christian message and the democratic way of life in Latin America, posits Frei.

The future for Latin America demands a new "civilization project" which must solve the social problems not through class conflict but rather through "a process that is progressive, ascendent, and integrative". The ascent of the common people is "obvious and irresistible". The creative force for a new society transcends the outmoded class consciousness idea. The masses are being integrated into the dynamics of history. Yet, notes Frei, in Latin America we find the sad spectacle of Christians who refuse to renounce their status quo and who even trade in their better values to "whoever can guarantee their security and privileges." Rightist authoritarian, "neofascist" regimes are on the increase with the excuse of combatting totalitarian communism, yet these rightist groups have no real "global vision of life and history"; they live from a negative, afraid of change. They use, says Frei, the same methods as totalitarian communism which they claim to be resisting. These authoritarian regimes stay in power by means of the secret police which repress all political opposition movements. The "greatest mistake would be to fall into that fatal trap" of accepting the dilemma of either "totalitarian" or "authoritarian" regimes of the left or the right.[11] We need institutions and modes of expression which give the poor masses participation.

Frei's certainty about the efficacious qualities of democracy relate to his rejection of 'politics as violence'. There are two major points that he finds must be taken into account: i) violent revolution does not guarantee any particular outcome; and ii) transformation is multidimensional. A change of government does not change many of the economic factors, provide an educated populace quickly, or change the infrastructure of the nation overnight.

b. Discourse
Frei's terminology

We shall first review some of Frei's terminology. When Frei speaks of *liberalism* he is aware of the two uses of the concept, namely in referring to *civic liberty* while a second use refers especially to *economic liberalism* in terms of the market system, often referred to by Frei as *laissez faire*. Liberalism has a hierarchy of values which places freedom (understood as individual liberty) first, and tends to view other values, such as justice or distribution, through its primary value. Frei often runs liberal, *laissez faire*, and capitalism together, using them interchangeably, whereby the central thought is that the individualistic and egoistic tendency he perceives in the same must be corrected by continual attention to the *'common good'*.[12] This latter goal can only be achieved, posits Frei, through integration of

---

[10]*Ibid.*, p.70.

[11]*Ibid.*, p.86ff.

[12]Debates around this sometimes centre on 'negative' and 'positive' rights. Cf. Douglas Rasmussen & James Sterba, *The Catholic Bishops and the Economy: A Debate (London: Social Philosophy and Policy Center, 1987).*

the now marginalized masses into the dominant social-economic-political structures. While capitalism commonly refers to private ownership and the values of competition leading to efficiency of production, when used in Latin America, *capitalism* often refers to 'foreign capitalism', 'dependent capitalism' (of the periphery on the centre). Capitalism is not so much an economic as a political concept for many in Latin America. Since the most successful private enterprises in Latin America tie into the 'domination by the dollar' and by activities of transnational corporations, Latin Americans often associate "privatization" with "foreignization" (cf.ch.I.IV.2). Frei overtly rejects capitalist materialism as a "philosophy" (by which he means that it causes distortions when thought of as more than a form of production and is allowed to wedge out other values).[13] While to a large degree he accepts several precepts that are part of the traditional definitions of capitalism, such as the private ownership of means of production, the need for efficiency in production stimulated by a competitive profit market, the importance of considerable freedom for the working of 'capital' and entrepreneurship, at the same time he always comes back to a critical reserve and shows appreciation for the counter arguments, such as the need for some government regulation of the common good, especially in relation to such areas as transport, public health, education, housing and agrarian reform. Frei's position is that of a social democratic striving towards the advantages of the 'welfare state' and for that reason he can make sharp statements about any ideology which maintains the present status quo in Latin America, whether that ideology be conservatism, repressive military regimes, or capitalism. Frei includes capitalism in this reactionary series to the extent that it combines with oligarchism, neocolonialism, and authoritarian repressions, or, as he also suggests: to the extent that the idolatry of 'capital' prevents social legislation. He is likewise critical of the "ideological vacuum" in the wealthy countries, by which he means the lack of real global vision for distributive justice. He often refers to the *consumer* society which, when contrasted to the squalor in many areas of the world, represents, for Frei, the dislocation of global resources. Frei does not, like some, propose the unmitigated conclusion that the best way to fight (foreign) capitalism would be with (local) capitalism; rather, he suggests that the dominance of the profit motive contains global dangers. As for *Marxism* and *socialism*, Frei is aware of the historical and theoretical variations. It remains a hindrance, however, that he does not take up sufficient dialogue with neomarxist and liberationist critique in Latin America. This is a hindrance since in Latin America the word 'Communist' has been rapidly and profusely applied to anyone who has spoken of social justice, and the differentiation Frei is capable of is not always to be assumed by the wider readership. Frei attempts to prioritize social justice and the communal good while avoiding the use of the term 'socialism' (using only the word 'social'). As for his references to *neofascism*, which he more often calls *authoritarianism*,[14] it is clear that he has in

---

[13]*Opción*, p.33: "La forma capitalista de producción no es una filosofía ni una respuesta a las grandes interrogantes humanas. Y aunque se haya demostrado eficaz en calificados aspectos económicos y en determinados países, no constituye de por sí lo que llamaríamos 'un proyecto de civilización'."

[14]*Ibid.*, p.115: "...en el caso de los latinoamericanos alrededor del 70% de su población se encuentra bajo regímenes eufemísticamente llamados 'autoritarios'."

mind the *military-oligarchies* which have abused the most basic human rights. This kind of critique of the political right would place Frei's book "centre-left" in the mind of many in Latin America. Finally, *democracy*, for Frei, includes *'formal democracy'* as a means of procedure and a strategy for renewal, as well as *'social-economic democracy'* whereby the 'common good' is sought through social legislation towards a welfare society. He speaks multidimensionally and would measure democracy according to several indices, such as political and ideological freedoms, health and education, landtenure, etc. His many statements about poverty and marginalization as needing primary attention illustrate this understanding of democracy and what he sometimes calls a *participatory society*.

Inadequacy of present ideologies

The hope for Latin America, according to Frei, is democracy, rooted in a philosophy which places human values first; this he calls *integral humanism* and a 'new ethic' (new in Latin America). Such an approach has roots drawing from Christianity, though Frei is careful not to be exclusive on such roots. We further see that Frei does not wish to identify all technical nor economic growth with 'progress'. If the 'human factors' are missing, such 'development' will not cure the great problems of poverty and exploitation, he suggests.

Frei speaks of the "feigned death of ideologies" (*la falsa muerte de las ideologí-as*). He often uses *'ideology'* synonymously with 'philosophy'. By 'ideology' Frei means that "systems of values"[15] and social movements have different ways of defining what is "good". Thus the "ideological vacuum" in the 'free West' is in itself a problem.[16] However, Frei also points out that there is, of course, an operative ideology in the West, namely consumerism. But a fuller philosophy is missing. He speaks of both Marxism and capitalism as sometimes taking on surrogate religious qualities.

In his second chapter he grants that Marxism "contains large doses of truth...has provided analytical tools...has highlighted the problem of human alienation...." But, also: "Marxism is fundamentally superseded".[17] However, Frei does not fully follow up on his *own* statement about the contribution of Marxism - even though that was a dominant question at the time[18] - nor explain if it has any contribution to make through its "large doses of truth" to the situation in Latin America. The result is that he by-passes liberation theology in all too sweeping terms.

While he is clear on exploitation, military expenditures and the increased 'neofascist authoritarianism' in Latin America, he also at various points emphasizes that "terrorism and armed struggle have in fact furnished an excellent pretext for the establishment of anti-insurrectional regimes". It is almost as if Frei places the blame on counterviolence as the source or justification for the institutional violence of the "national security" states. However, Frei does maintain an important insight

---

[15]*Ibid.*, p.22f. Cf.further Gordon Graham, *Politics in its Place: A Study of Six Ideologies* (Oxford: Clarendon Press, 1986).

[16]*Ibid.*, p.33.

[17]*Ibid.*, p.29f.

[18]cf.*Christentum und Marxismus - Heute* (Wien: Europa Verlag, 1966).

into the problem of violence, which he sees as a departure from truly creative politics. He also has sufficiently biting words concerning the status quo to prevent anyone from considering his aim to be merely cosmetic.

Frei's political ideological orientation is typically an example of what has been called a 'third way' or a 'third option', in Latin America.[19] The third way claims to propose an alternative to the worst excesses of both capitalism and Marxism as well as offer an alternative to Latin American military authoritarianism. However, critics say that the third way has no standpoint nor transforming strategy of its own and when in power will side with the dominant oligarchies. It does, indeed, seem that the very adeptness which the Christian Democratic political philosophy has acquired in pointing out ideological dilemmas easily leads to a sense of accomplishment which does not correspond with the results of their practice.

In Frei's analysis, the choice between repressive authoritarianism and revolutionary counterviolence in Latin America is a false dilemma: "that fatal trap". Frei is well aware that "grassroots organizations" have to be promoted along with "authentic democracy".[20] He rejects counterviolence; the means must already illustrate the end. Yet this raises the question whether 'revolution in freedom' - to use his term - is possible in the context of Latin American polarities.

2. Latin America at the Crossroads

a. Summary
A splintered continent

When Frei looks at Latin American reality he sees a "splintered continent". A basic political experience of Latin America is the "cycle of democracy - anarchy - dictatorship".[21] Known for its *caudillos* (strongman military leaders) and its oligarchies, Latin America now finds its proletariat and middle class active and the situation more complex. Democratic governments which advance reforms find themselves blocked by the rightist groups and then accused of 'reformism'[22] by the leftist groups. It is a facile explanation to put "most of the blame on outside causes". While foreign intervention is very real, this is not always the determining

---

[19]cf.Juan Luis Segundo, *El Hombre de Hoy Ante Jesús de Nazaret: Fe y Ideología* (Madrid: Cristiandad, 1982), p.338ff. Also, Enrique D.Dussel, *Historia de la Iglesia en América Latina: Coloniaje y Liberación, 1492-1983* (Madrid: Mundo Negro, 1983), p.410f. *Idem.*, "A Specious Alternative: The Third Way", in *The Church at the Crossroads* (Rome: IDOC, 1978), p.92ff. Juan Luis Segundo, *The Liberation of Theology* (Maryknoll: Orbis, 1976), p.90ff. A.Fierro, *El Evangelio Beligerante* (Navarra: Verbo Divino, 1975), p.86ff: "Liquidación del ideal de cristiandad".

[20]*Opción*, p.93f.: "La valoración de cada hombre, de ejercio pleno de sus derechos, la vitalidad de las organizaciones de base...buscar las instituciones y maneras de expresar las nuevas formas de una democracia más real y auténtica; incorporar a la gran masa de los trabajadores y al pueblo a la plenitud de sus responsabilidades para contar con la riqueza inagotable de su aporte, es caminar en el sentido y dirección de la Historia."

[21]*Ibid.*, p.118: "...numerosos e importantes países de América Latina han visto caer sus regimenes democráticos e instaurar nuevas formas de dictaduras. Este ciclo democracia-anarquía-dictadura, para recomenzar incansablemente, es una vieja experience latinoamericana...."

[22]*Reformismo* in Spanish has become a common term for stymied reform ideals that do not work in practice.

factor. Internal factors, such as a weak economy, leadership failure, and absolutization of power prepare the downfall of democracy in Latin America. At this point Frei criticizes certain priests who have turned to Marxism and forms of populism which have become demagogical and opportunistic, producing "such extreme tensions and such a pervasive lack of judgment that democracy was unable to survive". "The ruling classes have clung blindly and egoistically to their privileges."[23] The growing middle classes have not served the poor, but themselves. In earlier colonial history, Latin America seemed more advanced, more promising than North America. What happened? Latin America is a splintered continent. The regimes "based on force" had no vision of "effective community...which would have to be more open and decentralized". The goal of the ruling minorities was to keep themselves in power; they felt animosity toward accelerated social change which would destroy their privileges. Similarly, the new "national security" doctrine is not open to such changes. Lack of unity stymied progress.[24] The republican separation from Spain did not change the social-economic structures. The *latifundio* feudalism remained, and so did the social dualism of elite and poor masses. This class structure was intensified by the racial factor of indigenous peoples becoming subservient to the foreign colonists. Social rigidity ensued. Without social mobility there is no possibility of true transformation.[25] Bolívar already saw the problems.[26] Yet, suggests Frei, there is change taking place through industrialization and urbanization. There is release from church domination, which allied itself with conservative forces opposing transformation. Today the church is often the "chief defender of human rights and of the poor". In economics and infrastructure advances are being made. Education is spreading. However, the problems are immense when we consider the widening gap between the less and the more developed nations. One-third of the population in Latin America "live on the margin of life in dire poverty".

Theory of dependency

Frei then turns to the *dependency theory*, which sees that the less developed countries are dominated by the more developed ones. He notes various authors, as Cardoso and Faletto, Theotonio Dos Santos and André Gunder Frank (cf.ch.1.III-.2), also recording that there is considerable variation in the implications these and others draw from dependency. When put generally as a historical problem of a lack of independence, Frei says that such can hardly be questioned. The problems arise

---

[23] *Opción*, p.128.

[24] *Ibid.*, p.133f.: "...América Latina aparece desintegrada... es un hecho que ha faltado visión común y decisiones políticas de todos...."

[25] *Ibid.*, p.143ff.: "La estructura agraria perpetuó la antigua encomienda, transformada después en...latifundio...lo cual dio origen a un nuevo tipo de feudalismo...se creó una sociedad dual con clases separadas realmente por un abismo...por el trato entre 'patrón' y el 'trabajador'. ...No hubo, pues, en América Latina verdadera movilidad sino rigideces y contrastes sociales...."

[26] Simón Bolívar (1783-1830) was a key leader for independence in the revolt against Spain and held the ideal of a united Latin America. Before his death at age forty-seven, he wrote: "America is ungovernable. He who served a revolution ploughs the sea", quoted in Emilio Núñez and William Taylor, *Crisis in Latin America* (Chicago: Moody Press, 1989), p.71.

when discussing more exact definitions and aspects of the theories. The dependency perspective helps "to gain a better understanding of the whole Latin American process...but it has been found to be of very limited usefulness when used politically as an instrument for liberative action".[27] Acknowledging the reality of Latin American dependency, Frei adds that he objects to speaking of imperialism by the U.S.A. and Western Europe while forgetting the imperialism of the U.S.S.R. No one can deny the influence of the U.S.A. in Latin America, says Frei, but two exaggerated views exist: one believes that the U.S.A. is the "source of all ills", while the other looks to the U.S.A. as "object of unreserved admiration...and hope of financial aid". Yet it is true, he admits, that "the democracy in North America has always ended up allying itself with the privileged groups or dictatorships in Latin America that have little to do with democracy."[28] Frei continues: The U.S.A. tradition has been one of *unilateral decision-making* and "not the result of joint elaboration" with Latin America. Meanwhile, Latin America, especially because of its fragmentation, remains passive and dependent, content to seek loans to overcome the crisis of the moment, lacking political policy. Only if Latin America acts in concert for its own interests and with specific goals and dialogue, will the U.S.A. pay attention. Latin Americans have become aware that they have often "been victims of coercion and exploitation from North America". Now is the time to shape a new policy. "Some say that we are weak because we are dependent. But we could just as well say that our dependency stems from our weakness, from our inability to organize ourselves" as an integrated unit within the overall world picture.[29]

The recurring cycle

Frei returns to the theme of the "recurring cycle", noting that at the time of writing (1977) many of the democratic governments in Latin America had toppled in favour of military dictatorships. In Latin America it has been thought that "we could correct everything by trading in one government for another. ...In the course of a century and a half more than 190 constitutions have been drawn up in Latin America...." Those who "advocate revolution, violence, and complete change immediately, sacrifice freedom on the altar of their utopia. They thus support those who sacrifice freedom in the name of 'order' and 'security'". This is what happened in Chile, says Frei, referring to the changes from when he was president (1964-70) to the years of Salvador Allende (1970-73) and the coup which installed Pinochet (1973). The main cause for the collapse of democracy in Chile was not the military coup but rather the government's errors and lack of common sense, he suggests.[30]

The new wave of violence and subversion in Latin America, Frei believes, has

---

[27] *Opción*, p.167.

[28] *Ibid.*, p.169

[29] *Ibid.*, p. 177: "Algunos piensan que somos débiles porque somos dependientes. También podríamos pensar que la dependencia nace de nuestra debilidad, a causa de nuestra desintegración e incapacidad para organizarnos dentro de un cuadro mundial donde día a día gravitan más los que constituyen grandes bloques regionales de poder."

[30] *Ibid.*, p.183ff.

as its curious outcome that it encourages the dictatorial governments that react to this challenge. Violence is a "blind alley". Even though 'institutional violence' (top down) exists, we cannot "use violence to put an end to violence".[31] The revolutionary warfare has brought on the counter-revolutionary response of the 'doctrine of national security'. Torture, murder, negation of human rights are the result. Politics becomes warfare; government and the armed forces dominate all of life with the excuse of protecting "national security". Any great democratic country refuses "to let the military become a political power, much less subjugate the life of the nation to the demands of a domestic 'war' which through military-political action aims to first of all eliminate all subversives and then all dissenters. Yet... this is precisely the doctrine that has been exported to Latin America."[32] Repression is no solution: Latin America is presently faced with the "infernal circle" of "terrorism, counterinsurgency, and violence of all sorts". Civilization has always "aimed at...juridical norms". The task of politics "is to achieve a consensus;...politics is a failure if it can triumph only through the use of force". Politics should include all members of the community in an effort to achieve the "common good".[33] Rather than this "fatal dilemma" of violence, we need a "rational approach to liberation".[34] The "wild adventure...of the ultra-left and the ultra-right" who reject the electoral approach and choose for force and violence do not have the support of the people. Freedom presupposes justice; but justice is also based on freedom, as the "full exercise of human rights". Total revolution and violence do not liberate. Dictatorial regimes may establish order for a time, but offer no solution. Democracy, with its principles of humanism, is the only way out of the dilemma.

b. Discourse
The vicious circle

Frei looks at Latin American reality and sees a cycle of "democracy - anarchy - dictatorship" which impedes Latin American development. Politics is quite frankly partisan without a vision for *el bien común* (the common good). But does Frei consider carefully enough this cycle of democracy - anarchy - dictatorship? Could it not also be a case of dictatorship - counterviolence - dictatorship, or in some cases: dictatorship - revolution - democracy? It is clear that Frei assumes that democracy could function well if the extremists of right and left (who resort to violence) would stay within the democratic lines of procedure. However, this is to forget that democratic rights have not been functioning well for the opposition groups. It is to Frei's credit that he continually refers to this pattern of human rights violations; but his critique diminishes by appearing to assume that the repression is a reaction to subversive revolutionary activity rather than that the subversive revolutionary activity is a reaction to the long-standing repression.

---

[31]*Ibid.*, p.196.

[32]*Ibid.*, p.202.

[33]*Ibid.*, p.206: "La tarea política consiste precisamente en lograr el consenso, afirmar el sentido de la solidaridad, tratar de incorporar a todos los miembros de la comunidad en el esfuerzo por alcanzar el Bien Común."

[34]*Ibid.*, p.208.

It could be succinctly argued that much of Latin America has never gotten past a democratic facade or *la democracia restringida* (restricted democracy). When the way to the poll booth is strewn with corpses and when politicians, union leaders, development workers, journalists, professors and church leaders risk their lives when they encourage *concientización*, reform of landtenure or wages, where is democracy? We surely cannot expect Frei, who thinks of democracy in social, economic and political terms, to accept an uncritical use of the term "democratic government". Yet, it appears that he is using a double definition of democracy which leads to uncertain duplicity in his analysis. This is evidenced as follows:

i) The full definition of democracy for Frei is undeniably more equality in social, economic, political and educational terms. He is by his own confession a social-Christian democrat who is against conserving the oligarchic status quo and does not believe that a laissez faire liberal approach is sufficient for the necessary transformation.

ii) But when he builds on the thesis that "numerous nations of Latin America have seen their democratic governments crumble before the installation of new forms of dictatorship"[35], Frei does not seem to distinguish sufficiently the quality of democracy involved.[36]

Disunity and dependency

One of the weightiest factors that impede development, according to Frei, is disunity in Latin America as a region as well as internally in the dualism of oligarchy and masses. The oligarchies have been more orientated to Madrid and Miami than to the village next door. Social and economic dualism not only produces injustice, but impedes development. While acknowledging the high level of dependency in Latin America, Frei does not accept the "dependency theory" (cf.ch.1.III.2) as fully identifying the problem. The undeniable fact of dependency is for Frei a symptom of a deeper problem: "dependency stems from...our inability to organize...." We might then ask: Can the "periphery" develop within the shadow of the "centre"? Frei suggests that the key to transformation is that the internal problems, even when connected to external domination, must de dealt with internally.

Democracy and the military

Continuing his thoughts in reference to the "recurring cycle" Frei reminds us that since independence from Spain, Latin America has shown a lack of political coherence in some 190 constitutions during a period of a 150 years.[37] Whatever the reasons for this unsettled pattern, Frei frankly mistrusts the repressive rationali-

---

[35] cf.note 21.

[36] Of course, writing from Chile, where the 1973 coup against Salvador Allende, who was legitimately elected, brought Pinochet undemocratically to power, this view makes sense. But to apply this widely to Latin America is to invite the question: how can democracy crumble where it has never yet existed?

[37] *Opción*, p.183.

ty of the 'national security' states as well as the dialectical rationality of a left-wing revolution. They both spell violence for him, and neither has the key to humanizing transformation. We heard Frei say: "None of the great nations under democratic rule...let the military become a political power, much less subjugate the life of the nation to the demands of a domestic 'war' against all subversives and dissenters." Three points are salient here:

i) Important as this antirepressive challenge by Frei is, he might appear to be caught in a circle with no point of entrance or exit: how does Latin America eliminate what is already factual, namely military politics and the symbiosis of the military and the oligarchy? Democracy does not allow military rule; but what if military-oligarchy rule does not allow democracy?

ii) Frei says that great democratic nations do not allow the military to become a political power. However, he does not fully discuss the thesis that while the U.S.A. does not allow the military to dominate politics within its own borders, it has supported the very strategy of military political power in Latin America (see ch.II:I.6).

iii) Can Frei's statement above be reconciled with the role of the Christian Democrats at the time of the coup against Allende? Frei says that the collapse of democracy in Chile was due to the Allende government's errors. The facts are intricate, and include the role played by foreign pressures. Detailed studies reveal the following kinds of elements:[38]

    a. Frei's victory in 1964 was significant, receiving 55.7% of the votes.

    b. However, to have a reform programme and to implement it are two different things.

    c. Though Frei was the first Chilean president to implement agrarian reform, the plan was only 20% effective as to the number of peasant families helped. The moderate steps toward nationalizing the copper industry caused divisions within Frei's party. Some see the Frei reforms as holding considerable potential which failed because of a lack of national unity.[39]

    d. Allende of the socialist Unidad Popular party achieved marginal victory in the 1970 election because the Christian Democrats lost the conservative vote.

---

[38]cf.Gonzalo Arroyo, *Golpe de Estado en Chile* (Salamanca: Sígueme, 1974). Helio Gallardo, *Actores y Procesos Políticos Latinoamericanos* (San Jose: DEI, 1989), ch.2. Phillip O'Brien, ed., *Allende's Chile* (New York, 1976). Nathaniel Davis, *The Last Two Years of Salvador Allende* (London, 1985). Stefan de Vylder, *Allende's Chile: The Political Economy of the Rise and Fall of the Unidad Popular* (London, 1976). Arthur F. McGovern, "Chile under Allende and Christians for Socialism", ch. 6 in *Marxism: an American Christian Perspective* (Maryknoll: Orbis, 1981). Harold Molineu, "Allende's Chile", in *U.S. Policy Toward Latin America: From Regionalism to Globalism* (Boulder, Colorado: Westview, 1990), p.177ff. Gary W.Wynia on Frei and Allende in *The Politics of Latin American Development* (Cambridge: University Press, 1984), p.169-189. James R.Whelan, *Out of the Ashes: Life, Death and Transfiguration of Democracy in Chile, 1833-1988* (Washington: Regnery Gateway, 1989).

[39]John Sheahan, *Patterns of Development in Latin America: Poverty, Repression, and Economic Strategy* (New Jersey: Princeton University Press, 1987), ch.9.

e. Allende's goals included the nationalization of large enterprises such as the copper and automotive industry. He initially worked with full support by congress.

f. Allende doubled the rate of the agrarian reform plan and land expropriation.

g. After some seeming success, it soon appeared that government spending was outracing public revenues. A drop in the price of copper caused further problems. Agricultural production began to lag and there was rising inflation, which by 1972 was running at 163% per year.[40]

h. Opponents used these problems to crush the Allende regime. The U.S.A. blocked loans from the IDB and World Bank to Chile; the long truckers' strike was particularly effective in paralyzing the economy.

i. In September, 1973, the military "emboldened by Conservative and Christian Democratic protests and provoked by rising civil strife and economic chaos"[41] ended the Allende experiment by means of a coup.[42]

j. The resulting Pinochet regime which brutally transgressed human rights lasted from 1973-1989. Pinochet maintained power over the armed forces when the Christian Democrat Patricio Aylwin was elected in 1989.

k. Conclusions we may draw from Chile are: first, that a democratic path to redistribution cannot succeed if the nation becomes polarized; and secondly, the risk of U.S.A. economic boycott (or eventual military intervention) highly threatens the possibility of change.

3. Democracy as a historical project in Latin America

a. Summary
Basic ingredients

We need a "viable historical project", continues Frei, in order to restore democracy. 'Authoritarian' regimes rely too much on a 'strong arm', not because of rational arguments but due to such factors as fear of freedom and distrust of the majority - the common people. Here Marxist-Leninism and fascism meet.[43] The argument that says that underdeveloped countries are not ready for democracy is false; rather, "democracy is vitally required for economic, social, cultural and human development of peoples, as well as for their economic growth. Communities are organic entities that need room to discuss and settle conflicts. Authoritarian and totalitarian regimes try the simplistic solution, says Frei, of not listening to opposition parties, of promoting social inertia and the herd mentality, of controlling the press and other media. Such "simplistic primitivism" is "sheer negation of what the human condition and contemporary society should be". Today there are many centres of power, including multinational corporations, communication media,

---

[40]Molineu, *op. cit.*, p.183.

[41]Wynia, *op. cit.*, p.187.

[42]Lernoux, *Cry*, p.46: "Thus many of Chile's Christian Democrats came to rue the day they had encouraged the generals to overthrow Allende, since contrary to their expectations, they suffered as much repression as did the Socialists...."

[43]*Opción*, p.217.

partisan political groups and labour unions; none may be allowed to demand priority for "their special interest over those of society as a whole". The role of the government is to orientate but not dominate the various sectors of society. Government should "superintend the interests of the common good [for] ...social justice is the first victim of misgovernment".[44] Political parties must link the "grassroots citizen participation" (*la participación de las bases ciudadanas*) and the "decision-making process".[45]

Primary objectives

Social and economic planning is essential in today's world, also in Latin America, where half the population is under twenty-five. The population of Latin America will double, notes Frei, during the last quarter of the present century.[46] Full realization of democracy is not the same as "absolute freedom to consume", but gives priority to production and equitable distribution among the masses.[47] The idea of a Latin American common market could help pursue economic stability for the region. Further, the development of science and technology is essential. When some societies are ahead in rapid technological evolution and others lag behind, "equitable relations between the two...become almost impossible". It is a "false illusion to assume that inequality can be eliminated by...good-will.... It is a mistake to base one's hopes for a just system on human generosity". Both paternalistic governments and dictatorships rob organizations of substantive power. The only alternative is the right of association for labourers, peasants, intellectuals, etc., in the quest for justice. Organized labour is a key element. In Latin America some would promote *laissez faire* (*capitalismo liberal*) "to a degree that is no longer accepted in the countries where that doctrine originated". These countries have organized labour, whereas in Latin America the labour movement is without power or even is destroyed. There is every indication that *laissez faire* economics "intensifies and increases inequalities".[48] While foreign aid is indispensable,[49] a self-conscious democratic government will turn to creative efforts for development through a socio-economic model for Latin America. There must be redistribution of

---

[44]*Ibid.*, p.236.

[45]*Ibid.*, p.245ff.

[46]Population growth and projections in Latin America (registered in thousands) now run according to Núñez and Taylor, *Crisis,* p.110f., as follows:

1930	1950	1965	1985	2000	2025
107,408	164,810	249,125	404,806	546,395	778,662

[47]*Opción*, p.256f.: "La realización plena de la sociedad democrática no reside, entonces, en mantener una libertad absoluta de consumo, sino en dar preeminencia a la producción y distribución equitativa de los bienes básicos que permita a todos y cada uno de sus miembros alcanzar un mínimo de dignidad y una forma razonable de vida."

[48]*Ibid.*, p.270ff.

[49]Around the same time that Frei was writing other studies were more and more exposing the problems of foreign aid. See Willem Gustaaf Zeylstra, *Aid or Development: The Relevance of Development Aid to Problems of Developing Countries* (Leyden: Sijthoff, 1975), p.257, who concludes his book saying: "One can only guess how much harm has already been done to developing countries in the name of development aid." See also our ch.5:II.2 (The question of aid).

income and land.[50]   There can be no true development without investment in health, education and housing. "Our first priority should be to rescue the vast masses of the people from the intolerable poverty and misery...the decision to overcome poverty is an act of justice. It is also the precondition for further progress and development. It will raise millions of people to a new level of existence, turning them into a market for our economic expansion and a source of labour and active endeavour."[51]

A creative task

Frei concludes his book saying that it is necessary to strive for a pluralistic society that is communitarian and seeks justice. There must be greater participation by popular organizations. We must seek regional integration as well as a world community in order to confront problems and promote justice. There is "every reason", he says, "to believe we can build a better society" in Latin America. He ends with a number of points which can be summarized as follows:[52]

We must:

i)   combine freedom and responsibility;
ii)   maintain democratic elections and a plural society;
iii)   promote economic and political development according to human values rather than prestige, power and wealth;
iv)   encourage popular organizations and decision-making;
v)   reject simplistic views and violence;
vi)   overcome poverty through internal and regional integration;
vii)   pursue world community and global justice.

b. Discourse

Goals and means?

Democracy is for Frei the spreading of cultural power and responsibility: transformation of society must be multidimensional. *Liberation* depends on this *development*. But others will respond: does this development not depend on liberation from dependency and an oppressive situation first? For Frei, the *crux moralis* is not the choice between capitalism and socialism,[53] but rather between a human or inhuman society, which he then understands politically as the choice between a democratic and an undemocratic society. Frei's vision of democracy is that it gives expression to the popular will through the electoral system, through various party and labour organizations, and through the strengthening of intermediate groups. The question will always be: how do we move from 'here' to 'there' on

---

[50]*Opción*, p.276f.

[51]*Ibid.*, p.280: "Tomar la determinación de derrotar la miseria significa un acto de justicia, y es asimismo la condición para el progreso, pues en esa forma se incorporará a un nuevo plano de existencia a millones de personas que serán mercado para la expansión de la economía y fuente de actividad y trabajo."

[52]*Ibid.*, p.296ff.

[53]cf.Juan L.Segundo, "Capitalismo-socialismo, crux theologica", p.223ff in Rosino Gibellini, *La Nueva Frontera de la Teología en América Latina* (Salamanca: Sígueme, 1977).

the chess board of transformation? Is conscientization enough to produce democratization? Already when Frei was writing there had been a significant call for a new international economic order, as well as the advance of the dependency thesis which argues that Latin America is locked into a spiral of debt and economic crises from which the global economic order prevents it from emerging. Frei, while recognizing the factor of dependence, does not fully address the question as to what extent this factor affects the possibility of internal transformation.[54] However, he has a progressive line running through his presentation when he emphasizes the necessity for regional cooperation.[55] It can, at the same time, be asked if he has not empowered democracy with a little too much "magic", a little too "simplistic" faith, as he suggests of other ideologies.

The strong statements Frei makes about "redeeming the masses" from misery as a primary task[56] could be called 'Frei's option for the poor'. This is seen by Frei in development terms and a quest for the influence of popular organizations. At the end of his book he refers to what he apparently as yet feels to be the Achilles' heel of his hopeful option, namely: that neither "goodwill" nor "human generosity" will by themselves produce a just system. The alternative, he says, is the formation of strong associations in area of labour, among the peasants, and among intellectuals.

Since the time that Frei wrote there has been a return to formal democracy and considerable turning to privatization, but there is every evidence that behind this facade the poor are carrying the burden.

II. OVERVIEW

1. Typical features of Frei's political ethics

a. *The gospel and politics*
  i)   The gospel connects to the political via Christian values which in turn must be historically mediated.
  ii) Frei does not develop theological themes, such as sin, redemption, kingdom of God, but refers to political-ethical categories, such as: justice, equality, violence, poverty.
  iii) He appeals to Christian humanism as an important pillar for democracy, though he recognizes this is not the only one.
  iv) Frei often warns of the long-standing tradition of ideological identity between Christianity and the ruling class leading to the exploitation of the poor.
  v)   Neither the church (institution) nor theology are assigned an overt role in the political.

---

[54]Luciano Tomassini, *Introducción a la Teoría de las Relaciones Internacionales* (San José: FLACSO - Facultad Latinoamericana de Ciencias Sociales, 1988).
[55]cf.Gonzalo Martner, coord., *América Latina Hacia el 2000: Opciones y estrategias* (Caracas: Nueva Sociedad, 1986), p.236.
[56]*Opción*, p.279: "La tarea de redimir a estas grandes masas de la situación de miseria insoportable en que se encuentran debe constituir la primera prioridad."

b. *Democracy*
i)   This is the concept Frei uses most: it refers to a procedural method, and also to
ii) distribution of opportunities and resources.
iii) Frei sees the root of many problems in Latin America in the historical pattern of *paternalismo*[57] whereby the state, patron, church and army have played a role, maintaining a rigid social system without sufficient functioning of intermediary institutions.
iv) Frei emphasizes popular organizations.
vi) The needs of the people, for example the urgency to end poverty, are political priorities, according to Frei.

c. *Capitalism*
i)   Frei rejects the *laissez faire* approach. While accepting the capitalist contribution within the context of a mixed economy, he criticizes capitalism as a philosophy.
ii) Capitalist materialism has led to exploitation in Latin America.
iii) Frei does not accept the fact of external dependency as sufficient for clarifying underdevelopment, which he sees as stemming from colonial patterns of *paternalismo* and lack of regional organization. (The counterargument is that the colonial roots to this pattern are by definition part of external dependency.)

d. *Marxism*
i)   Includes 'many truths'.
ii) At the same time it is said to be 'superseded'.
iii) Frei considers liberation theology's turn toward Marxist analysis ideologically inappropriate.
iv) He emphasizes the priority of eliminating poverty, and understands this in developmental, not in class struggle terms.

e. *Repressive authoritarianism*
i)   Frei sometimes uses the term 'neofascism', but most often speaks of 'authoritarianism' and 'military regimes'. He sharply critiques the "national security" doctrine in Latin America.[58]

---

[57]Eduardo Frei Montalva, "Paternalismo, Pluralismo, y Movimientos Reformistas Cristiano-demócratas en Latinoamérica", in William D'Antonio & Fredrick Pike: *Religión, Revolución y Reforma: Nuevas Formas de Transformación en Latinoamérica* (Barcelona: Herder, 1967), p.67ff.: "La esencia del espíritu con que Latinoamérica fue descubierta, conquistada y colonizada es algo que podríamos llamar 'paternalismo'. El sistema era rígido y social y económicamente proyectado a través del 'encomendero', que no solamente era el propietario de la tierra, sino también el curador de las almas que vivían en ella. ...El rey, la Iglesia y Dios estaban aliados en la conservación de este orden. ...La debilidad de las funciones intermedias en la educación y la enseñanza de la responsabilidad - la familia, el municipio, la cooperativa, el sindicato, la provincia - ha distorcionado monstruosamente esa lucha por el poder."

[58]Frei, contrary to Jean Kirkpatrick and Ronald Reagan, rejects the dilemma of choosing

ii) He does not think that counterviolence will help topple authoritarian regimes, since they have grown more repressive in the face of subversion.

iii) Frei does not fully bring to light the role of the U.S.A. in relation to Latin American military regimes.

f. Strategy for change

i) Frei makes a strong appeal for nonviolent transformation. The circle of violence is a 'fatal trap'.

ii) He recognizes the existence of institutional violence, but says that counter-violence is not the way to eliminate institutional violence. We must walk a political road.

iii) Transformation must be toward a pluralistic society and the spreading of power and responsibility.

g. Development and liberation

i) Development helps bring liberation. He can speak of a 'rational' approach to liberation, whereby 'rational' means a democratic development strategy.

ii) Frei rejects an equating of economic growth with progress.

iii) He thinks that the concept of liberation must have deeper ethical-spiritual roots than any materialist philosophy (capitalist or Marxist) can provide.

iv) Development and liberation need well-functioning organizations in all areas of society.

2. Strengths of Frei's viewpoint

a. Frei attempts an approach which is critical of both capitalism and Marxism.

b. He has an eye for the multidimensional factors involved in underdevelopment and injustices.

c. Frei values democracy and has a realistic sense of the institutional basis necessary for progress.

d. It is clear that he wants to link political transformation to grassroots participation.

e. In his political ethics Frei places a practical emphasis on both production and distribution. He can be critical of both foreign capitalism and the lack of production and unity in Latin America.

f. Frei believes that the 'common good' ('human values'), with an emphasis on the need to conquer poverty, should take precedence over prestige, power, wealth and violence.

3. Ambiguities in Frei

a. Given the vested interests in the status quo, Frei does not explain how to move from a democratic facade (*la democracia restringida*) to the social democracy he favours.

b. Frei seems at times to presuppose that the circle of violence begins by

---

between 'authoritarian' or 'totalitarian' government. Cf.Jean Kirkpatrick, "Dictatorship and Double Standards" in *Commentary*, Vol.68, No.5, November 1979.

the subversive left, more than by the reactionary right.
   c. Frei by-passes a sufficient discussion of Liberation Theology's contribution to Latin America.
   d. While critical of the U.S.A and its unilateral decision-making, Frei somewhat underplays the theme of dependence.

III. CRITICAL APPRAISAL OF CHRISTIAN DEMOCRATIC POLITICAL ETHICS IN LATIN AMERICA

Even strict critics recognize considerable merits in the early stages of the Christian Democratic movement in Latin America, especially because it clearly challenged the old oligarchic order of things. But it is one thing to have a theory about a new dawn for development and democracy, and it is another thing to see that actually take hold in the face of reactionary forces and the battle against domination (internal and external). In this section we present a review of some critical appreciations and challenges for Christian Democratic political ethics.

1. Edward J.Williams: Latin American Christian Democratic Parties

In 1967 Edward J. Williams of the political science department of Marquette University wrote an up-date on Christian Democratic theory in Latin America at a time when the recent arrival of Christian Democrats to power through Eduardo Frei's election to presidency (September 1964) gave the topic considerable buoyancy.[59] Williams' study aims to provide a description and an evaluation of the movement. We shall first consider some of his pertinent remarks and then listen to his own evaluation at that interesting juncture for Christian Democratic political ethics in Latin America. The following section headings are combinations from Williams' chapter titles.

a. Origins and theoretical foundations

Williams states that Christian Democrats see themselves as a "third force" in Latin America, attempting to draw on political theory neither fully of the right nor left. Political party organization in Latin America has traditionally been little more than pressure groups which identified through personal ties with the aristocracy or with the newly developing commercial sectors. The factor of *caudillismo* (strongman leadership) has been typical in the midst of weak programmes.[60] The catalyst for Christian Democratic party foundation is often traceable in Latin America to Catholic university students who "had been nurtured on the social doctrines" of the Vatican. Ideological splits in the other parties and "increasing opposition to authoritarian and dictatorial regimes has created additional support for the movement."[61] Williams credits the following as moulding Christian Democratic thought:

---

[59]Edward J. Williams, *Latin American Christian Democratic Parties* (Knoxville: University of Tennessee Press, 1967).
[60]*Ibid.*, p.6.
[61]*Ibid.*, p.17.

i)   the *Church* through the papal encyclicals;
ii)   French philosopher *Jacques Maritain* and a number of early European Christian Democrat founders;
iii) rival *Social Democratic* movements;
iv)   *indigenous cooperative* movements;
v)   influence from Christian Democratic movements in *Europe*.

Williams notes an "aura of messianic mystique" which has accompanied the rise of the Christian Democrats, who have claimed that they will put persons in the centre of political justice, rather than monetary gain.[62] Their stated aim of replacing liberal democracy by (Christian) social democracy has not been lacking in colourful slogans, such as "the age of social justice" and "revolution without violence". They claim to promote revolution by which they mean *structural changes*: the goal may be revolutionary, but the method is evolutionary. At the same time they seek a renewal of Christian principles and a critique of the dominant ideological choices. They can state in the tradition of Maritain that "the real dilemma is Christianity or materialism, be it capitalistic or communistic materialism".[63] Williams says: "Christian Democratic thinkers consider the 'hidden hand' of classical liberal theory absurd". But he also suggests that "in their analysis of capitalism, Latin Americans generally, including Social Christians, paint a caricature of the system" of capitalism.[64] However, he admits that both foreign and internal capitalism have given Latin America an entirely different outlook on capitalism than many northern viewers hold. In any case, since Christian Democrats see political authority as "vested by God in the community as a whole", this leads to democracy rather than despotism. Their idea of institutionalized pluralism places a check on state omnipotence.[65]

b. Policies and programmes

Whatever the actual achievements, Christian Democratic theory places considerable emphasis on welfare and the organization of labour. It believes that "class conflict will end when all...are made property owners", and that the means of production should (eventually, through reforms) become more owned by those who work.[66] Williams portrays Christian Democratic programmes as proposing some fundamental reforms, including patterns of agrarian ownership, the organization of the market with stable prices, infrastructural improvements in transportation, support of cooperatives, and attention to educational opportunities and integration of the Indian population. One of the planks in the Christian Democratic platform is price stabilization among the Western nations whereby raw materials exported from

---

[62]cf.Eduardo Frei Montalva, "The Aims of Christian Democracy", *Commonweal, LXXXI (Oct.9, 1964), p.65.*
[63]Williams, *op.cit.*, p.41.
[64]*Ibid.*, p.45f.
[65]*Ibid.*, p.61ff.
[66]*Ibid.*, p.104.

Latin America would not continue to lose out to price gains in manufactured goods. Christian Democratic proposals place a high emphasis on "providing the necessities for all, even if it must be at the expense of the affluent". One of the main ways of seeking transformation is tax reform. Private property is seen as a good, but the limiting factor of the *'common good'* means that private property should yet have a social function. Christian Democrats often speak of the reform of enterprise so that it will be more based on co-participation, co-determination, and co-ownership. Since economic development is needed to realize social justice, Christian Democrats seek industrialization, whereby the government is expected to take a major part in this effort. However, private initiative is also emphasized as a motor of economic activity. There is room for nationalization and expropriation of, for example, (i) key industries of primary national importance; (ii) areas where private industries will not or cannot meet the demands of the common good; and (iii) uneconomically utilized property. Of special importance seems to be the Christian Democratic emphasis on regional integration and unity for Latin America whereby they typically encourage a stronger common market. They are also among those calling for regional parliamentary union. Preference is given to multilateral rather than unilateral settling of regional and international disputes. They are critical of U.S.A. policies which have thwarted "genuinely progressive social and political movements" and "bolstered dictatorial regimes".[67] The approach taken to wider political matters is thus structural rather than purely according to the "realism of strength".[68]

c. Relations with the military, the church, and with other parties

Williams speaks of that "unholy trinity": the traditional alliance between the military, the church, and the oligarchy. However, he also discusses the complexity of the problem and sees that the church has moved away from the old authoritarian regimes toward identification with the masses.

The Christian Democratic movement has been critical of both military politics and church traditions. No doubt this critical stance gave the movement popular appeal in its earlier stages. Frei, in the line of a 'New Christianity' and 'integral humanism' could speak of Spanish Catholicism as lacking concern for social problems, too individualistic, even evidencing "mental narrowness" and a "poverty of style" in relating the spiritual to the social.[69] The willingness to challenge the old patterns in a pro-popular stance helps account for the rise of the Christian Democratic movement. Christian Democratic parties are parties of the centre; the perception of their stance as being, now centre-left and now centre-right, however, changes from country to country and from time to time. They have attracted a very

---

[67]*Ibid.*, p.153.

[68]Venezuelan Christian Democrat, Rafael Caldera, for example, has said that principles of social justice "obligate the economically strong countries with repect to the economically weak". Cf.Rafael Caldera, *La Idea de Justicia Social Internacional y El Bloque Latinoamericano* (Santiago de Chile: Editorial del Pacífico, 1961), p.23.

[69]Eduardo Frei, *La Política y el Espíritu* (Santiago: Ediciones Ercilla, 1940), p.196. Also, Eduardo Frei, "Notes on the Catholic Church and Development" in *Latin America: Evolution or Explosion?* Mildred Adams, *ed.*, (New York: Council on World Tensions, Dodd, Mead & Co., 1963), p.197.

heterogeneous electorate. They often seek collaboration and coalition with other parties, most naturally according to political theory with the Social Democratic parties and with those who have a sense of "popular vocation" toward the masses. However, trying to reform the political process on a continent where "the *caudillos* and the colonels who shoot their way into the presidential chair are no longer the effective agents of all political change",[70] remains a challenge for any transformation ethic.

Having summarized from Williams, let us now hear his own evaluations.

d. Handicaps to the movement
We may outline Williams' critique as follows:

i) *The messianic bent*
Williams perceives a certain zeal and optimistic vitality which, on the one hand, may give the movement considerable élan, while on the other hand it may be aiming much higher than the results it brings. In fact its "mystique" could go so far as to ironically cause it to forget that "the postulation of heaven on earth is theological heresy as well as bad social and political theory". Williams astutely observes a problem here of supposed "easy and harmonious resolution of the social, economic and political conflicts" which is "surprising if one contrasts it with Catholic emphasis on the corrupting influence of original sin".[71] In any case, the enthusiasm will not be enough: the people will judge it by whether it fulfills its promises.

ii) *Ideological lacunae*
Williams also questions the relationship between the authentically pluralistic society Christian Democratic theory favours and the equally emphasized planned economy: there is a challenge here to really develop mediary institutions because of the "penchant for dynamic, active central government, which has been so characteristic of Latin America."[72] It is possible that corporatism could promote on-going democratization but there are factors which militate against success in this, for the doctrine can be misused to maintain inequities. Is it also possible that Christian Democratic critique of capitalism does not see that "the alienation of man is not necessarily the result of capitalism but of the bigness that the modern industrial system necessarily implies"? There can be no return to "the idealized community of the Middle Ages". The *social* benefits of communitarianism will according to Williams "not necessarily have the *economic* effects that many optimistic Christian Democrats envision".[73]

Also to be counted among the lacunae is the problem of connecting "well-

---

[70]John J.Johnson, *Political Change in Latin America: The Emergence of the Middle Sectors* (Stanford: University Press, 1958), p.viii.

[71]Williams, *op.cit.*, p.231.

[72]*Ibid.*, p.233.

[73]*Ibid.*, p.236.

developed philosophical ideas to day-to-day tactical considerations". In a word, Williams suggests that the movement is too deductive and impeded by: a) the heterogeneity of the parties; b) the difficulty of moving from religious ethics to plans of action and political programmes; and, c) rapid change of the practical problems. He writes: "The well-known Latin American affinity for the philosophical and abstract makes very clear and present the danger of losing contact with the realities of politics. Neither Christ nor Maritain, sadly enough, offer concrete programs to solve concrete problems: over-reliance on either in the political arena can spell disaster."[74]

iii) *The revolution*

The high goal of the Christian Democratic movement is social and economic transformation of Latin American society, called *Revolución en Libertad*. But the sober question must be asked: "Is the revolution possible and is it possible under Christian Democratic aegis?" Political programmes must show efficiency and imagination, all the while avoiding "the undeniable corrupting influence of power...and opportunist elements". The revolution cannot succeed without popular support and without practicality; central is the question as to whether "democratic measures can achieve the radical aims which the movement seeks". Can "recalcitrant opposition from strongly entrenched sectors of Latin American society" be overcome through democratic processes? The movement will either

> "...choose to abide by Christian and democratic methods which it has outlined, and probably be relegated to the impotent position of middle-class reformers, or it will forsake the much-heralded means in favour of radical reforms that create basic tensions in society if not overt violence, repression, and authoritarianism. Either alternative is a corruption of the optimistic Christian Democratic politic and a failure to attain the promise of *Revolución en Libertad*. Moreover, either decision would probably spell profound internal dissension within the parties.... Neither their theory nor their practice indicates that the Latin American Christian Democrats will be successful revolutionaries."[75]

e. Assets of the movement

Having summarized Williams' critical remarks we may now listen to what he perceives as strengths of the Christian Democratic movement in Latin America.

i) *Ideology and heritage*

The ideological bent may serve Christian Democratic parties well in Latin America, since now personalist *macho* politics is on the wane and Latin Americans, always interested in ideas and philosophical approaches, may find considerable appeal in Christian Democratic programmes. Further, their newness and nontraditional character may help. One advantage is that Christian Democracy, less than some other (imported) ideologies, "does not imply a break with the Catholic,

---

[74]*Ibid.*, p.240.
[75]*Ibid.*, p.257f.

humanistic value system of the Latin American cultural tradition."[76] Christian Democracy can build on values of personal worth (*dignidad de la persona*), so intrinsic to the Latin American value system, on an emphasis of intermediate groups, and on positive state leadership in a tradition where the state has been the integrating factor.

ii) *Reputation of the parties, electoral appeal*

Williams says that "perhaps the most heartfelt desire of the masses is for honest, conscientious government". While Christian Democracy, like all political movements, may be misled by incompetents and opportunists, it does have some repute for the "integrity of its leadership". In several countries it has passed through "the prestige of political martyrdom".[77] It also knows how to make use of its position in the centre of the political spectrum, whether for forming governmental or opposition alliances. Christian Democratic parties seem to have strong support exactly in the sectors of the electorate which may grow in future influence, including such areas as women, youth, peasantry and the middle sectors.

Along with its Catholic heritage and connections with the European experience, the Christian Democratic movement is sometimes seen as an alternative to what in Latin America has been perceived as "the Communist threat". This role, however, is not unambiguous, for it could both lead to more support as well as suffocate the movement, since more is needed than a negative identity. Guessing - in 1967 - about the future, Williams sees the Christian Democratic movement as reaching no "Social Christian sweep of the continent", but growing here and there in importance.

Let us now consider the more recent view coming out of Latin America.

2. Pablo Richard: The political organization of Christians in Latin America

So much has happened in Latin America since Williams wrote, not the least being the rise of Liberation Theology. It is important to hear the critique of Pablo Richard and like-minded who in a short article give what has become an influential attitude among many Christian leaders who reflect on the political task of Christians in Latin America today.[78] Richard, born in Chile (1939) and professor in the department of theology at the National University of Costa Rica, begins his article by noting that Latin America is both *poor* and *Christian*. Reflection today about the relationship between those two factors leads toward new ways of political responsibility. The old patterns of Christendom and that of the (New Christianity) Christian political party-idea are no longer considered useful or legitimate. Yet to avoid too much individualism here, Richard continues to speak of the importance of the public contribution of Christians "as Christians" toward the political liberation-project of the poor. The churches should be helping Christians find their role

---

[76]*Ibid.*, p.267.

[77]*Ibid.*, p.271ff.

[78]Pablo Richard, "De Politieke Organisatie van de Christenen in Latijns-Amerika", in *Concilium: De Kerk en de Christen-Democratie*, 1987 - 5, p.22ff.

among such challenges. As to the Christian Democratic movement, Richard provides an analysis of, a) its opportunity; b) its crisis; and c) adds suggestions for a new model for political contribution by Christians.

a. Opportunity

Starting around 1930 and up to about 1960 the rise of the Christian Democratic movement in Latin America had some *positive consequences* for Christians of that time, says Richard, since it provided a *reforming* project that had the name of seeking *popular development*. This was in contrast to the earlier *oligarchic* and authoritarian project. The rise of the Christian Democratic project was simultaneous with such changes as industrialization, democratization, modernization and urbanization. Drawing on the *European* tradition and the *social teaching* of the Vatican, the Christian Democratic movement had considerable political possibility because of the following:

i)   The *interclassist* character of the movement, which draws mainly on the middle sectors and some popular sectors, in contrast to the old oligarchic tradition;

ii) Its *reformational and developmental* ideology which loosened it from the traditional struggle between conservatives and liberals, with openness toward the social question;

iii) The *popular* opening, drawing on middle and "popular" sectors, but, says Richard, "without breaking with the dominant capitalistic system";

iv) The *new political institutionalization* which is more democratic and allows for greater participation than the old oligarchic forms did.[79]

b. Crisis

Richard sees the Christian Democratic movement enter a crisis after about 1960 whereby its project becomes distorted. The reasons for the changes were: (1) inherent weakness in the *reforming popular-development* project; (2) the rise of a *new model of domination*, which economically excludes the popular sectors and follows the authoritarian national security doctrine which prevents political action by the middle sectors; (3) the rise of a *new model of the church within the popular movement* ('church of the poor').[80] The results of this crisis of missed opportunity for the Christian Democratic movement, are seen as:

i)   The Christian Democratic movement now ends up *legitimizing* the new domination model and terrible repression, as in El Salvador and Guatemala where "the army has the power and the Christian Democrats are the ideological blanket".

ii) This legitimizing role confuses the church's political possibilities since people still expect results which the Christian Democratic movement cannot supply.

iii) This brings the Christian Democratic movement in conflict with the *political*

---

[79] *Ibid.*, p.23.
[80] *Ibid.*, p.24.

project which arises from the popular movement and in conflict with the Theology of Liberation, says Richard.

c. A new model for political contribution by Christians

Considering the failure of the Christian Democratic movement, it is important to offer a new model, since "for Christians the *collective demand for political efficiency* of faith remains important in a continent that is poor and Christian."[81] Richard suggests:

(1) A new model must be based on the *political project of the liberation of the poor*. The reforming developmental project "no longer exists". The "reasonable alternative is the historical project of the poor". Any model of Christian political organization should root us more firmly in the project of liberating "the people".

(2) A new model must go beyond the *New Christianity (nueva cristiandad) model* in which the church still sees itself as a partner with political power. Richard supposes that the world has been viewed too much as under the church (sacralization model) which explains the former need "for Christian institutions: Catholic school, Catholic university, Catholic labour union, Christian peoples' movement and also a political party of the church and in her service". Rather than such a model of political influence, the church, says Richard, "must only lean on the power of her faith, hope and love; on the power of the gospel". With this spiritual power the church enters the world of the poor like a yeast with the liberative power of the gospel.

(3) The new model must be aligned with the present *renewal movement of the church* which is expressed in official documents as well as in the *comunidades de base* movement. While the new model cannot yet be defined, the rich variety of renewal during approximately the past fifteen years, says Richard, looking especially at his experience in Central America, leads him to suggest not so much a theory but certain *historical elements* which are a basis for the new model, namely:

i) The *common practice* of Christians and non-christians within the liberation project of the poor, which leads to new contacts, respect, discovery and cooperation in a revolutionary political praxis. Quoting Ernesto Cardenal, the suggestion is made that since the majority are Christian, and since, however, Christianity was formerly misused to promote reactionary politics, if the same Christian impulse is channeled into the revolution, then the "Latin American revolution will be insurmountable".[82]

ii) The existence of a *spirituality, a pastoral practice and a theology* which accompanies the Christians in the new political project.

iii) The *political diaconate of the church of the poor* is important. This is a kind of political task which includes: a) *political forming* in the basic communities

---

[81]*Ibid.*, p.26.
[82]*Ibid.*, p.27.

which help people discern political choices; b) the attempt to renew the *social teaching of the church* with priority given to the liberation of the poor (without, however, becoming a "Christian political theory" or "political party programme"); c) the political service of the church in regard to liberation of the poor can help by creating *specialized groups* and committees which facilitate the Christian participation in the liberation project.

Richard repeats that this is quite different than a Christian party practice, but also different than a purely individual response, since it is a "programmed and thought-out step by the church". Christians then participate in the liberation project without forsaking their Christian communion and the church accompanies them in their political engagement through an adequate spirituality, pastoral practice and theology. There is a public Christian contribution to be made to the liberation project of the poor.

3. Otto Maduro: Christian Democracy and liberation

In the same issue of *Concilium,* Otto Maduro, born in Caracas, Venezuela (1945), and author of numerous articles and several books on liberation, writes a critical essay, entitled: "Christian Democracy and the choice in Latin American Catholicism of liberating the oppressed".[83] Maduro begins with noting the limited influence of the Christian Democratic movement, which has achieved power in Chile, Venezuela, El Salvador and Guatemala, but in most of the rest of Latin America is of limited importance or even of no influence. More than this, the movement now faces the challenge of a number of other options in social-political life, including Christians orientated toward the political left who seek something different than Christian Democracy has attained.

a. Latin American Christian Democracy: roots and promises

Maduro sees the European Christian Democratic movement as arising in a church which was weakened by the loss of the bourgeoisie and later the workers, whereby the church "felt threatened by both the liberal anticlericalism of the bourgeoisie and the socialistic rejection of religion". The political answer of Christian Democracy is a "project of the New Christianity" movement, which was supposed to be an alternative to both the old ideas of the Middle Ages and the new ideas of liberalism. It was later popularized in Latin America, but attracted mainly some of the "growing middleclass, Catholic, white, urban, adult, male, intellectual" sector.[84] While the movement performed a critical function by speaking of a "new social utopia...integral humanism...a third way between capitalism and socialism", it missed, according to Maduro, a social-economic analysis of capitalism and sufficiently concrete political plans.

In Latin America the 'European answer' was attempted by organizing leading laity in 'Catholic Action'; what started as Catholic parties grew into Christian

---

[83]*Concilium: De kerk en de christen-democratie,* 1987 - 5, p.89ff.
[84]*Ibid.*, p.91.

Democracy.[85] Maduro says that while it as yet had no power and was a rising opposition party, the Christian Democratic movement developed "a powerful, critical up-to-date and sometimes radical tendency". It could be critical of national and international capitalism, the military dictators and the oligarchies. At the same time it developed an anticommunist tendency as well. It attracted supporters thus from the left and the right at a time when many were enthusiastic about the idea of development and modernization in Latin America.

b. Failure of power

Once the Christian Democrats came to power they felt the pull from different sides. For several reasons the movement proved incapable, according to Maduro:

i) Christian Democrats have never properly "acknowledged social reality as conflictive" but relied on the conviction of "harmony between the social classes", as well as between the Third World and the capitalistic dominant nations.

ii) There is an "almost total separation between the principles they preached and the politics they practiced".

iii) Christian Democrats lack alternative programmes to overcome the misery and dependency so typical for Latin America.

iv) There is an overweight of middleclass professionals and intellectuals within the party structures who do not identify sufficiently with the popular classes;

v) There has been insufficient recognition of the corrupting influence of power and wealth, and a "rather naïve" conviction that the "political-religious faith of Christian Democracy is sufficient to overcome these temptations".[86]

The Christian Democrats, contrary to their "theoretical dreams" were soon to discover that they couldn't please both the employers as well as the workers and unemployed. Once in power, the Christian Democratic 'third way' became but a weak "dependent capitalism". Too close to U.S.A. policies, the movement lost the support of the more nationalistic sectors in Latin America. Maduro posits that the Christian Democrats suffered the delusion (common with the Left as well, he adds) "that through the 'taking of power' the radical change would be immediately possible."[87] They have now lost the perspective of long term change and practice a politics of pragmatic power, on the side of capitalism.

c. The Latin American Church: surpassed Christian Democracy: new actors and answers

Maduro confirms that the 'development-politics' supported around the time of the Kennedy administration are now seen to be a debacle, for "economic dependence, inflation, unemployment, malnutrition, illiteracy, the concentration of capital in the

---

[85]cf.in the same issue of *Concilium*, Franz Horner, "Kerk en christen-democratie", p.29ff.
[86]Maduro, *op.cit.,* p.93.
[87]*Ibid.,* p.94.

hands of few...have *increased the frustration and the protest* of the oppressed."[88] The Christian Democrat movement has gradually become more and more an *enemy* power against the rising popular sectors. In the meantime the critique of capitalism in church encyclicals and by the Latin American bishops, as well as the creative avenues of the basic ecclesial communities and Liberation Theology, have now surpassed the answer given by the Christian Democrats. While the latter were once at the forefront, they are now left behind by the new social movements. "The church has taken notice and embraced the rise of the popular classes as *subject of their own history* - in the church and in society...." The "preferential option for the poor" more and more typifies Latin American Catholicism of our time. But the Christian Democratic movement has not caught the vision, suggests Maduro.

From around 1960 those who worked and lived with the poor began to grasp a different understanding of poverty, more *structural, critical, and engaged* than had been the traditional view by the church and even by Christian Democrats. As the vision on poverty changed, many kinds of studies, movements and forms of conscientization were pursued for promoting solidarity with the poor. There arose new ways of *thinking, expression, organization, and worship* which reflected the new commitment. Popular organizations began to take on political implications. The Christian Democratic parties began to lose support through splits toward the political left, including through the formation of new groups such as the *Cristianos por el Socialismo*.[89] The emphasis on a liberation option for the poor and oppressed brought Christians and Marxists into closer contact. The church became suspect by the dominant powers while the Christian Democrats appear more and more to be part of Latin American dependent capitalism and allied with the influence of the U.S.A. in Latin America.

d. Provisional conclusions by Maduro

Characteristic for the changes during the last twenty-five years in Latin America, says Maduro, is the *rise of the oppressed sectors as historical subject*, creatively and effectively both in the church and society. The passive patience and the fatalistic inertia are gone, also partly through the influence of the *aggiornamento* since John XXIII, and processes of change in production, communication and experiences in political democratization. Also important is the contribution of the ecclesial grassroots movements and the Theology of Liberation. The church is listening more and more to the poor, while the economic, political and military powers are less and less trusting of the church, which in turn means that the oppressed find the church more powerful and believable among them while the dominant powers are in turn more repressive against the liberation actions of the church. The Christian Democrats now appear on the defensive and form a part of the capitalist system: they have "stopped having a Christian meaning", and those Christians who vote for them do not do so out of Christian but rather out of "purely pragmatic reasoning". The Christian Democratic movement was at one time instrumental in calling forth a theological dialogue on political justice, but has now

---

[88]*Ibid.*, p.95.
[89]cf.note 4.

abandoned it for mere pragmatism. The new project is that of the poor as historical subject: the Theology of Liberation and the *comunidades eclesiales de base* are a creative part of the new liberation process. The Christian Democratic movement has not wanted to recognize this liberation process nor the *new way of understanding the relationship between faith and politics*. This new understanding by Liberation Theology neither wishes to be "reduced to a purely political movement", nor does it want to "sacralize a specific political option". In fact, "liberation theology is thus not a 'political theology', but a theological reflection whereby *also* politics can be critically analyzed. ...Theology of Liberation wants to be a reflection on faith from out of the experience of liberation of the oppressed...."[90] It has more aims than the strictly political and the politics it does encourage is a flexible plurality that must be critically evaluated. It involves, according to Maduro, a critical revision of the Christian life in the midst of, and in the service of, the experience of the liberation of the oppressed.

4. Short evaluation of Williams', Richard's and Maduro's views

Williams' study is informative though now dated. It is valuable to look back and see what was said then in comparison to what might be said now. Of particular interest is Williams' relatively early drawing together of the perceived handicaps and assets of the movement. It also remains a view from the outside. It may be noted that some of his critical questions, especially as to *tensions* in the movement between different positions, whether more socially radical, more capitalist or more corporatist, and the *optimism* Christian Democrats seemed to have about changing society, as well as the danger of drifting into power *pragmatism*, all returns in the sharp critique of Richard and Maduro. These latter, in turn, also recognize some moments of positive contribution by Christian Democracy, but emphasize that it has missed the new turn to the oppressed as historical subject. They bring into question some of Williams' positive points as well, especially because of changes since the time that Williams wrote. For example, whereas Williams can speak of integrity of leadership, Richard and Maduro speak of pragmatic cooperation with oppressive powers.

Richard's and Maduro's stance have all the advantages of hindsight, as well as contextuality. They analyze problems of Christian Democracy, especially when it has achieved power, and though Maduro indeed says that delusions of swift changes once in power are "common with the Left" as well, this point is perhaps not given due weight. However, we would also have to admit that the left, as in the case of Castro in Cuba, Allende in Chile, and the Sandinistas in Nicaragua, all have had to contend with forceful external pressure by the U.S.A., whereas the opposite can be said of the Christian Democrats when in power. Richard and Maduro's critique of Christian Democratic regimes in El Salvador and Guatemala is to the point. We shall hear more on this in chapter five.

Richard appears to move rather quickly from the political to the church and surprisingly seems to place a Christian approach to politics back under considerable theological and church tutelage again, especially when he speaks of the new

---

[90]*Ibid.*, p.99.

liberation project as a "programmed and thought-out step by the church". While it is not really Richard's intention to fall back into theological and church tutelage over the political, the wholesale abandonment of Christian party formation may have the result of overloading the theological with political expectations. Further, Richard fails to say if there is any guarantee that another new model will not fail as easily as past models have failed. One might also wonder if Richard is too negative toward reform-development models, whether the "historical project of the poor" is sufficiently defined, and if it is too late for the Christian Democratic movement to regain the lost élan, perhaps through listening to this very critique by Liberation Theology.

It will be evident that the critique by Richard and Maduro cannot easily be gainsaid, and when they ask of the Christian Democrats whether they have tied their Christian identity to political pragmatism, this question must be faced and answered honestly. We are brought back to the basic question: what strategy for change is best in Latin America and how does this relate to a Christian view on political ethics? The two Christian movements of Christian Democracy and Liberation Theology are not in agreement on this, and not always sufficiently in dialogue, either. The articles by Richard and Maduro are, however, an important attempt toward open debate.

5. Resulting points and questions for Christian Democratic political ethics:

i)   Christian Democratic political ethics has envisioned transformation for Latin America.

ii) Many are disappointed by what is perceived to be a gap between political theory and political practice by Christian Democrats.

iii) When in power Christian Democrats have problems controlling the oligarchy and the military (as do other governments).

iv) The middle position can be perceived as no position. It also has coalition possibilities with either side. However, the original vision of combatting poverty is too easily abandoned for pragmatic politics.

v)   Can the Christian Democratic movement afford to ignore the challenge of Liberation Theology, or will it listen to its critique and compare views and strategies?

Transition to chapter four

Having seen in some detail the ethics which underpins Frei's vision on democratic hope for Latin America, and also having reviewed some of the inner tensions within his presentation and questions that arise when we listen to critics of Christian Democracy, we may now turn to the more recent movement which has presented a new challenge in Latin America: Liberation Theology. We shall be interested in comparing the analysis which Gustavo Gutiérrez has made of Latin America and his answer of liberation to what we have just studied from Frei's perspective. In what ways do these two positions differ or perhaps overlap? Are they completely incompatible, or do they together point to perspectives yet to be completed?

CHAPTER FOUR

OPTION FOR THE POOR?

"The decade of *developmentalism* is over and we are now
inaugurating the decade of *liberation*.
...liberation is the new name for development."

(Symposium on Liberation Theology)[1]

Introduction

In this chapter we shall give a summary of Gustavo Gutiérrez' *Teología de la
Liberación* (1971) in section I, with special attention to the theme of development
and liberation. In section II we look more closely at statements in later works by
Gutiérrez which affect our field of inquiry. We provide a perspectival overview in
section III, looking back to Frei as well, and then in section IV we listen to
Michael Novak's critique on the dependency perspective, in order to deepen the
discussion.

I. *TEOLOGIA DE LA LIBERACION*

1. Theology, development and liberation

a. Summary
Theology

Gutiérrez begins his book with an overview of the nature of theology, which is
"of necessity both spirituality and rational knowledge". It is also a "critical
reflection on praxis". Such a modern definition, says Gutiérrez, has roots that go
back to Augustine's *The City of God*,[2] which examines the signs of the times and
their challenge for the Christian community. Orthodoxy is to be balanced by
orthopraxis. This leads to a definition of theology as a self-critique of our basic
principles. This will include economic and socio-cultural issues. Theology is...

> "...the theory of a definite practice. Theological reflection would then necessarily be a
> criticism of society and the Church insofar as they are called and addressed by the Word
> of God; it would be a critical theory, worked out in the light of the Word accepted in
> faith and inspired by a practical purpose - and therefore indissolubly linked to historical
> praxis."[3]

Theology is 'second-step' critical reflection. To be relevant, it must start with
"facts and questions derived from the world and from history", instead of "using

---

[1]Gustavo Pérez, *Simposio sobre Teología de la Liberación* (Bogotá: Editorial Presencia, 1970),
vol.II, p.4.
[2]Augustine, *The City of God*, Gerald G.Walsh, *ed.*, (New York: Doubleday, 1958).
[3]Gustavo Gutiérrez, *Teología de la Liberación, perspectivas* (Lima: CEP, 1971), p.34.

only revelation and tradition as starting points". Critical theology thus "fulfills a liberating function for mankind and the Christian community, preserving them from fetishism...idolatry...narcissism". Theology of liberation is not merely a new theme, says Gutiérrez: it is a *new way* to do theology. Theology no longer merely reflects on the world, but wants to transform the world, becoming part of the struggle against oppression and for the building of a just society - open "to the gift of the Kingdom of God".[4]

Development and liberation

Today we are aware of the unequal development around the world, continues Gutiérrez. The purpose of economic activity can be defined as "wealth", but also as "well-being". Development can be considered in terms of *economic growth*, but also as a *total social process* which includes socio-political-cultural aspects. The first attitude is typically the capitalist approach, while the second is the perspective of social scientists concerned with the Third World, and has a more ethical approach or concern for human values, notes Gutiérrez. In this latter element Christian-inspired and Marxist-inspired approaches can be seen as two humanist (promoting human values) perspectives. Since *development* needs to be truly defined (to include more than mere economic growth), we can better speak of *liberation*. The term development has been criticized in Latin America by calling it developmentalism (*desarrollismo*) and reformism (*reformismo*), to point out that change within the present structures is not enough: the structures have to be challenged. The poor countries are now aware "that their underdevelopment is only the by-product of the development of other countries".[5] Accordingly, true development for the poor countries can only come through breaking the domination by the rich countries. Liberation means a social revolution that breaks such dependence and allows the change toward socialist society.

It was the CELAM II meeting of the Latin American bishops (Medellín, 1968) that for the first time in Roman Catholic theological circles emphasized liberation instead of development. Summarizing his second chapter, Gutiérrez remarks that *liberación:* i) expresses the conflictive aspect of transformation; ii) refers to a dynamic understanding of history; and iii) is closer to biblical-theological roots than is the idea of development (*desarrollo*), which "to a certain extent limits and obscures the theological problems implied in the process designated by this term [development]". These three elements are interdependent within our understanding of "the saving work of Christ". They help us avoid a spiritualistic (idealist) approach as well as avoid a shallow short-term view.[6] The revolutionary situation in the Third World is not content with superficial '*reformismo*'. Liberation means an end to the present status quo and domination. The fuller theme is really: *oppression-liberation*. The *very meaning of Christianity* is in question in our

---

[4]*Ibid.*, p.15.

[5]*Ibid.*, p.51: "Los países pobres toman conciencia cada vez más clara de que su subdesarrollo no es sino el subproducto del desarrollo de otros países...."

[6]*Ibid.*, p.68.

approach to what it means to be Christian in our social praxis.[7]

Liberation means release from the domination of the capitalist countries. Latin America is in "the midst of a full-blown revolutionary ferment" due to "the untenable circumstances of poverty, alienation, and exploitation". Those with the most fruitful approach to liberation in Latin America recognize the need for socialism, though there is diversity in this, and a search for indigenous socialist paths are underway. Gutiérrez stresses that private property must be subordinated to the social good. Though the model is yet to be defined, it is said that it must be a democratic socialism. He speaks favourably of the hope for socialist change in Chile. [Writing in 1971 he could not have known of the coming coup in 1973 against Allende and the installation of Pinochet].

Conceptual clarity

Before entering into discourse on the above, we must be clear about some fundamental definitions which Gutiérrez has in mind, which we may state as follows:

i) The rejection of *developmentalism*

'Developmentalism' (*desarrollismo*), synonymous with 'reformism' (*reformismo*) and with the modernization model,[8] are concepts Gutiérrez uses to refer to a reductionist view of development (*desarrollo*) which thinks in terms of economic growth but not in terms of social services,[9] and is correspondingly weak both in ethics ("attention to human values") and in politics (it misjudges the complexity of the problem and the conflictive aspects).[10] Developmentalism has failed in Latin America because it leaves the unjust structures in tact and does not bring true transformation to the lot of the poor.

ii) Theory of *dependency*

Gutiérrez takes the stance that the situation of dependency is the "starting point for a correct understanding of underdevelopment in Latin America." The major challenge for social sciences in Latin America is "the study of the typical dynamics of dependency". Dependency is a "key element for interpreting Latin American reality". Specifically, the mode of insertion of Latin America into the world economy has brought dependence upon the industrialized nations and continued the subjection to external domination, both economically and politically.[11]

---

[7]*Ibid.*, p.80.

[8]*Ibid.*, p.51: "Desarrollismo pasó así a ser sinónimo de reformismo y modernización. Es decir, de medidas tímidas, ineficaces a largo plazo, cuando no falsas y finalmente contraproducentes para lograr una verdadera transformación."

[9]*Ibid.*, p.47f.

[10]*Ibid.*, p.117: "No tenía suficientemente en cuenta los factores políticos y, lo que es más grave, se mantenía a un nivel abstracto y a-histórico.... La óptica desarrollista y modernizante impedía, pues, ver tanto la complejidad del problema, como los inevitables aspectos conflictuales del proceso, tomado en su conjunto."

[11]*Ibid.*, p.118ff: "Esta situación inicial de dependencia es, pues, el punto de partida para una correcta inteligencia del subdesarrollo en América latina." Gutiérrez quotes from F.H.Cardoso,

iii) Liberation as a *total social process*

At the heart of the concept of liberation for Gutiérrez is the persuasion that humanity must be freed from all kinds of oppression, whether political, economic, ethical or spiritual. (Gutiérrez also speaks of three levels of liberation - cf.point 2, below.) In relation to the question of poverty and development, it must be taken into account that liberation is a total social process which involves all the aspects of life in society.[12] The liberation movement in Latin America, in regard to political transformation, specifically means the "break up of the status quo", which ties into the "domination exercised by the great capitalist countries" and their allies, the Latin American elites, "who control the national power structures".[13] The social revolution, which aims at having the marginalized share in the freedom, opportunities, and wealth presently reserved for the few, means the democratization (in the full sense of including the popular classes) and re-evaluation (in the sense of emphasizing human values, personhood and participation) of society.

Different paradigms: *Christendom, New Christianity, Prophetic model*

Gutiérrez turns to the question of relating faith to society. One of the ways of relating faith and temporal reality was Christendom, in which the task of the church was thought to include the guiding of temporal realities which lack autonomy. The categories of the Christendom mentality are today dysfunctional, he notes. A second approach, which through Jacques Maritain came to be known as the New Christianity, tried to incorporate some modern democratic elements. The main goal of the New Christianity idea was to build a society inspired by Christian principles. The strategy for this was especially through Christian organizations. Maritain made an attempt to distinguish, without separating, the two spheres (*dos planos*) of church and world. The world thereby emerged as autonomous from ecclesiastical authority. The role of the church is then that of "evangelization and the inspiration of the temporal sphere". Gutiérrez sees an advance in responsibility through this "distinction of spheres" view, whereby "Church and world, each in its own way" contribute to the edification of the Kingdom of God.[14] However, the New Christianity (*Nueva Cristiandad*) model soon lost its vitality. Even though it was begun by a socially concerned vanguard, it is now in the hands of conservative power groups in Latin America, says Gutiérrez. This includes the Christian Democratic movement. He suggests that it is now better that the church, in a radicalized

---

Desarrollo y Dependencia (Buenos Aires, 1970): "Las relaciones de dependencia suponen la inserción de las estructuras de modo específicamente desigual: la expansión del mercado mundial creó relaciones de dependencia (y de dominación) entre naciones...el sistema de dominación *externa pasa a ser vivida como interna.*"

[12]*Ibid.*, p.48: In the liberation perspective "el desarrollo es visto como un *proceso social global* que comprende aspectos económicos, sociales, políticos y culturales. ...Enfocar el desarrollo como un proceso social global compromete necesariamente, para algunos, dimensiones éticas, lo que supone, en última instancia, una atención a valores humanos."

[13]*Ibid.*, p.126f.

[14]*Teología de la Liberación.*, p.90: "Los planos están así claramente diferenciados. La unidad estará dada por el reino de Dios; iglesia y mundo contribuyen, cada uno a su manera, a su edificación."

situation, speak more directly - as for example at Medellín-1968. An appeal to the "two spheres" idea has led the church to remain silent on, and appear to legitimize, dictatorial and oppressive governments.

The church now looks the reality of Latin America and the need for transformation directly in the face. The church's role includes such features as *prophetic denunciation* of injustice and a *conscienticizing evangelization* that leads to true humanization. The church must become a poor church, through simplicity of life-style in a spirit of service, free from seeking prestige.

The *Rockefeller Report (1969)* voiced a patronizing concern about the role of the church, says Gutiérrez, when it suggested that like the young, the church may have an idealism about revolution which lacks definition as to governmental system and is guilty of the enthusiasm of first converts (in this case, to Marxism).[15] Yet now we see that the changed situation for the church in Latin America includes persecution, murder of priests and laity, the silencing of the Catholic press. The church is now making "an authentic political option". While Vatican II dealt in terms of underdevelopment, CELAM II recognized the neocolonialism and viewed things from the standpoint of the poor countries.

b. Discourse

Gustavo Gutiérrez has made an original contribution to Latin American theology, a contribution that has been in progress for some decades, without thereby pretending to develop a complete system. The emphasis most important for Gutiérrez has been to seek a contextualized theology in the face of the bitter poverty and repression which so many in Latin America experience on a daily basis. It is easy to jump to conclusions about Gutiérrez' views and miss the way his thinking relates various factors (such as social analysis and theology, faith and praxis, context and utopia), so that some make a caricature out of his intentions.[16] We hope to listen carefully to Gutiérrez' own perspective. We shall limit our discourse to elements most important to our focus on political ethics. Thus we make no evaluation on many other rewarding aspects, and certainly not on the whole, of Gutiérrez' theology.

There is no doubt that Gutiérrez casts the bid high when he opens his first chapter of *Teología de la Liberación*, for he speaks of nothing less than a new way of doing theology. Theology now includes a "critical reflection on society and the Church" and "tries to be part of the process through which the world is transformed". His opening gambit is bold and clear: development(alism) has failed; it is

---

[15]cf.*The Rockefeller Report on the Americas* (Chicago: Quadrangle Books, 1969), p.31.

[16]It is well known that early reactions were disturbed by certain concepts used by Gutiérrez, such as class struggle, socialism, revolution, so that he was accused of views he did not hold. In our opinion we see two factors at work in this: first, some analysts jump hastily to conclusions when they meet concepts they dislike; secondly, most concepts carry many connotations and must be clarified, especially when taken from one area, such as philosophy or sociology, and introduced into another area, such as theology and ethics. We must emphasize that such concepts are often quite remolded by Gutiérrez due to his own use of these, through the searching for both a contextualized understanding and Christian normativity. For a recent discussion on the context, coherence, and development within Gutiérrez' theology, see especially Jacques Van Nieuwenhove, *Bronnen van Bevrijding: Varianten in de Theologie van Gustavo Gutiérrez* (Kampen: Kok, 1991).

time for liberation.

A first question to be asked is whether Gutiérrez is accurate in saying that development (economic growth, reform, and modernization) have failed.[17]

Our answer is that the facts of poverty and malnutrition so widely spread in Latin America would seem to speak for themselves. That the poor are many is definitely a very brutal fact. Factors often mentioned by development and liberation analysts[18] include: i) even when the GDP improves, this is not necessarily passed on to the poor (i.e., one must consider the social indicators); ii) economic growth does not keep pace with the population growth in many parts of the region; iii) agricultural export products have not kept pace with the cost of imported manufactured products; iv) transnational companies have a disproportionate weight to many local companies and even governments;[19] v) the impoverishment has continued and even worsened for many parts of the region since the "oil shock" (1973) and the "debt crisis" (1981) leading to present "economic adjustments" which intending development are presently increasing the impoverishment of many.[20] Analysts of all political and economic persuasions, though disagreeing on policies, do agree on the fact of the "crisis". Thus we conclude that Gutiérrez is accurate in saying that development has failed, and is correct in using this fact as a mayor premise in his perspective on liberation.

Secondly, we saw above that the situation of dependency is presumed to be "the starting point for a correct understanding of underdevelopment in Latin America". How does the inclusion of the dependency paradigm function in Gutiérrez' liberation perspective? We shall briefly discuss three features:

i) Poverty is seen by Gutiérrez as a *structural problem of domination and oppression.* Since the fact of dependency cannot be denied, an alternative is to find reasons for dependency other than because of external exploitation. However, those who argue that dependency comes from internal problems, cannot ignore the fact that the pattern of internal problems has roots in colonial and neocolonial history. We might at this point recall that Frei (ch.3:I.2.a.) challenged the idea of 'we are weak because we are dependent' with the thought: 'we are dependent because we are weak' in political-economic organ-ization. Judging by how the debate on this matter has stirred minds and pens (and hearts), it is worth considering whether there are some elements of truth on both sides of the argument, and also whether there are (ideological) presuppositions which

---

[17]Some take the position that development has not yet been truly applied (cf.section IV on Michael Novak).

[18]cf.Gonzalo Martner, *coord., América Latina hacia el 2000: Opciones y estrategias* (Caracas: Nueva Sociedad, 1986). *Idem., El Desafío Latinoamericano: Potencial a desarrollar* (Caracas: Nueva Sociedad: 1987).

[19]cf.Leslie Sklair, *Sociology of the Global System* (London: Simon & Schuster, 1991). An often cited example is that of the ITT (International Telephone and Telegraph Company) spending hundreds of thousands of dollars to campaign against Salvador Allende in Chile. cf.Michael J.Kryzanek, *U.S.-Latin American Relations* (New York: Praeger, 1990), p.130.

[20]cf.Fernando Enrique Cardoso, *et.al., The Crisis of Development in Latin America* (Amsterdam: CEDLA, 1991). Alcides Hernández Chavez, *coord., Deuda Externa y Crisis en América Latina* (Tegucigalpa: Guaymuras, 1988).

easily mislead us.

ii) The dependency perspective is *not compared* by Gutiérrez with other theories on poverty and wealth. That is regrettable, since a comparative description of sources of poverty could have strengthened his reasoning for giving the dependency perspective ample room or even priority over other perspectives on poverty (which is often alternatively ascribed, for example, to a lack of certain ingredients, such as entrepreneurial efficiency and technology). At the same time we judge that Gutiérrez obviously has a strong case for saying that poverty in Latin America is embedded in oppressive structures which create and maintain poverty.

iii) *Capitalism* is viewed as part of the problem and *socialism* as part of the answer. What is capitalism for Gutiérrez? It is especially "dependent capitalism" (*capitalismo dependiente*), or foreign domination, intertwined with an oppressive oligarchic system.[21] To argue that what is needed is "democratic capitalism" in Latin America (cf.section IV on Michael Novak) is at best to present an important element, but not to deal with the colonial/neocolonial history of the region, nor with the question of the world system. What, correspondingly, does Gutiérrez understand by socialism? A democratic (especially 'popular') political ethics which give priority to basic human needs and participation by the marginalized (who are 'nonpersons' in the present system). Such socialism is in an experimental stage in Latin America.[22]

Thirdly, we have seen that liberation is a multidimensional concept for Gutiérrez, which is deeply cultural and spiritual.[23] We shall continue to inquire about the unity and variety of meaning he gives this concept, and especially about the relation this bears to his view on political ethics. We have already seen that liberation for Gutiérrez ties into political ethics in a qualitative way, inspiring a concentration on "human values", and not merely on economic growth. Further, the social revolution Gutiérrez seeks will open up space for the popular sectors, the oppressed people, and allow them to participate democratically in freedom, in education, in health care, and in the wealth which is presently reserved largely for the elite.[24]

Fourthly, Gutiérrez is clear in presenting three historical models of relating faith to culture. The vision of Christendom (unified around the church) has become

---

[21]Gutiérrez does not draw a distinction between the Iberian feudal mercantilist system and neocolonial capitalism, since both of these profit from the dependency of Latin America. While he might have said more about the possibility of internal industrial-welfare capitalism, this does not seem to provide an option (cf.the summary below, section II.2: "International capitalism"). As with Frei, so also with Gutiérrez, the word capitalism tends to mean a consumer society built on exploitation and an unbalanced global situation which has forgotten human values so that extreme riches and extreme poverty exist side by side.

[22]*Teología de la Liberación*, p.148ff: "Hacia una transformación de la realidad latinoamericana."

[23]*Ibid*, p.61f: "Concebir la historia como un proceso de liberación del hombre, es percibir la libertad como conquista histórica;...Esto implica no sólo mejores condiciones de vida, un cambio radical de estructuras, una revolución social, sino mucho más: la creación continua, y siempre inacabada, de una nueva manera de ser hombre, una *revolución cultural permanente.*"

[24]For a discussion of social revolution in Gutiérrez, cf.Jacques Van Nieuwenhove, *op.cit.*, p.60ff.

dysfunctional in modern times where the independence of spheres and on-going democratization of decision-making dominate. The New Christianity ideal, expressed in the Christian organization strategy, activated the laity; however, a weakness, says Gutiérrez, is that it fell into a status quo mentality. Politically, its expression in the Christian Democratic movement missed a consequent turn toward the popular classes (the poor) and did not arrive at sufficient prophetic and structural critique of injustice.

Now, it is a common question - we saw this also with Frei - to ask whether Liberation Theology, in trying to re-unite faith and politics in a liberative praxis, can avoid ideological blindness. By 'ideological blindness' we mean, for example, to accept theories on transformation without sufficient examination of reality. Such theories might be: socialism (or capitalism) knows best; or, for example, that the end of dependency means the end of poverty and oppression. In regard to the first, Gutiérrez recognizes the need for a democratic, self-critical socialism;[25] in regard to the second, he sees the task as much more creative than merely ending injustices; it also involves the building of a qualitatively different society[26] (and even a better humanity). In so far as liberative praxis is true to the perspective of Gutiérrez, it will be characterized by openness to self-critique and may not, therefore, be accused by critics to be entirely 'ideologically tainted' in an a priori manner.[27] By way of example: that he emphasizes the reality of the class struggle, must be seen in the light of the failure of an interclass answer in Latin America, and the ongoing impoverishment (often under the name of liberal democracy).

2. Faith and the new humanity: encountering God in history

a. Summary
The gospel and politics
Today, continues, Gutiérrez, salvation is not seen as other-worldly, but relates to the transformation of every aspect of human existence: it is "intrahistorical...and guides history to its fulfilment".[28] Just as faith 'desacralizes' creation, so the Exodus from Egypt 'desacralizes' social praxis. 'Humanization' is part of the process of salvation. The dilemma between "either spiritual redemption or temporal redemption" comes from "Western dualistic thought (matter-spirit), foreign to the biblical mentality". The "liberating action of Christ", says Gutiérrez, is at the heart of the struggle for justice. Overcoming the old dualism, however, must not lead us

---

[25]*Ibid.*, p.129: "Entre los grupos y personas que han levantado la bandera de la liberación latinoamericana, la inspiración socialista es mayoritaria y representa la veta más fecunda y de mayor alcance. No se trata, sin embargo, de una orientación monolítica. Una diversidad, teórica y práctica, empieza a diseñarse. Las estrategias y tácticas son distintas y, en muchos casos, hasta divergentes."

[26]*Ibid.*, p.131: "Procurar la liberación del subcontinente va más allá de la superación de la dependencia...es, más profundamente...una verdadera revolución cultural."

[27]The Vatican document by the *Congregation for the Doctrine of the Faith* (August 1984), on "Instruction on Certain Aspects of the 'Theology of Liberation'", warns about "borrowed concepts of an ideological inspiration". This, however, must of course be applied to all ideologies, capitalisms as well as socialisms.

[28]*op.cit.*, p.194ff.

to sacralize certain ideas on 'progress' and 'development'. Sin becomes evident in oppressive structures, as the Medellín Conference pointed out, notes Gutiérrez. Though the Kingdom of God is more, it includes political liberation. A spirituality of liberation is needed: "a concrete manner, inspired by the Spirit, of living the Gospel". It must be a contemporary commitment. A spirituality of liberation means *conversion* to the neighbour, the oppressed and exploited. Conversion includes the socio-economic and political: "without a change in these structures, there is no authentic conversion".

We come, then, says Gutiérrez, to the old question of "the relationship between Gospel and politics". Today, there is a "new political theology". When challenged by the Enlightenment and later by Marx, theology reacted by privatizing the life of faith abstracted from the social world. We must now "de-privatize" faith. The new political theology will not mix politics and religion as in the past; yet it will - along with the church - be an instrument of social criticism, serving the liberation of humanity. The church (and not just the individual Christian) becomes "the subject of the praxis of liberation". The church must thus find a new self-awareness in order to so function.

Turning to Jesus, Gutiérrez suggests that there has been an "iconization" or a theological abstraction of his life, which places it outside of history. Then it is alleged that Jesus was apolitical. However, Jesus confronted the groups in power, both the political and religious leaders. Accordingly, "Jesus is opposed to all politico-religious messianism which respects neither the depth of the religious realm nor the separate identity of political action".[29] The gospel's political dimension does not refer to a particular political option, but is in itself subversive to established powers of wrongful domination, pointing us to a society of solidarity and justice.

Three levels of liberation

Gutiérrez also speaks of *utopia*. Popularized by Thomas More's work of the same name, it has also come to mean a "lack of realism". But today its subversive element is again recognized. It can be related antithetically to history: Thomas More described a future society without private property, money or privileges. Utopia functions as denunciation and annunciation (Freire). Or, says Gutiérrez, we can also think of Marcuse's "Great Refusal".[30] *Utopia* spurs on to historical praxis and a new social consciousness. It is imaginative and dynamic, while contrarily, *ideology* masks the established order and is dogmatic. Gutiérrez speaks of three levels of liberation: i) economic, social, political liberation; ii) creation of a new humanity and a society of solidarity; iii) liberation from sin, communion with God and neighbour. The first relates to scientific rationality; the second to utopia or historical projections; the third to faith. It is only through utopia that faith and politics are correctly related. To posit an immediate relationship is to "seek from

---

[29]*Ibid.*, p.301: "Jesús es opuesto a todo mesianismo político-religioso que no respeta ni la hondura de lo religioso ni la consistencia propia de la acción política."

[30]cf.Hebert Marcuse, *Reason and Revolution* (Boston: Beacon Press, 1968); *idem., One-Dimensional Man* (Boston: Beacon, 1968).

faith norms and criteria for particular political options", while in reality these options must be based on rational analysis of reality; on the other hand, to posit that faith and politics are not related leads to political opportunism. Utopia, so understood, does not make us dreamers but radicalizes our political commitment. Christian hope keeps us open to the gift of the Kingdom; then we do not absolutize any stage of history or any revolution.

b. Discourse

Gutiérrez' emphasis on integral salvation that relates to "the whole person" and by implication to all aspects of life, can only be welcomed. He correctly sees the unacceptability of the old dilemma between "either spiritual redemption or temporal redemption", expressed in "Western dualistic thought (matter-spirit), foreign to the biblical mentality".[31] That, gladly assumed, we shall not go into the challenges of his soteriology as such, but rather consider how he relates faith to *desarrollo* and *liberación*. And indeed, he soon says that certain ideas on "progress" and "development" must not be sacralized. This is certainly a needed warning, given what seems to be an almost perennial persistence of the status quo to seek the blessing of the church. Does Gutiérrez equally see the danger of sacralizing liberation-theory? He does, in fact, build in important limiting guidelines, saying that political liberation "is not *the* coming of the Kingdom, not *all* of salvation".[32] It would by no means be correct to say that he reduces the gospel to the political. Nor does he wish to 'sacralize' (theologically legitimize) specific political choices. His speaking of three levels of liberation has the merit of keeping the relation between the gospel and politics indirect. Gutiérrez, does, however, wish to emphasize the demands of the gospel for justice. Conversion to God, Gutiérrez says, is conversion to the neighbour, with an emphasis on the oppressed and exploited neighbour. In order to keep an open (creatively dialectical rather than ideologically closed) relationship between gospel mandate and politically liberative praxis, Gutiérrez speaks of utopia as the means for relating faith and politics. We thus arrive at a dynamic epistemology which undergirds Gutiérrez' view of liberative transformation; we shall briefly summarize what we see as the essential role played by the following elements of his epistemology: i) praxis as a walking in the truth; ii) the poor as subjects of their own history; iii) the role of the utopian aspect.

Praxis

We have already seen how Gutiérrez defines theology at the very beginning of his book as a critical reflection on historical praxis. Praxis, for Gutiérrez, involves doing the truth, or walking in justice.[33] This ties into a "new way of doing theology", which protests against injustice and seeks a new and fraternal society.[34]

---

[31] *Teología de la Liberación*, p.222f.

[32] *Ibid.*, p.240: "Puede decirse que el hecho histórico, político, libertador *es* crecimiento del reino, *es* acontecer salvífico, pero no es *la* llegada del reino, ni *toda* la salvación."

[33] cf.Jacques Van Nieuwenhove, *Bronnen van Bevrijding*, p.40ff: "Kritische Theolgie en Historische Praxis".

[34] *Teología de la Liberación*, p.40: Liberation theology is "una teología que no se limita a pensar el mundo, sino que busca situarse como un momento del proceso a través del cual el

It is in the doing of the will of God (also in a situation of oppression that cries out for justice) that we encounter truth through a conversion to God and to the neighbour. That said, how do we more specifically arrive at such a liberative praxis? The following two points are key concepts for Gutiérrez.

The poor as subjects of their own history (epistemological privilege)

It is to be noted that Gutiérrez has a central emphasis on the poor as subjects of their own history, i.e., also of their own transformation. Said shortly: since the dominant minority, the oligarchy, benefits from the status quo, we may not expect them to be the subject of transformation, acting against what they understand as their own interest. Besides that, to focus on the powerful as subjects of history is too paternalistic towards the poor and marginalized. Gutiérrez combines the liberation of the poor with the right of the poor to finally have a voice in their own history. It is, of course, well known that critiques of material dialectical thinking often question the ability of class consciousness to avoid its own forms of ideological reification.[35] Another critique is that since it is generally admitted that the poor are too powerless to effect the necessary changes, or even too alienated to have a vision of transformation, revolutionary leaders are necessary. But these revolutionary leaders are also theorists, and we are thus back at the basic question of theories of change (for example, a classist theory overagainst an interclass theory; or, for example, a material technical approach overgainst a material dialectical approach). Has Gutiérrez entered this maze unaware, accepting ready-made concepts on the poor as subjects of the revolution?

We do not judge this to be so. He does make choices among the possible political-economic-ethical perspectives, including the discussion of ideologies (as systems of thought and even of a certain trust). But it must also be recognized that Gutiérrez has built in a number of limiting aspects which show that he is aware of the problem of defining the new transformation. He points out the many forms of socialism, thus avoiding oversimplifying reifications on this point. He limits the scope of class consciousness by drawing on normative principles from the gospel, such as justice and love for the neighbour. He has on-going openness and critique as an essential part of all praxis. Here the utopian aspect of historical transformation plays a creative role.

The importance of the utopian dimension

We arrive at an element easily glossed over by negative critics of Liberation Theology, namely the question of ideology and transformation. Said shortly: according to Gutiérrez, the utopian dimension of praxis has the critically-creative power to subvert the accepted status quo, and to mobilize toward a qualitatively

---

mundo es transformado: abriéndose - en la protesta ante la dignidad humana pisoteada, en la lucha contra el despojo de la inmensa mayoría de los hombres, en el amor que libera, en la construcción de una nueva sociedad, justa y fraternal - al don del reino de Dios."

[35]As J.S.Reinders puts it, in *Violence, Victims and Rights: A Reappraisal of the argument from institutionalized violence with special reference to Latin American liberation theology* (Amsterdam: Free University, 1988), p.145: "In my opinion, the claim to the epistemological privilege of the poor is in danger of excluding the subjects of liberation from moral criticism."

transformed society.[36] The utopian aspect is thus anti-ideological and also keeps liberative transformation itself from becoming ideological (uncritically self-serving and dogmatic).

There is another possible critique we should mention in this context. Those who begin with individual responsibility and see social problems largely in that perspective, tend to suspect socialist utopian perspectives as largely soft on personal responsibility, as if these 'utopians' expect to build a new humanity merely by changing the structures.[37] While this critique has its own contribution, we may as yet reply in line with Gutiérrez: i) individual identity and even our understanding of good and evil are intertwined with social consciousness and structures; ii) attention to the 'social question' does not thereby imply inattention to more personal dimensions of transformation (personal spirituality is important for Gutiérrez and has gained in emphasis in his writings); iii) an individualistic approach to poverty in Latin America would have to ignore many aspects of historical-empirical reality.

All this does not preclude further questions on Gutiérrez' selection and understanding of political-economic concepts within his transformation ethics. Such a question might be: why does Liberation Theology present a material dialectical approach without much encouragement on a material technical approach to poverty and transformation? The reply, in short form, appears to be: development has failed without liberation. Another question is whether Gutiérrez' focus on oppression and his discussion of the utopian dimension detracts from emphasizing the empowering and enabling structures of human freedom.[38] Yet Gutiérrez clearly calls for organization of the poor and democratization of society. His critique of social structures includes a searching for better and more just structuralization of human society, locally, regionally, and internationally. Again, it might be asked if a fuller comparison could not have been made of political-economic paradigms.[39] While that would have been of interest, it remains true that Gutiérrez points to the principial direction in which he believes Latin America should move: namely toward justice, understood in the sense of full human rights for personhood, participation in society, and better distribution of available resources.

---

[36]cf.Van Nieuwenhove, *op.cit.* p.65f.: 'Utopie en bevrijdende praxis'; and *passim.* Also, Raúl Vidales y Luis Rivera Pagán, *La Esperanza en el Presente de América Latina: "El Discernimiento de las Utopías"* (San José: DEI, 1983). Horacio Victorio Cerutti Guldberg, "Para una Filosofía Política Indo-Ibero Americana: América en las Utopías del Renacimiento", in Hugo Assmann, Enrique Dussel, *et al.*, *Hacia una Filosofía de la Liberación Latinoamericana* (Buenos Aires: Bonum, 1973).

[37]cf."Instruction on Certain Aspects", iv.15.

[38]cf.Rebecca S.Chopp, *The Praxis of Suffering: An Interpretation of Liberation and Political Theologies* (Maryknoll: Orbis, 1986), p.145f.

[39]Unlike E.F.Schumacher, Gutiérrez does not refer to the possibilities in their full range. cf.*Small is Beautiful: A study of economics as if people mattered* (London: Sphere Books, 1974), p238, where Schumacher lists the following eight schematic models:

1.Freedom	2.Freedom	3.Freedom	4.Freedom
Market Economy	Planning	Market Economy	Planning
Private Ownership	Private Ownership	Collectivised Ownership	Collectivised Owner.

5.Totalitarianism	6.Totalitarianism	7.Totalitarianism	8.Totalitarianism
Market Economy	Planning	Market Economy	Planning
Private Ownership	Private Ownership	Collectivised Ownership	Collectivised Owner.

3. The Church: sacrament of history...and poverty

a. Summary

Gutiérrez continues his story: The church must be "uncentered". While the early church favoured freedom in society so that it, too, could survive, the christianization of society after the fourth century led to church-centeredness and finally to "outside the church there is no salvation", so that "to be for or against Christ came to be fully identified with being for or against the church". Religious liberty was lost. With the rupture of Christendom in the modern period the church needs to find a new posture. It is now evident that "the prevailing capitalist society in Latin America has made the institutional church into a part of the system and the Christian message into a part of the dominant ideology."[40] The church has been but a "piece of the system". The social-political role of the church must change. Some now fear a "Constantinianism of the Left".[41] But if the church truly casts its lot with the oppressed and exploited, it will divest itself of power and thus of a privileged ideology. The question is not whether the church must use its influence, but rather the question is: "for or against the established order", which is largely a repressive order in Latin America. The church, as a sacrament of history (historical sign of liberation) is called to *denounce* every dehumanizing situation and give a "radical critique of the present order". Since the church's position in Latin America is public, its denunciations must also be public. Similarly, the church *announces* love, communion, and personalization.[42]

Class struggle

Gutiérrez also refers to the presence of the class struggle as a cardinal world problem that the church must face. To deny this problem is to avoid viewing things as they are and as they are experienced by those who have been marginalized. To ignore the fact of class struggle is to be deceived. Groups in power think that those who speak of class struggle "advocate" it, whereas to recognize it as a fact, says Gutiérrez, is not to invent it nor endorse every expression of it. Those who propose an "interclassist doctrine" are in fact classist and reflect the view of the dominant class. To announce the love of God for all people is not to avoid conflict and confrontation, nor does it mean to preserve a fictitious harmony or false reconciliation. Rather, as Girardi has said: "Love for those who live in a condition of objective sin demands that we struggle to liberate them from it. The liberation of the poor and the liberation of the rich are achieved simultaneously."[43] Love for

---

[40]*Teología de la Liberación*, p.342.

[41]One can think here of what A.Fierro writes in *The Militant Gospel* (Maryknoll: Orbis, 1977), p.75, where he notes "a new Christian political mythology fed by the lexicon of the leftist. ...Christians seem to be looking for a new Constantine, embodied now in the guerrilla fighter rather than in an emperor."

[42]'Personalization' and 'integral humanization' are categories that dominate in Roman Catholic philosophy, especially since Maritain and Mounier, as well as in the social encyclicals and the Christian Democratic vocabulary. Cf.Carlos M.Manjarrés & Antonio G.Fraile, *Fe Cristiana y Mundo Moderno: Religión y Moral Católica* (Madrid: Paulinas, 1985), p.91ff.: "Tema 8: Los humanismos del siglo XX ante la fe cristiana". Also E.Mounier, *El Personalismo* (Buenos Aires: Editorial Universitaria, 1987; trans. of *Le Personnalisme*, Paris, 1950).

[43]Gutiérrez quotes from J.Girardi, Amor cristiano y lucha de clases (Salamanca: Sígueme,

the oppressors means to liberate them from themselves as oppressors, thus to combat the oppressive class. To "love our enemies" does not eliminate "the radicalness of the combat against them". The church itself is split by the social divisions and cannot place itself beyond the question of oppression. Unity - as a gift of God and as an historical conquest by humanity - is the "result of overcoming all that divides people".[44]

Poverty: solidarity and protest
i) Since Vatican II the theme of poverty has been recovered. Poverty first of all means *material poverty*. Some Christians give this a positive value. But it leads to a subhuman situation. In the Bible poverty is a central theme: it is a scandalous condition contrary to human dignity and to the will of God. Poverty is not the result of fate but of oppression. Gutiérrez quotes Amos 2:6,7 and lists numerous other texts. The Bible speaks of concrete ways of avoiding poverty, as in Israel's legislation "to prevent the accumulation of wealth and the consequent exploitation"; this included the pardoning of debts and return of property.[45]
ii) There is also *spiritual poverty*, about which there is much confusion. A 'spiritualistic' approach defines the poor person as one who is unattached to material goods - even though one does possess them. But spiritual poverty is better defined, says Gutiérrez, as "openness to God". This spiritual poverty means to entrust ourselves to God and is called "blessed" in Matthew 5:1. It is the "precondition for being able to receive the Word of God", says Gutiérrez, and is not a question of indifference to the goods of this world. Luke's "blessed are you poor" (6:20), is not the "canonization of a social class". Nor is it meant to sacralize misery and injustice by preaching resignation. Rather, as material poor, they are now blessed because the Kingdom of God is being "received in history" - and "this implies the reestablishment of justice in this world".

1971).

[44]Gutiérrez rewrote this section on "Christian Fellowship and Class Struggle", in the new edition calling it "Faith and Social Conflict". He says that the original section "gave rise to misunderstandings that I want to clear up. I have rewritten the text in the light of new documents of the magisterium and by taking other aspects of the subject into account". *cf.A Theology of Liberation*: 15th Anniversary Edition (Maryknoll: Orbis, 1988), p.156. A comparison of the original section and the new section shows that while the first emphasized the reality of the class struggle, the second puts an emphasis on the importance of Christian love. However, also in the new edition Gutiérrez repeats that the class struggle is a reality. He appeals to John Paul II's encyclical *Laborem Exercens*, quoting passages which show that the problem is one of structures, the ownership of property, and the class conflict of interests between 'capital' and 'labour', as well as a problem of personal conflict, since, as *Laborem Exercens* (14) says: "It is obvious that, when we speak of opposition between labour and capital, we are not dealing with abstract or 'impersonal forces' operating in economic production. Behind both concepts there are persons, living, actual persons; on the one side are those who do the work without being the owners of the means of production, and on the other side those who act as entrepreneurs and who own these means or represent the owners." In the new edition Gutiérrez adds in a footnote: "It is enough to say that the determinist approach based on economic factors is completely alien to the kind of social analysis that supplies a framework for the theology of liberation."

[45]cf.Leviticus 25. Robert Gnuse, *Comunidad y Propiedad en la Tradición Bíblica* (Estella: Verbo Divino, 1987). Marcelo de Barros & José Luis Caravias, *Teología de la Tierra* (Madrid: Ediciones Paulinas, 1988).

iii) A third meaning is: "poverty as a commitment of solidarity and protest". "Christian poverty" does not mean to idealize material poverty, but rather is solidarity *with the poor* through a protest *against poverty*. The ideal is not to become poor, but to eliminate poverty. Today, poverty is a political effect of exploitation. To accept "Christian poverty" is to side with the oppressed and to put one's life in danger in Latin America. The church can only preach "spiritual poverty", openness to God, if it makes itself poor (commits itself to the poor) in order to protest against and reject poverty.[46]

b. Discourse

The church in Latin America must relate to the context of social revolution, affirms Gutiérrez. That is clear. Yet the question remains: how and with what vision? Gutiérrez offers us two choices: the church must decide whether it is "for or against the established order", whereby the established order is described as exploitive, capitalistic, caught in dependency, lacking in human rights, and so forth. The church (Roman Catholic or Protestant) could hardly choose for such an exploitive order. Yet, actively and silently it has often done just that in the past history of colonialism and in present neocolonialism. It is to the credit of Liberation Theology that it has sought to turn the tide and is without doubt a major factor in on-going conscientization.

The question of how the church and theology can best go on contributing to liberation raises three further questions we would like to mention in relation to the above:

i) Does Gutiérrez lose the possibility of a mediary role for the church by evoking a class oriented analysis in his theology? We answer that 'class' must be understood in the Latin American context. The dominant class has been maintained in its position through factors which include colonial history, army politics which often ignores basic human rights, and international capital, as well as U.S.A. foreign policy (cf.ch.2.I.6). Latin America cannot be understood without taking class structure into account. While the mediary role of the church is important, it must not lead to evasion of describing the actual structures and calling for the kinds of changes necessary.

ii) Does his class struggle emphasis perhaps tend toward a negation of the negation without relating this sufficiently to building blocks of reconstruction? To this it may be said that while it is true that Gutiérrez does not tackle the question of reconstruction in a completely systematic way, he does mention enough to point in the direction of popular democracy, restoration of human rights, incarnation of human values into the political-economic system, and on-going social critique and transformation.

iii) In spite of many good insights is there perhaps a hindering streak of undifferentiated thinking, so that the role of the church at times seems to be that of

---

[46]For an overview on the history of poverty, cf.Paul Christophe, *La Historia de la Pobreza* (Estella: Verbo Divino, 1989).

assuaging the lack of vital political party alternatives? We answer that Gutiérrez is careful to keep the relationship between church and politics (cf.above on
utopia) indirect, that is, dialectical rather than ideological. Further, his liberation theology does not intend to replace the task of political-economic analysis
nor the task of political parties and other organizations. We could better say
that Gutiérrez had the courage to place on the agenda a topic being ignored in
too many parts of society.

In his last chapter we find keen insights on poverty. Gutiérrez has pointed clearly
to the fact that the economic problem (development) is very much tied into a
political problem (liberation). Of importance is to recognize that he intends to make
some quite principial statements about the Christian calling to do justice, but he
does not pretend to provide a full map on social ethics. There are points at which a
more comparative method may help a theology of liberation.[47] The strength of his
vision - and that is a great good - is that the church and Christians must become a
prophetic voice of conscientization on the exploitative situation of the *non-person*.

II. DEPENDENCY IN GUTIERREZ' LATER WRITINGS

1. Introduction

When Gutiérrez first published *Teología de la Liberación* in 1971, defining
liberation in contrast to modernization theory, he was aware of limits to the
paradigm of dependency.[48] Looking back over twenty years we see that the
modernization/dependency debate has not stood still nor has Gutiérrez' attitude to
this sociological mediation remained the same. Especially since *perestroika* the
rethinking of the dependency theory is and will be affected by the status of the
political left in Latin America.[49] The fact of dependency remains; the interpretation may change. In his 1971 *Teología de la Liberación*, Gutiérrez accepts the idea
that underdevelopment in Latin America can best be understood from the *dependency* viewpoint. This is a constitutive element of his liberation perspective. He is
likewise strong on the idea that *external* dominating factors lead to *internal*
domination and dependency,[50] a point to be restated strongly in *La Fuerza*.

---

[47]Rebecca Chopp, *Praxis of Suffering*, p.146, suggests: "Gutiérrez has, as yet, failed to make
the essential link between human consciousness and institutional structures within his own
philosophy of history". Also, Wogaman, *Christian Perspectives on Politics*, p.60: "One can
read through the work of many liberation theologians without finding much discussion on
postrevolutionary political institutions." However, we must not by-pass the clear intention of
Gutiérrez to favour popular organization of the people and a democratic socialism which will
empower the poor to participate fully in society.

[48]For example, *Theology of Liberation*, p.87, where Gutiérrez quotes Cardoso, saying that
"The importance of analyzing the problems of the peripheral countries in terms of dependence,
as we understand it, requires an effort to avoid new reifications...."

[49]Robert Carty, "Latin American leftists look ahead", *Latinamerica Press*, vol.22, no.36,
October 4, 1990, p.7: "Like believers who have just lost religion, Latin American leftists are
looking for new ideas, new models, even new words to define themselves."

[50]*Teología de la Liberación*, p.118ff. Cf.Arthur F.McGovern, "Dependency Theory, Marxist
Analysis, and Liberation Theology" in Marc H.Ellis & Otto Maduro, *The Future of Liberation
Theology: Essays in Honor of Gustavo Gutiérrez* (Maryknoll: Orbis, 1989).

In 1979 Gutiérrez published *La Fuerza Histórica de los Pobres*, which is a collection of eight essays, published separately in the years "between Medellín and Puebla". We shall review how he there speaks of dependency and liberation, and also of international capitalism.

2. *La Fuerza Histórica de los Pobres* (1979): *The Power of the Poor in History*

In *La Fuerza* Gutiérrez takes another look at the causes of the present situation in Latin America. He affirms that the "most important change" in the new understanding of Latin America is the awareness that underdevelopment is "primarily due to economic, political, and cultural dependence on power centres that lie outside Latin America".[51] Later on he says that the problems go too deep to speak of mere reforms: "...we speak of social revolution, not reform; of liberation, not development; of socialism, not modernization of the prevailing system." And in the same context he again mentions dependency and the idea of the Latin American system being best understood as "dependent capitalism".[52] He also takes note of the influence of the industrial revolution. While it gave an unprecedented transformation, it has also included the aggravation of contradictions which are "now at the point of international crisis".[53]

In his essay *Teología desde el reverso de la historia (Theology from the underside of history)* included in the same volume, Gutiérrez again mentions the dependency theory, noting that earlier research perhaps failed to sufficiently point out that the confrontation is not primarily between nations and continents whereby centre and periphery are understood geographically, but in terms of power between social classes; into this basic conflict other factors enter, such as nationalism, race conflict, and the role of the multinationals. When asked during a conference in the same year (1979) about the use of the dependency theory, Gutiérrez replied that liberation theology should not be reduced to one of its aspects which it sees as a helpful means to understand social reality. He said that such social analysis will probably change for liberation theology in the future, but at present there is "no other alternative" social theory "for studying the situation in Latin America".[54]

---

[51]Gutiérrez, *La Fuerza Histórica de los Pobres* (Salamanca: Sígueme, 1982), p.41: "El subdesarrollo como hecho global aparece cada vez más claramente y, ante todo, como la consecuencia de una dependencia económica, política y cultural de centros de poder que están fuera de América latina. La dinámica de la economía capitalista lleva simultáneamente a la creación de mayor riqueza para los menos y de mayor pobreza para los más."

[52]*Ibid.*, p.63: "Dependencia externa y dominación interna marcan las estructuras sociales de América latina. ...la formación social latinoamericana [ha sido] un capitalismo dependiente, y prever la estrategia necesaria para salir de esa situación."

[53]*Ibid.*, p.67.

[54]Quoted in Jacques Van Nieuwenhove, *ed.*, *Bevrijding en Christelijk Geloof in Latijns-Amerika en Nederland* (Baarn: Amboboeken, 1980), p.142. At the same conference, Gonzalo Arroyo presented an evaluation of the dependency theory, *Ibid.*, p.55ff: "Afhankelijkheidstheorie, een geldige bemiddeling voor de bevrijdingstheologie?", in which he distinguishes this position from analysis which suggests that Latin America is underdeveloped because of: i) a slowness to use capital, know-how and technology; ii) traditional society problems (feudal); and iii) the dualist society problem lacking integration of the market. These understandings are inadequate, says Arroyo, because Latin America is too dependent on the industrialized centres to achieve transformation.

La no persona : the nonperson

In the same essay on *Theology from the underside of history*, he makes a ringing appeal which so typifies his urgent theology, saying: our question is not that of "progressive theology", namely, how to talk about God in an adult or autonomous world; no, the question of liberation theology is how to communicate to the person without human rights, the *nonperson*, that God is love. This hermeneutic of the "other history" and the history of "the other", reread from the side of the poor, is a necessary and still new way of mediating the gospel.[55] Thus the focus of Gutiér-rez' liberation theology is quite clear: the poor are questioning the "economic, social, and political order that oppresses and marginalizes them" as well as "the ideology that is used to justify this domination". Specifically: "Their questioning seeks to go to the very root of the misery and injustice which is experienced in Latin America and other parts of the world. This is why they take the road of social revolution and not of reformist half measures. This is why they go in search of liberation, not developmentalism; they call for socialism, not some moderniza-tions of the present system."[56]

The gospel and ideology

Gutiérrez continues to affirm that "Christ's liberation cannot be reduced to political liberation" though it is certainly "present in concrete historical and political liberating events." This, however, does not mean that we can move directly from theology to politics; rather, there must always be social and political analysis ("mediations") to avoid "religious messianism".[57] Political activity, he notes, has its own demands, laws and mechanisms which must be understood. Similarly, "the gospel message is a message that can never be identified with any concrete social formula", for the gospel challenges all our "historical incarnations". To evade this point is to "backslide into ideology, to justify a determinate social situation".[58]

International capitalism and new forms of domination

In his essay "La fuerza histórica de los pobres",[59] from which the collected essays in this volume take their name, Gutiérrez sees the rise of the popular movement answered by new repressions from the dominant system. We may summarize his points as follows:[60] i) though economic crises are part of the

---

[55]*La Fuerza*, p.259.

[56]*Ibid.*, p.246.

[57]*Ibid..*, p.85: "La liberación de Cristo no se reduce a la liberación política pero se da en hechos históricos y políticos liberadores. No es posible saltar esas mediaciones. De otro lado la liberación política no es un mesianismo religioso, tiene su autonomía y sus leyes, ella supone análisis sociales y opciones políticas bien determinadas...."

[58]cf.Bernard Höfte, *Bekering en Bevrijding: De betekenis van de Latijnsamerikaanse theologie van de bevrijding voor een praktisch-theologische basistheorie* (Hilversum: Gooi & Sticht, 1990), p.244ff, where he records the attempt of liberation theologians to come to terms with the "epistemological autonomy" of both the social and the theological sciences. This has been dealt with by Clodovis Boff in *Theology and Praxis: Epistemological Foundations* (Maryknoll: Orbis, 1987).

[59]Originally published in shorter form as an introduction to *Signos de Lucha y Esperanza. Testimonios de la Iglesia en América latina 1973-1978* (Lima, CEP 1978).

[60]*La Fuerza*, p.104ff: "Una nueva forma de dominación".

capitalist system, economic growth after World War II led to an optimism about transcending such crises; ii) transnational companies, seeking ever greater profit, moved manufacturing operations to Third World countries, where low wages were exploitable; iii) the methods of decapitalizing the poor countries became more sophisticated; iv) the military arms industry went together with concentration of technology in a few nations; v) the U.S.A. dominated the control of a large portion of the world's food supply; vi) the distance between poor and rich countries, periphery and centre, keeps on growing, showing that international "capitalist development is of its very nature detrimental to the masses" (*"carácter esen-cialmente excluyente del desarrollo capitalista"*); vii) since about 1970 there are signs of a crisis in capitalism; viii) capitalism keeps fighting its decline by brutally devaluating the contribution of the world's labour force; ix) the poor nations are caught in this circle of misery because of their dependency upon the foreign capitalist system.

When we ask about democracy, Gutiérrez says in the same context: i) Lately there has been a growing application of the "ideology of national security" in Latin America. These regimes - supported by international capital and its policy ideals - use the cruel repression of economic and military force to prevent the popular classes from gaining any changes.[61] ii) The international capitalist system has a "new face of domination" through "restricted democracy" (*la democracia restrin-gida*) and through the defense of limited human rights. This amounts to a liberal defense of "formal liberties and individual rights, but leaves in tact the existing profound social and economic inequality."[62] iii) This misses the deeper question of misery and the social conflict underlying the social question. iv) A "democratic opening toward the middle sectors" is not sufficient: there must be a change in the situation of the popular classes: "only from the place of the poor" can the problem be rightly seen and transformed.

3. Teología y ciencias sociales (1984): *Theology and social sciences*

In this essay Gutiérrez attempts to clear up some misunderstandings of his intentions. We should recall that this appeared after criticism from the Vatican.[63] Gutiérrez makes an effort to show that he is not to be counted among those overly captivated by Marxism. He speaks of taking recourse to sociology as a means for

---

[61]*Ibid.*, p.108: "Los regímenes de seguridad nacional no son sino una expresión de lo que el imperialismo capitalista y las clases dominantes han considerado necesario para imponer sus nuevas condiciones a las clases populares, y para contener los intentos de cambio...."

[62]*Ibid.*, p.109f.

[63]In March 1983 the *Congregation for the Doctrine of the Faith* published "Ten Observations on the Theology of Gustavo Gutiérrez" which accuse Gutiérrez of a reductionist theology which builds in too much Marxism ("Ten Observations", reprinted in Hennelly, *Liberation Theology: Documentary*, p.348-350). Gutiérrez replied that he had repeatedly warned against reducing the gospel to the political aspect and that the critical use of Marxist analysis is not the same as acceptance of its ideological perspectives (cf.Gustavo Gutiérrez, "Criticism will Deepen, Clarify Liberation theology", p.419-424 in Hennelly, *op.cit.*). The Vatican *Instruction on Certain Aspects of the 'Theology of Liberation'"* (Ratzinger report, August 6, 1984) says: "it is difficult, and perhaps impossible, to purify these borrowed concepts... certain forms of liberation theology...use in an insufficiently critical manner, concepts borrowed from various currents of Marxist thought."

knowing social reality better, for understanding the situation of the poor and the causes of that situation, for sketching with more precision the challenges to the announcement of the gospel and theological reflection in Latin America.[64] He wants to make clear that the function of this "recourse to social analysis" is to pursue an "understanding of a situation and not in order to study issues considered more strictly theological". He thus cuts off all charges of reducing the theological to the sociological. Turning to the theme of dependency, he reminds us that he had stressed ten years earlier in a meeting of CELAM that while dependency is a fact, a theology of liberation should be critically attune not only to dependency theory and its variations, but also to other types of analysis, avoiding generalizations.[65] He further shows that his originally stronger tie to dependency theory was not Marxist, since Marx could say that the more industrially developed countries display for the underdeveloped ones their own future (capitalism precedes socialism), whereas the theory of dependence insists that such supposed linear development is nothing but an 'eurocentric' idea.[66] In fact, the use of dependency theory, which he admits was "very present in the first works of the theology of liberation", does not mean that liberation theology must always be bound (*enfeudarse*) to this theory: "In the context of theological work, [the theory of dependency] is simply a means to know social reality better."[67] This kind of statement shows Gutiérrez' integrity in seeking whatever means helps us understand social reality and poverty in Latin America. We might comment, however, that this does not exclude the question of whether it is not rather uncritical to say that dependency theory functions as "merely a means", since it has led to position choices on so many features in his writing.

4. Expanding the view: new horizons?

In 1988 Gutiérrez wrote an introduction to the new edition of *A Theology of Liberation*, called "expanding the view", which shows considerable shifting of focus. He looks back on his original writing on liberation as a twenty year old "love letter to God, to the church, and to the people to which I belong". While still standing behind the basic commitment, he calls for continued refinement. This has direct repercussions on the relationship between development and liberation.

The theory of dependency inadequate
Gutiérrez emphasizes that the complex world of poverty calls for more than one-

---

[64]Gutiérrez, *Teología y ciencias sociales*, p.72, in Joseph Ratzinger, Leonardo Boff, Gustavo Gutiérrez, *et al.*, *Teología de la liberación: Documentos sobre una polémica* (San Jose: DEI, 1984.)

[65]*Ibid.*, p.75: "...la teología de la liberación tiene en cuenta este hecho de la dependencia y es imposible, al mismo tiempo, no tener en cuenta la teoría de la dependencia. Y la tiene en cuenta *con su sentido crítico*. Sin embargo, la teología de la liberación debe ser más atenta a estas variaciones y a estas críticas en la teoría de la dependencia, evitar generalizaciones, enriquecerse con otro tipo de análisis y de niveles."

[66]*Ibid.*, p.77.

[67]*Ibid.*, "Además el empleo (critico como hemos visto) de la teoría de la dependencia no significa enfeudarse definitivamente en ella. En el contexto del trabajo teológico, ella es simplemente un medio para conocer mejor la realidad social."

dimensional analysis, for "being poor is a way of living, thinking, loving, praying, believing, and hoping, spending leisure time, and struggling for a livelihood".[68] Amid the many aspects of poverty, one must look for the causes, he reminds us. And then it is boldly said: "It is clear, for example, that the theory of dependence, which was so extensively used in the early years of our encounter with the Latin American world, is now an inadequate tool, because it does not take sufficient account of the internal dynamics of each country or of the vast dimensions of the world of the poor." This is a mayor concession which shows that Gutiérrez is self-critically willing to strike at a constitutive element which went into the very definition of liberation in juxtaposition to 'developmentalism' (though we have shown that liberation meant much more than this for Gutiérrez). He adds: "As far as poverty is concerned, an important transformation is undoubtedly taking place in the social analysis on which liberation theology depends to some extent. ...The economic dimension itself will take on a new character once we seek things from the cultural point of view; the converse will also certainly be true."[69]

This carefully stated openness to a more multidimensional approach to poverty could open the door to a reassessment of the relationship between liberation and development. For, what usually typifies development theory in its critique of liberation-dependency theory, is the stress on cultural values and on understanding economic underdevelopment through "internal dynamics": economic, but also political, educational, technical, and spiritual. Liberation theory has the merit of bringing more attention to the political and international structural factors, something often reduced in development theory. Gutiérrez' phrase: "from a cultural point of view" could indicate a new step toward a synthesis of liberation theory and development theory. Northern readers have been quick to notice this shift.[70] We must add a word of caution, however. The distance Gutiérrez takes from dependency theory does not imply that he now is about to accept 'developmentalism', or what we saw earlier to mean reform, modernization and development strategies which in fact have not alleviated poverty.

What does the turn to culture mean for Gutiérrez? It does not mean that he has turned to a position of suggesting that the technically dominated culture of western capitalism is the answer for Latin America. Rather, he wishes to place more emphasis on the indigenous culture of the people in Latin America. This can be seen as part of the three stages Gutiérrez' thought has moved through, namely:[71] i) starting (1968-73) with an emphasis on economic-political liberation (a critique of

---

[68]New edition of *A Theology of Liberation* (Maryknoll: Orbis, 1988), p.xxi.

[69]*Ibid.*, p.xxiv.

[70]As strong a critic as Michael Novak, defender of "democratic capitalism", can say concerning Gutiérrez' shifting on the dependency theory: "This open-mindedness is admirable" (*Will It Liberate?* chapter seven: "What dependency? Who are the Poor?, p.132). As McGovern states it, *Liberation Theology and Its Critics*, p.137: "In recent years, some liberation theologians, like Gutiérrez, have all but disavowed dependency 'theory'. ...It offered no solution to Latin American problems. Rupture with the capitalist North might bring independence, but not development. Dependency theory offered no direction for creating new structures. It oversimplified the problem...."

[71]Van Nieuwenhove, *Bronnen*, develops this structural understanding of Gutiérrez' *via theologica*.

111

historical praxis); ii) he then turned (1974-77) to more emphasis on the praxis of the people (including various forms of giving the poor a voice and organization); iii) more recently (1978...) he has concentrated on a theology of the self-interpretation of the people (including a pronounced emphasis on the God of life). Thus, turning to cultural arguments has especially the characteristic of turning to the right of the poor to exist and to think, to organize, and to also maintain their own cultural identity.[72]

It would be a mistake for those who side with the modernization idea more than with the dependency idea to welcome this shift without considering the following: now that Gutiérrez has stated that the dependency *theory* is not as useful as he first thought, we are still left with the growing problem of the *facts* of dependency. As Peter Berger writes:

"...capitalist penetration in the Third World today is largely supported by evidence. ...growing economic dependency of poor nations upon the rich (as reflected in mounting debts, deteriorating terms of trade and balances of payment, vulnerability to decisions made by governments and nongovernmental bodies in the rich nations) - all these are not inventions of Marxist ideologists, but empirical facts readily available to any objective observer. ...The Latin American critique of 'developmentalism,' ...is thus correct in what may be taken as its central proposition - that underdevelopment can only be understood if one understands the basic facts of dependency. Total identification of the two phenomena (*subdesarrollo* = *dependencia*) is clearly an exaggeration...."[73]

Many of those who do not accept what to them seems an overwrought critique of capitalism in the dependency theory do not therefore deny the economic, technical, political and military dependency features in many parts of Latin America.

III. PERSPECTIVAL OVERVIEW

1. Typical features of Gutiérrez' political ethics
The following points help us see the relationship and the discontinuity between Frei (Christian Democracy) and Gutiérrez (Liberation Theology) in their political ethics.

a. The gospel and politics
i)   Whereas for Frei the gospel connects to the political via a philosophy of *Christian humanism*, Gutiérrez approaches the political by means of a *critical theology of praxis.*
ii) Frei finds a liberal-democratic ethic insufficient and appeals to a social-democratic approach inspired by Christian values, with eradication of poverty as a priority. Gutiérrez appeals to a revolutionary-democratic (popular) analysis and programme (*proyecto*) understood as transformation from the

---

[72]*La Fuerza*, p.113: "Derecho a existir y derecho a pensar". Cf.Van Nieuwenhove, *op.cit.*, p.136f "Optie voor de armen", and ch.v: "Una canción posible".
[73]cf.Peter L.Berger, *Pyramids of Sacrifice: Political Ethics and Social Change* (New York: Basic Books, 1974), p.54.

underside of history, with the first feature being the necessity of a preferential option for the poor.

iii) Church and theology are to take an overt prophetic stance in political change in Latin America, according to Gutiérrez, while Frei expects a prophetic stance more from Christians in politics rather than predominantly via the church and theology.

iv) Frei sees the Christian position as interclassist; Gutiérrez sees the option for the poor as more explicitly a class question. This means that only from the place of the repressed poor can the true (conflictive) nature of the situation in Latin America be seen and a sufficient (empowering of the poor) answer be found.

b. Democracy

i) Whereas Frei's favourite word is *democracy* (understood in a wider social-economic sense), Gutiérrez' is *liberation* (understood in a popular - thus fully democratic-socialist sense).

ii) Gutiérrez speaks of the failure of "restricted democracy" and does not use "democracy" as a central concept the way Frei does.

iii) A popular approach for Gutiérrez means that the grassroots organizations, the parties and unions which struggle for the right of the marginalized to participate in the social process, are the key to transformation. The *comunidades de base* movement is an important expression of popular participation within the church and Christian action.[74]

iv) For Gutiérrez an 'option for the poor' replaces what he sees as the "undemanding" concept of "a badly understood 'common good'."[75]

c. Capitalism

i) Gutiérrez refers to capitalism in categories of imperialism, dominance and dependence, and exploitation of the poor, and thus views capitalism as the major source of social-economic-political problems in Latin America.

ii) Because of capitalist exploitation, liberation from dependency is needed.

iii) Gutiérrez does not, like Frei, criticize Latin America for a lack of entrepreneurial development.

iv) Gutiérrez' critique concerns Latin America's being the object of northern capitalism, which is interwoven with the dominant classes of Latin America. He does not investigate the possible importance of becoming the subject of capitalist development (if only as a stepping stone toward socialization), because he sees no room in the present global economic system for that kind of development, and also because 'more of the same' is not the answer.[76]

---

[74]Gutiérrez, *La Fuerza Histórica de los Pobres*, p.128: "Sólo desde la base, desde el movimiento popular, desde las comunidades cristianas populares es posible ver lo que hay de permanente, profundo e irreversible en el proceso histórico latinoamericano y de vivo en la iglesia."

[75]*Teología de la Liberación*, p.79: "poco exigente terreno de un mal entendido 'bien común'."

[76]cf.the summary above, section 2: "International capitalism and new forms of domination".

d. Marxism and Socialism

i)   According to Gutiérrez, Marx(ism) makes an important contribution to social criticism, especially in exposing the exploitation done by capitalism.

ii) Marxism provides a "scientific understanding of historical reality".[77]

iii) Gutiérrez finds that Marxism helps us see the "*fact* of misery and exploitation"; this is not the same as accepting Marxism as an *ideology*.[78] Frei, however, while acknowledging some Marxist insights, is more predisposed to assume that the ideological aspects of Marxism are more often than not part of what Marxists call scientific.

iv) Gutiérrez, though using Marxist-leaning concepts, has been more anticapitalist than Marxist.[79]

v)   A reading by others, such as José Míguez Bonino, understands that Gutiérrez has summarized the objectives of the project for liberation as follows: "a) societal appropriation of the means of production; b) societal appropriation of political power; c) societal appropriation of freedom; and d) the creation of a new social consciousness."[80] Gutiérrez is flexible on the strategy for "societal appropriation", as long as it transforms the present repressive and exploitive situation and redistributes opportunities and goods so that the presently marginalized may live and be recognized as persons.

e. Repressive authoritarianism

i)   Gutiérrez has in common with Frei an open critique of the "national security" military-oligarchy regimes in Latin America.

ii) He is more silent than Frei concerning the value or the danger of counterviolence.

iii) More than Frei, Gutiérrez exposes the connection between the U.S.A. and Latin American authoritarianism.

f. Strategy for change

i)   Gutiérrez points out that traditional electoral democracy isn't working. Frei believes that electoral democracy is the only route out of "that fatal dilemma" of violence from the right and the left.

---

[77]*Teología de la Liberación,* p.57. Cf.also Gutiérrez, *Teología y ciencias sociales,* section B.2: "Aspectos ideológicos y análisis marxista". Rebecca S.Chopp, in what is an appreciative discourse, can even say: "Gutiérrez seems, at times, to [be] ...adopting rather than critically adapting Marxist categories", p.60 in *The Praxis of Suffering: An Interpretation of Liberation and Political Theologies* (Maryknoll: Orbis, 1986). For a balanced discussion, cf.John R.Pottenger, *The Political Theory of Liberation Theology: Toward a Reconvergence of Social Values and Social Science* (New York: State University Press, 1989), ch.3: "The Marxist-Christian Tension".

[78]*La Fuerza Histórica de los Pobres,* p.206.

[79]Even the stong emphasis on some kind of socialism to replace capitalism has been relativized, so that Gutiérrez can now say that "socialism is not an essential of liberation theology; one can support liberation theology or do liberation theology without espousing socialism" (cf.McGovern, *Liberation Theology and Its Critics,* p.148). This reflects gradual changes along the way, as we also saw in regard to the importance he gave to the dependency theory, and then later relativized in regard to other factors.

[80]José Míguez Bonino, *Toward a Christian Political Ethics* (London: SCM, 1983), p.77. Cf.Van Nieuwenhove, *Bronnen,* p.60f.

ii) There is no real acknowledgment in Gutiérrez that the bourgeois classes could be a liberating force.[81]

iii) For Gutiérrez, transformation includes class struggle and conflict concerning human rights. For Frei the struggle is toward political reforms.

iv) The new society, according to Gutiérrez, involves the creation of a "new humanity". The popular revolution leads to a kind of socialism, not entirely defined, but it will avoid the problems that arise from private appropriation of what is rightly communal wealth.[82] Frei, in turn, speaks of a "new philosophy" of values, and improvement in production and social legislation.

g. Development and liberation

i) According to Gutiérrez, liberation is now a prerequisite for development in Latin America: "*dependencia* and *liberación* are correlative terms".[83]

ii) Liberation is a multidimensional concept, not reducible in Gutiérrez to economic or political categories alone. His later writings have stressed this even more.

iii) Liberation needs spiritual roots.

iv) For Gutiérrez, liberation and development come especially through popular grassroots movements, not from the top down.

v) Frei, however, finds that liberation can only come through better development, along the route of a renewed social vision, democratic reforms, regional cooperation, and technical modernization.

2. Ambiguities in Gutiérrez

a. Gutiérrez did not, originally, distinguish sufficiently between the *fact* of dependency and the *theory* of dependency.

b. While Gutiérrez' view of capitalism rightly points to real and drastic forms of exploitation, he does not present a comparative view on sources of poverty and sources of wealth.

c. Sociology is to help a theology of liberation "know social reality better",[84] but Gutiérrez does not highlight the various sociological choices of perspective nor always remain clear on the need to decode the philosophical-ideological frameworks and connotations involved.[85] A comparative approach acknowl-

---

[81]cf.Harvey Cox, *Religion in the Secular City: Toward a Postmodern Theology* (New York: Simon & Schuster, 1984), p.133-165.

[82]*La Fuerza*, p.63: "Sólo la superación de una sociedad divida en clases, sólo un poder político al servicio de las grandes mayorías populares, sólo la eliminación de la apropriación privada de la riqueza creada por el trabajo humano, puede darnos las bases de una sociedad más justa."

[83]*Teología de la liberación*, p.113: "Dependencia y liberación son términos correlativos. Un análisis de la situación de dependencia... lleva a desear conocer mejor sus mecanismos; permite también poner de relieve las aspiraciones más profundas que están en juego en la lucha por una sociedad más justa."

[84]*Teología y ciencias sociales*, p.72.

[85]While taking into account what at the time was a new impact by the dependency theory, Gutiérrez, however, calls this theory "simply a means" (*simplemente un medio*) for knowing social reality in Latin America better. This would seem too innocent a view for what Gutiérrez repeatedly calls a critical theology and a rigorous scientific social analysis. His later "expanding the view" recognizes this problem. According to William R. Garrett, "Liberation Theology and

edging strengths and weaknesses of sociological mediations would be helpful. (cf.ch.1.III.4).

3. Strengths of Gutiérrez' Political Ethics

a. Gutiérrez faces up to the failure of development strategy in Latin America.

b. In his prophetic approach to justice, Gutiérrez causes the church to take seriously the problem of exploitation of the marginalized 'nonperson'.

c. His reawakening of church and theology shows the ideological captivity of past approaches.

d. He begins where the problem is most accute, with the majority, the popular longing for change, the underside of history.

e. In Gutiérrez one finds the urgency of the great command of love for God and the neighbour, combined with important elements of a theology of the cross, of suffering, and a theology of life which strikes at the political and theological status quo.

f. For Gutiérrez, human values take precedence over the facade of formal democracy and forms of *desarrollismo* which do not liberate.

g. He can reply to capitalist-leaning critique that the wealthy nations must be educated in the matter of social justice, rather than blindly holding to the "rightness of profit".[86]

IV. MICHAEL NOVAK'S CRITIQUE ON LIBERATION THEOLOGY'S ECONOMIC ETHICS

1. *The Spirit of Democratic Capitalism*

In 1982 Michael Novak published *The Spirit of Democratic Capitalism* in which he attempts to point out grand errors in socialist-liberationist thinking. We shall retrace some of his key pronouncements, leaving aside (because of our posing of a specific problem) much that is otherwise of value, and illustrating especially that section of his thought which relates to the development/liberationist point of comparison, especially in relation to the modernization/dependency theme.

Novak takes us along a route in which key concepts become the "market economy", "democracy", "economic growth", "practicality", "progress for all", "liberal ethics" and so forth. He is clear in his view on Latin American liberation theology and on the papal encyclicals. A sweeping word in the introduction of his book sets the star for the course: "It is surprising that the authoritative documents of the Roman Catholic church, including the encyclicals of recent popes, proceed

---

Dependency Theory", in Richard L.Rubenstein & John K.Roth, *eds.*, *The Politics of Latin American Liberation Theology: The Challenge to U.S. Public Policy* (Washington Institute for Values in Public Policy, 1988), p.187: "The fate of liberation theology is inextricably tied to the enduring cogency of dependency theory." This, however, would seem too quick a conclusion, first of all, because the factual state of repression and poverty continues, and secondly, because Gutiérrez has gone on to emphasize other themes in new ways, such as the failure of limited democracy, the God of life, and the right of the poor to their own cultural identity over against systems which marginalize and kill.

[86]cf.Marie Augusta Neal, "God and Society: A Response to Liberation Theology", in Ellis & Maduro, *The Future of Liberation Theology*, p.295.

as if democratic capitalism did not exist."[87] This, however, does not prevent Novak from dedicating his book "In homage to Pope John Paul II". In Novak's opinion, Roman Catholic social ethics have been strong on distributive justice and weak on economic development. This is to be explained according to historical roots:

> "In the long Catholic ages, Catholic thought was fashioned to deal with a static world. It was, properly, fascinated by distributive ethics; it ignored questions of production. Secondly, its attitudes toward money were based on premodern realities. It did not understand the creativity and productivity of wisely invested capital. Thirdly, it took justifiable pride in the sense of community it succeeded in inspiring even within the rather inhospitable world of feudalism. Its satisfaction with the organic sensibility of medieval society and with its sense of the order of being and the hierarchical society allowed it to overlook the structures of domination inherent in feudal relations."[88]

Those who are calling for democratic socialism and are "hostile to capitalism" are "vague about future economic growth. Their strength lies in the moral-cultural system, their weakness in political and especially in economic analysis." He admits thereby that democratic capitalism's very successes in the political and economic order can undermine it in the cultural order, especially through corruptions of affluence, advertising and moral weakness, structural irresponsibility, the lust for power, envy, consumer taste-levelling, and so forth.[89] Over against these weaknesses there is the great advantage of sustained economic growth. Novak relates Max Weber's analysis of six elements of "the capitalist spirit": 1) free labour; 2) reason (practical intelligence); 3) continuous enterprise (planned, organized, evaluated); 4) separation of workplace and household; 5) invention of corporate law; 6) dynamics of cities and towns. Novak, however, does not share Weber's pessimism about the capitalist spirit producing "an iron cage", since capitalism has "multiple types of rationality" which include innovative answers to the problems it raises: "The spirit of democratic capitalism is the spirit of development, risk, experiment, adventure. ...In differentiating the economic system from the state, it introduced a novel pluralism into the very center of the social system."[90]

A theology of economics

In the third section of the book, entitled "A Theology of Economics", Novak takes to task what he sees as Roman Catholic and Latin American anticapitalist leanings. A perusal of Roman Catholic social encyclicals since Leo XIII shows an attempt at finding a "middle way" between individualism and collectivism, says Novak. However, this approach to economics seems to have become "suspended in air" and rather abstract and utopian without real practical guidance.[91] Equally

---

[87]Michael Novak, *The Spirit of Democratic Capitalism* (New York: Touchstone, 1982), p.21.

[88]*Ibid.*, p.25.

[89]*Ibid.*, p.32ff.

[90]*Ibid.*, p.48.

[91]*Ibid.*, p.247ff: "Resisting socialism and standing outside democratic capitalism, Catholic social teaching...occupied a sort of utopian ground - literally, no-place. ...The record of wholly

challenging is Novak's turning toward Third World problematics in chapter XVI, "Guilt for Third World Poverty". He argues that developed nations are not the cause of poverty in the poor nations. The causes of poverty in Latin America are rather factors such as rapid population growth, the landtenure system, the moral-cultural system, and lack of entrepreneurship because of state mercantilism.[92]

Centre and Periphery

Novak rejects the idea of centre and periphery as an explanation of underdevelopment and poverty. He says that while centralization and the lack of differentiation has been a problem in socialist societies, the centre-periphery analysis is ironically used to critique democratic capitalism; yet it is the latter that has been successful in creating more and more centres of economic activity and development. The result, says Novak, is that Liberation Theology rejects development theory and reform as just so much *desarrollismo* (developmentalism). While liberation theologians have "much to say about poverty" they have little understanding "about the causes of wealth".[93] Unfortunately, the dependency theory hides factors which a theology of development should point out, namely the cultural ones. The difference between Catholic and Protestant lands is well established; and that traditional difference in development seems due to cultural factors involving punctuality, the ability to compromise, the idea of worldly life as a spiritual vocation. Latin cultures seem to "oscillate between anarchy and hierarchy" without the ability to establish functional efficiency. Sustained economic development comes through science, technology and economic organization; or as some Latin American analysts have also said, "internal structures common to Latin American and Iberian countries are the fundamental obstacles to overcoming underdevelopment".[94] In a word, Novak's view concerning liberation theologians is that:

> "...their rage against the existing order and against foreign multinationals prevents them from thinking *institutionally* about how to devise checks and balances... They have not thought *theologically* about the vocation of laymen and laywomen in the world, particularly in commerce and industry. They have not discerned the spiritual hunger of the commercial and industrial classes...for a theological vision of daily work. They have not seen how the three strongest institutions in Latin America - the clergy, the military, and the traditional landholding class - may be checked by the growth of a new middle class based in commerce and industry."[95]

2. *Will It Liberate? Questions About Liberation Theology*

Catholic countries in the history of economic and social development is not entirely laudable."

[92]*Ibid.*, p.279. Quoting a 1969 statement from the Catholic bishops of Peru in which they say "we are the victims of systems that exploit", Novak responds: "Do they wish to enjoy the wealth of other systems without having first learned how wealth may be produced and without changing their economic teachings?"

[93]*Ibid.*, p.293f.

[94]*Ibid.*, p.305.

[95]*Ibid.*, p.313. In *Will It Liberate? Questions About Liberation Theology* (New York: Paulist Press, 1986), p.22, he puts it thus: "The fact seems to be that Latin American economies are *pre*-capitalist, disproportionately state-directed. The three leading social classes are government officials, landholders, and the military."

After the above orientation to the thought of Novak we may keep short the references to his 1986 book, *Will It Liberate?* Already in the introduction Novak provides a challenge to Latin America:

> "Liberation theology says that Latin America is capitalist and needs a socialist revolution. Latin America does need a revolution. But its present system is mercantilist and quasi-feudal, not capitalist...the poor...are held back by an ancient legal structure, designed to protect the ancient privileges of a pre-capitalist elite. This elite invents virtually nothing, risks virtually nothing, takes virtually no new initiatives. It is parasitic.... The elite needs to yield place to the talented millions among the poor who show greater imagination, initiative, inventiveness, and creativity. ...When law is aimed at liberating the poor for economic activism, *only then* has a capitalist revolution begun...."[96]

Novak says that revolutionaries will have to learn to create new wealth instead of huge armies.[97] And he later notes: "Already in 1776, Adam Smith had predicted that Latin America would eventually end in poverty and tyranny...because the Latin American experiment consisted in reconstructing an ancient order, that of the Holy Roman Empire: a mercantilist view of wealth as gold and silver, an economy based chiefly upon a landed aristocracy, and the unity of church and state."[98] He devotes a chapter to the dependency theme in which he concludes that it is not so much external dependency as internal systems of inertia that prevent development. He says that Gutiérrez misunderstands economics because he looks at capitalism through the interpretation of Marx who wrote in the *Communist Manifesto*: "The lower middle class, the small manufacturer, the shopkeeper, the artisan, the peasant...they are all not revolutionary but conservative. Nay, more, they are reactionary, for they try to roll back the wheel of history."[99] After a lengthy section on the constitution of liberty through the "liberal ethic", Novak gives us his thesis in short: "Nothing so lifts up the poor as the liberation of their own creative economic activities."[100]

3. Evaluating Novak's critique

Novak's reply to liberation ideas based on dependency theory and what he calls utopian socialism is hard-hitting precisely because the liberation position was hard-hitting on the flaws of liberal ethics and capitalism. His arguments often seem to contain persuasive elements and he writes with clarity of presentation. His contribution undeniably is a challenge to put things in perspective. There is much in what he says that gives thought about practical answers to poverty, especially from the view point of "institutional inertia". Yet his presentation also seems flawed by avoiding a closer look at the effects of colonialism and neocolonialism. A particularly aggravating problem is that he does not deal with the limits to growth thesis.

---

[96]Michael Novak, *Will It Liberate?*, p.5.

[97]*Ibid.*, p.31.

[98]*Ibid.*, p.39.

[99]*Ibid.*, p.146.

[100]*Ibid.*, p.217.

He has little problem justifying the fact that a small proportion of world population uses an ever higher percentage of global resources,[101] since those users are also largely the producers of world wealth. He writes,

> "[The assertion is made that]...a small fraction of humankind uses a large fraction of the earth's resources, and that poverty results for millions. Is this in fact true? A special kind of human culture is required for the production of wealth. Not every organization of society or culture is suited to such production. Indeed, only a small fraction of the earth's population *produces* the larger part of the world's wealth. ...It is not empirically true, either, that "the poor are getting poorer." In longevity, medical care, and nutrition, the modern production of wealth has raised the levels of the entire population of the world...."[102]

This, however, by-passes the structuralist complaint about the Third World poor serving as the world proletariat. It is not empirically correct to say that the levels of the *entire population* of the world have been raised. This is to miss the moral point of Liberation Theology (when it speaks of a preferential option for the poor), for the impoverished cannot wait for the 'trickle down' system to reach them. Novak says little about global ethics. He does not deal adequately with "the case against capitalism" in a way which opens up the discussion to the ambivalent influences of monopolization, relations between the rich and the poor nations, the longer term results of consumerism, the relationship between capitalism and military interventionism, and such typical factors a critique of capitalism calls for.[103]

His view on Roman Catholic economic and political ethics deals with historical realities that must be taken seriously. His critique on this has many concordant voices who have dealt with the sociology of the corporative model,[104] and the anti-liberal reactionary elements of Iberian Catholic influence in Latin America. While by way of putting the matter in short form, it has been called a difference

---

[101]According to Peter De Vos, Loren Wilkinson, *et al.*, in *Earthkeeping: Christian Steward-ship of Natural Resources*, (Grand Rapids: Eerdmans, 1980), p.66: "...the United States has only 6 percent of the world's population but consumes approximately one-third of all the world's resources."

[102]Michael Novak, "Liberation theology and the Pope", *Commentary*, June 1979; reprinted in Hennelly, *Liberation Theology: A Documentary History* (Maryknoll: Orbis, 1990, sec.25.

[103]cf.Arthur F.McGovern, ch.4: "The Case Against Capitalism", in *Marxism: An American Christian Perspective* (Maryknoll: Orbis, 1981).

[104]Alfredo Fierro, *El Evangelio Beligerante,* p.82: "El corporativismo místico produce efectos conservadores. ...La invocación de la corporatividad social sirve siempre para que los miembros que cumplen las funciones más modestos, pero necesarios, no se subleven." cf.Roger E.Veke-mans, "Desarrollo Económico, Cambio Social y Mutación Cultural en Latinoamérica", in W.D'Antonio and F.Pike, *Religión, Revolución y Reforma* (Barcelona: Herder, 1967), p.245ff: "Nuestra hipótesis de trabajo es que existe una correlación entre el subdesarrollo económico, el extremismo social y la espiritualidad eticorreligiosa latinoamericana. ...Las categorías religiosas se salen de su verdadera órbita y comienzan a dirigir el mundo profano. ...se espera una 'gracia' que pueda derramar sobre uno mismo algún individuo privilegiado y poderoso. ...Y la autoridad o el centro de poder...se comporta si fuera omnipotente. Actuando por consideracio-nes interpersonales y no según un objetivo funcional, la autoridad tiende a hacerse cómplice de la transgresión por el hecho de acceder a la violación de la norma y al establecimiento de la excepción, y conceder la indulgencia suplicada. Estos procedimientos abren el camino al paternalismo y a la dictadura."

between the Roman Catholic and the Protestant ethic, it must at the same time be stated that we are speaking of Iberian Catholicism of a certain epoch, intertwined with so many historical factors,[105] and not thereby assuming that Roman Catholicism is always the same; indeed, as we saw in the second chapter, the progressive changes in the social encyclicals show a different side to the matter.[106]

However, Novak does not ask whether the more pragmatic 'Protestant ethic' has perhaps also proven insufficient in the long-run by providing an uncritical opening to other *'isms'*, such as the rationalization of individualism and consumerism. Granted the correctness of Novak's critique of Iberian Roman Catholic cultural impact in Latin America, he unfortunately does not evaluate Protestant's cultural problems in the same way[107]. The Puritan frontier ethic[108] which led to so much 'development' in North America has also led to new forms of captivity and not just to liberation. This is very much the "irony" which attends ideologies.[109] Novak does not deal adequately with the spiritual groundproblem that accompanies the fact that "the Protestant Reformation stressed individual salvation, based on individual interpretation of Scripture" which for good and ill connects all too readily with the market economy which sees "human existence as basically individual" and then also has the tendency to reduce relationships between these individuals to economic transactions.[110]

Novak is right in reminding liberation theology that a cultural analysis could help clarify the roots of poverty,[111] whereby more attention is paid to the weak infrastructure, population growth, low production, corrupt governments and other factors which enter into underdevelopment. But he does not take seriously enough

---

[105]Howard J.Wiarda puts it quite sharply in "Social Change, Political Development, and the Latin American Tradition" in Peter Klarén & Thomas Bossert, *Promise of Development: Theories of Change in Latin America* (Boulder: Westview Press, 1986), p.209f.: "Latin America may thus be viewed as a fragment of Southern European and Iberian culture and civilization of approximately 1500. The time period and the Iberian heritage were especially important in shaping Latin America's future. In terms of the history of Western civilization, Latin America was founded on a basis that was precapitalistic, preenlightenment, pre-Protestant Reformation, prescientific revolution, and prerepresentative government. ...The major institutions transferred to the New World were 'feudal', not 'modern'".

[106]As Leonardo Boff says in *Church, Charisma and Power: Liberation Theology and the Institutional Church* (London: SCM, 1985), p.44: "We must recognize that in the past few years, especially after Vatican II, extremely important steps have been taken. Just as the Church previously took on Roman and feudal structures, it is now taking on structures found in today's civil societies that are more compatible with our growing sense of human rights. This is the often argued 'democratization of the Church'."

[107]Protestantism had a keen economic spirit, as Weber and Tawney point out and as recognized, for example, by Robert L.Heilbroner, *The Making of Economic Society* (Englewood Cliffs: Prentice-Hall, 1980). Novak does not offer much to correct the run-away motif, when "seeking money becomes a work of devotion *ad majorem Dei gloriam*" and when "the fetish of money is an object of devotion", as said by Franz Hinkelammert, *Las Armas Ideológicas de la Muerte* (San José: DEI, 1981), p.32

[108]De Vos, *et al., Earthkeeping*, ch.10: "Economics: Managing our Household".

[109]Reinhold Niebuhr, *The Irony of American History* (New York: Scribner's, 1952), p.13: "The Christian idea of the significance of each individual in God's sight becomes, in bourgeoise civilization, the concept of a discrete individual who makes himself the final end of his own existence."

[110]De Vos, *op.cit.*, p.165.

[111]cf.also Max L. Stackhouse, *Creeds, Society and Human Rights: A Study in Three Cultures* (Grand Rapids: Eerdmans, 1984).

the possibility that economic growth has become a pseudoreligious belief within capitalist culture.[112] In his often well-phrased description of why development must not be lost sight of amid the cry for liberation, Novak, who takes the U.S.A. as the best example of progress, does not inquire into the long history of U.S.A. interventions in Latin America and the siding of capital with the repressive regimes. In fact, Novak seems to slide into using what can be called a 'dictionary of denial' about the unilateralist approach to diplomacy (which so often degenerates into hegemony and strong-man interventionism).[113] In other words, Novak fails to really see U.S.A. liberal-capitalism the way Latin Americans see its role in Latin America.

To this we must add that he does not imagine that an answer to the present Latin American turmoil might need the liberationist impulse before it can ever reach the opportunity to develop. Novak gives democratic capitalism a universally redemptive role which seems contrary to the results of dependent capitalism in Latin America.[114]

We can learn from Novak's insights on cultural and institutional aspects of development. However, while Novak takes considerable care to have his market system rooted in what he calls a moral-cultural system, and rightly so, the irony in Novak's position is that these values are added to the market system from the outside and are not really part of it. There is every danger that the transactional profit relationships of the market will continue to dominate international relationships according to profit-motivated decisions, to the detriment of other values, such as the eradication of poverty.[115]

V. A FUTURE FOR LIBERATION THEOLOGY?

We cannot but end with a sign of hope. Gutiérrez himself has moved toward a wider understanding of Liberation Theology, one which places emphasis on life rather than ideology. His "expanding the view" is a testimony of moving on to a

---

[112]cf.Bob Goudzwaard, *Aid for the Overdeveloped West* (Toronto: Wedge, n.d.).

[113]cf.Michael P.Hamilton, *ed.*, *American Character and Foreign Policy* (Grand Rapids, Eerdmans, 1986). In one of the essays, "Formative Events from Columbus to World War I", Robert L. Beisner says: "A nation [U.S.A.] born in the first modern anticolonial revolution, its people self-identified as pioneering anti-imperialists, became imperialists themselves. ...Imperialism by any other name, they persuaded themselves, is *not* imperialism. ...American imperialism in the past ninety years has commonly been aimed at suppressing or rechanneling the revolutions of other societies. ...tension between practice and rhetoric...confuses not only the leaders of other nations but ourselves as well. At what cost, we are still learning."

[114]Roelf L.Haan, "Christian Belief, Marxism, and Rich and Poor Countries," in John C.Vanderstelt, *ed.*, *The Challenge of Marxist and Neo-Marxist Ideologies for Christian Scholarship* (Sioux Center, Iowa: Dordt College, 1982), p.119: "The fact is that the underdeveloped world does not pass through this path of 'preparation for growth' to 'growth'. Nor does it obey the neoclassical theory...which states that the inflow of capital will, *through growth*, turn the debtor countries into creditors! ...the world is not a reflection of capitalist apologetic economic theory."

[115]cf.Eugene R.Dykema, "Wealth and Well-Being: The Bishops and Their Critics", in Charles R.Strain, *ed.*, *Prophetic Visions and Economic Realities: Protestants, Jews and Catholics Confront the Bishops' Letter on the Economy* (Grand Rapids: Eerdmans, 1989)), p.52f.

more comprehensive way of including development themes. Today we see theologies of life (which include the pursuit of human rights under repressive regimes) and of economic relinquishment trying to deal with an adequate theological approach to justice and the worldorder.[116] The development (modernization) and dependency (liberation) themes are at present still in discussion, and will surely remain so, given the facts of dire poverty. As one challenge - and a very powerful one - along the way, theological and Christian ethical-political reflection on poverty and justice, peace and development, may not by-pass the testimony of Gustavo Gutiérrez.

Summary and transition to chapter five

After our 'posing of the problem' in the first chapter, we traced elements of the history of Latin America, intertwined with the papal encyclicals and the political ethical challenges of recent decades. We saw the increased inclusion of the dependency perspective and Third World poverty in the encyclicals. At the same time we heard voices in Latin America calling for a more radical critique of the dominant system within Latin America, as well as a critique of world economic structures. In our third chapter we listened to Eduardo Frei and to critique on the Christian Democratic approach. It appeared that while Frei has several strengths in his ethical theory, including a sincere desire for transformation, a weakness is that it presumes less polarization in society than actually in fact exists in Latin America. In the present chapter we saw how Gustavo Gutiérrez struggles to find a perspective on transformation for Latin America, and we also saw the kind of critique this has invited, especially as to the relationship between theology and socio-politico mediations, and the need for a comparative view on socialism and capitalism, with a focus not just on distribution, but also on sources of wealth. However, we hasten to add that the strength of Gutiérrez' perspective is that he has, more than many others, drawn the attention to the importance of making an option for the poor, and wishes to begin where the need is greatest. In several ways, as our perspectival overview suggests, Frei and Gutiérrez complement each other's analysis. Next we turn to a regional study which shall once more focus our attention on the historical realities to which both development and liberation are attempting an answer.

---

[116]Pablo Richard, "Liberation Theology: A Difficult but Possible Future", p.502ff. in Marc H. Ellis & Otto Maduro, *eds.*, *The Future of Liberation Theology*, section 3: "Economics and liberation theology". Also, Marie Augusta Neal, *The Just Demands of the Poor: Essays in Socio-theology* (New York: Paulist Press, 1987).

CHAPTER FIVE

CENTRAL AMERICA: TRANSFORMATION IN FREEDOM?

"I am a true political leader...because I am here without your votes."

Ríos Montt[1]

"So tonight I ask you to do what you have done so often in the past. Get in touch with your representatives and senators and urge them to vote yes. Tell them to help the freedom fighters [Nicaraguan *contras*] - help us prevent a Communist takeover of Central America."

Ronald Reagan[2]

---

[1]Quoted in James Dunkerley, *Power in the Isthmus: A Political History of Modern Central America* (London: Verso, 1988), p.493. He also quotes Ríos Montt as saying: "We declared a state of siege so that we could kill legally."

[2]Ronald Reagan, "Address to the nation on March 16, 1986", reprinted in Mark Falcoff & Robert Royal, *eds.*, *The Continuing Crisis: U.S. Policy in Central America and the Caribbean; Thirty Essays by Statesmen, Scholars, Religious Leaders, and Journalists* (London: U.S.A. Ethics and Public Policy Center, 1987), p.18.

"...I've always thought that the Cold War when it was on was one of the most bizarre wars in history because wherever you had the Americans, they created Communists and wherever you had the Communists they created anti-Communists. So that really the Cold War became the question of whether the Americans would create more Communists than the Russians would create anti-Communists."

Malcolm Muggeridge[3]

Introduction

After having listened to and raised questions about the political ethics of Frei and Gutiérrez, we now turn to a regional study which includes inductive analysis in order to draw together some factors that enter into the daily reality of the fact that the poor are many. As we noted in our introductory chapter, our turning to Central America cannot be done as if either Frei or Gutiérrez were providing a specific analysis of that region. They consciously write of Latin America with full realization that regional adjustments are necessary. We also are mindful that some inductive specificity is in keeping not only with the methodological changes in the Social Encyclicals, as well as a necessary basis for Christian Democratic political existence, but also that Liberation Theology has thrown out the strong challenge for a contextually located approach to praxis. Our focus is on a historical review of factors with which political ethics must wrestle in order to understand the region. In many ways, the crisis in Central America during the 1980s has led to more understanding of the problems of both development and liberation. Our choice to deal with the region, rather than one country, is motivated by the realization that a comparison between the countries shows them to be pieces of the same jigsaw puzzle. The jigsaw that separated them after colonial history had given rise to a society of peasants and landlords was a kind of oligarchic provincialism which led neither to regional unity nor to development for the masses. We survey this in part I, while part II deals with the problem and challenge of transformation, whereby we review some dominant factors in the crisis of development and liberation. We conclude the chapter with a historical chronology for the region. Some may wish to refer to this "appendix" earlier rather than later.

I. PROFILE OF THE ISTHMUS: HISTORICAL OVERVIEW

1. From Independence (1821) until the 1870s

The conquest of Central America by Spain was complete by 1545, though the administrative structures were still being put in place. Central America was to remain undeveloped for the coming centuries, its level of production and education lagging behind many other areas in Latin America. Society was very bipolar, with political and economic power in the hands of the few and distinct divisions between the conquistadorial oligarchy and the peasants. There was a kind of cultural

---

[3]Malcolm Muggeridge, *The End of Christendom* (Grand Rapids: Eerdmans, 1980), p.34.

genocide as the conquered indigenous peoples lost the fabric of their communal identity without a way of adequate integration into the society in formation. By 1810 when the independence movement began in Mexico, Central America had about 1.5 million inhabitants: of these, 900,000 were Indian; some 450,000 were *mestizos*; 100,000 were white; about 20,000 were black and *mulatos*.[4] Today the region is approaching 30 million and still has a high rate of population growth.[5] Indigenous population has always been more concentrated in Guatemala; Costa Rica formed an exception from the beginning with a more dominant Spanish population. When Napoleon imposed French authority over Spain in 1810, independence movements began to grow in Latin America. Central America declared independence on September 21, 1821, first in union with Mexico and a year later forming a federation. This federation was, however, quite paralysed by struggles between the liberals and conservatives. While the liberals were against church privileges and favoured religious toleration, republicanism and economic liberalization, the conservatives were on the side of strong central government and church privileges (which included the tithe, landholdings, educational influences, and the intermingling of state and Christendom). The vision of unity for the region under ideals of freedom and political virtue, especially promoted by the Honduran, Francisco Morazán (1792-1842), failed, and in 1838 the regional congress declared the provinces separate entities free to find their own form of government. Since then the region has indeed often been more divided than unified, leading to continual impediments to political and economic transformation. Up until the 1870s Central America was dominated from the old capital centre of Guatemala, which tried to impose a conservative direction. This included the colonial vagrancy laws (which allowed for forced labour); yet the common lands of the Indians were still somewhat protected. Debt peonage by advancing loans with labour obligations to the Indians was common. Economics continued along a feudal-mercantile course without any adequate labour code, peasant or worker organization, which could raise the rural wages.[6]

Manifest Destiny

Meanwhile neocolonial hegemonic ideas of Manifest Destiny and the Monroe Doctrine were having profound effects, first through filibuster adventures and then through systematic expansion and control, which continually influenced Central America through a combination of economic, political and military pressures. USA Secretary of State (later president) John Quincy Adams, concluding treaties with Britain and Spain in 1818-19, expounded the *Manifest Destiny* idea which viewed the USA as protector and rightful dominator of the Americas, this ideology being based on the belief that the USA had created the best political-economic system and

---

[4]cf.Thomas M.Leonard, *Central America and United States Policies, 1820s-1980s* (Claremont, California: Regina Books, 1985), p.2.

[5]The region is expected to reach 37 million by the end of the 1990s. cf.Edelberto Torres-Rivas, coord., *América Central hacia el 2000* (Caracas, Nueva Sociedad, 1989), segunda parte: "La población centroamericana", p.76.

[6]For an overview cf.James Dunkerley, *Power in the Isthmus*, ch.1: "The Formation of a Liberal Regime, 1820-1910".

was called to enlighten other nations. The spirit of Manifest Destiny led to the appropriation of half the territories of Mexico in 1846-48 and after the Spanish-American war (1898) the annexing of the Hawaiian Islands, the Philippines, Puerto Rico, and then the Panama Canal Zone (1903).

President James Monroe formulated an unilateral policy, later called the *Monroe Doctrine*, in his state of the Union message to Congress on December 2, 1823, saying that "...the American continents...are henceforth not to be considered subjects for future colonization by any European powers.... We should consider any attempt on their [the European powers'] part to extend their system to any portion of this hemisphere as dangerous to our peace and safety."[7]

At the end of the 1840s when the California gold rush began there was renewed talk of building a canal across the isthmus by Lake Managua in Nicaragua where Cornelius Vanderbilt's Transit Company at the time was transporting thousands who traversed Nicaragua to the Pacific. Among the more sensational political adventures in Central America during these years was the attempt by a group from the liberal party in Nicaragua to gain control by inviting some soldiers of fortune led by the filibuster William Walker to help them, but Walker took control of Nicaragua for a year, proclaiming himself president in 1856. This mock government was officially recognized by the U.S.A. But Walker was driven out and later captured in 1860 and executed.[8]

2. 1870s - 1930: oligarchy and liberal regimes

During this period we find a rapid integration into world markets through the agroexport basis of especially coffee and bananas. This dependency on one or two major crops per country set the pattern for years to come. This was the era of liberal reforms comprised of a series of changes and laws which brought the region, to some degree, out of the feudal era and into a first stage of capitalist changes, but without social improvements for the vast majority. As more land was taken from the Indians for export use, this not only put more land in the hands of the oligarchy, but at the same time provided labour, since the less land there was for the Indigenous and *mestizo* peasant communities, the more obliged they were to seek work as day and seasonal labourers. The general economic changes of this era have sometimes been called a move toward *mercantile capitalism* (not industrial capitalism) through a rapid rise in trade (coffee, bananas, cotton), without a change in the *mode of production*; the peonage system remained: it was still preindustrial, without labour organizations, and peasant based. The wages did not rise, as they are expected to do in industrial capitalism characterized by the presence of organized labour. We find thus the contradictory situation of more agroexport production and the rise of the profit motive, with on-going impoverishment for the

---

[7]For a summary of the many Monroe Doctrine corollaries, cf.Ernst E.Rossi & Jack C.Plano, *The Latin American Political Dictionary* (Oxford: Clio Press, 1980), p.231ff.

[8]cf.Lester D.Langley, *Central America - the Real Stakes: Understanding Central America Before It's Too Late* (New York: Crown, 1985), p.13. Also Lars Schoultz, "Nicaragua: The United States Confronts a Revolution", in Richard Newfarmer, *ed.*, *From Gunboats to Diplomacy: New U.S. Policies for Latin America* (Baltimore: John Hopkins University Press, 1984), p.117.

popular classes who had less and less land available. This was accompanied by an acceleration in the deculturization and disintegration of the indigenous Indian way of life. The general availability of cheap labour without labour organization led to exploitive subsistence wages which continue to be a great problem today. The one exception to the common pattern has been Costa Rica, which had little indigenous population and no mining; the land was settled by a system of homesteading and the landtenure system was more equally divided there than in the other areas of the region. Costa Rica also led the way in education, continuing to raise its percentage of literacy in contrast to the other countries.

Neocolonialism: dollars and gunboats

The first major USA investments in banana production and the corresponding land and tax concessions to the companies began at the turn of the century, after the Spanish-American war of 1898, leading to a quite systematic dependence of Central America on this northern neighbour. Price controls by foreign companies, markets and even foreign transport, land grants, broken promises, tax evasions and too much political power all did their part. Speaking of Isthmus relationships with the United Fruit Company, it has been said:

> "The suspicion would always remain, and was often justified, that corrupt leaders had sold out the national patrimony at a cheap price. UFCO did not invent unsavory politics in Central America. But it contributed to them by engaging in miscrupulous business practices that had been banished in its home country."[9]

We then enter what has been called the era of large-scale investments and large-scale interventions. This also is known as the "Big Stick" gunboat and dollar diplomacy, which had the marines landing time and again to align the region with USA interests. Theodore Roosevelt, who became U.S.A. president in 1901, spoke of walking softly and carrying a big stick when it came to matters in the Caribbean and Central America. In the 1904 Roosevelt Corollary of the Monroe Doctrine the president said that in the case of "flagrant" and "chronic wrongdoing" by Latin American nations, the U.S.A. must "however reluctantly...exercise an international police power".[10] The result has been tallied as follows:

> "A brief summary of the most important of these armed interventions will give some idea of their scope. From 1899 to 1933 Nicaragua was virtually a protectorate of the United States, and for more than twenty years of that time the country was under military occupation. Aid was given to a rebellion in Panama and that province was 'taken' from Colombia in 1903. The Dominican Republic was under absolute United States control between 1905 and 1924 and was occupied by Marines for ten years; Haiti was under military occupation from 1915 to 1934; between 1907 and 1925 there were six armed interventions in Honduras; Mexico was invaded several times between 1846

---

[9]Richard A.Nuccio, *What's Wrong, Who's Right in Central America? A Citizen's Guide* (New York: Roosevelt Center for American Policy Studies, 1986), p.16.

[10]cf.Rossi & Plano, *Latin American Political Dictionary*, p.235. Also, Richard McCall, "From Monroe to Reagan: An Overview of U.S.-Latin American Relations", in Newfarmer, *op.cit.*, p.15-34. Also, Nuccio, *op.cit.*, p.16f.

and 1916, including the bombardment and occupation of Vera Cruz in 1914...."[11]

It is claimed that by 1910 the USA investments in Mexico and Cuba were so high that a small group of USA investors actually controlled more of the local productive industry than the Mexicans and the Cubans did in their own country.[12] The USA marines were stationed in Nicaragua from 1912 until 1932 with only a short time out. This historical knowledge leads to the thesis that where USA intervention has been heaviest, the anti-USA and anti-capitalist reaction has also been heaviest.

Sandino: the beginning of anti-imperialism

While it is sometimes proposed that anti-USA sentiments come from Communist infiltration, the fact is that the USA interventions were in themselves sufficient to lead to anti-USA feelings. This was clearly the case in Augusto César Sandino's guerrilla campaign in Nicaragua (begun in 1927): it was a *nationalist protest*. Sandino had a limited anti-imperialist programme that focussed on the withdrawal of U.S.A. troops. Indeed, he lay down the struggle when those troops were removed in January 1933. However, he was betrayed and assassinated in February 1934 by the Guardsmen of Anastasio Somoza García. His ideas were heterogeneous, and though influenced by Augustín Farabundo Martí who founded the Communist Party in 1930 in El Salvador, Sandino could call himself a political liberal; he spoke not so much of class struggle as of "Indoamerican liberation" and thought in terms of multiclass transformation.[13] Sandino was the one clear and sustained protest to USA imperialism at the time and a foreboding of things to come. One of his famous sayings (when USA General Hatfield demanded that he surrender, offering guarantee for his safety) was: *Yo quiero patria libre o morir -* "I want a free country or death."[14]

During this period Central American politics remained oligarchical. The illiterate masses were not permitted to vote. The agroexport model grew in volume. The bipolar society and the exploitation of cheap labour continued. There was a gradual emergence of the beginning of a small middle class and urbanization. But the majority were *campesino* peasants; there was almost no industrialization and thus no industrial proletariat.

3. 1930s - 1970s : economic crisis, dictatorship, failed reform

When the economic depression arrived it hit the almost single crop dependency economies of Central America in a catastrophic way, leading to social crises, protests and repressions. The trade on raw commodities tumbled and left Central America with no income. This pushed the already poor population into desperation and we find a wave of social unrest, the formation of left wing parties and social

---

[11]John A.Crow, *The Epic of Latin America* (Berkeley: University of California, 1980), p.686.

[12]Crow, *op.cit.*, p.685, where he lists statistics.

[13] cf.Dunkerley, *Power*, p.70-74.

[14]cf.Philip Berryman, *The Religious Roots of Rebellion: Christians in the Central American Revolutions* (London: SCM, 1984), ch.4: "Free Country or Death!: Sandino, Somoza, and the Church". For documents and letters by Sandino, cf.Robert Edgar Conrad, *Sandino: The Testimony of a Nicaraguan Patriot, 1921-1934* (New Jersey: Princeton University Press, 1990).

consciousness with a corresponding growth in state repression and increase in terror. Long standing dictatorial regimes took hold in the 1930s whose main goal seems to have been the holding back of any new social action or any increase in participative politics by the popular sectors. We may speak of *exclusionary* rather than *inclusionary* politics during this reactionary period, whereby state response (whether repressive or accommodating) becomes an important factor in the decades ahead.[15] Dictatorships during these years were: in El Salvador, Maximiliano Hernández Martínez (1932-44);[16] in Guatemala, Jorge Ubico (1931-1944); in Honduras, Tiburcio Carías Andino (1932-48); in Nicaragua, the Anastasio Somoza García regime, which outlasted them all (1936-56), continuing through his sons Luis Somoza ("elected" president in 1957) and Anastasio Somoza Debayle ("elected" president in 1967), leading finally to the revolution in 1979. These repressive dictatorships struggled to preserve an archaic system under stress by the economic crisis. It has been said of these four dictatorships: "...the methods of power were strikingly similar: censorship of the press, exile or jail for the opposition, pervasive police control, special privileges for the prominent coffee producers, and generous treatment of the interests of foreign corporations."[17] Once again, Costa Rica was the exception which weathered through without such drastic repressions. By the end of World War II we see a swing back to moderation and a decade of reforms. Costa Rica led the way here in a conscious turn to social democracy under José Figueres, who accelerated government reforms in health care, education, and social services. This direction, along with industrial diversification, has continued in Costa Rica. Even the dictatorial regimes in the other Central American countries had to submit to changes, if only, as irony will have it, because they supposedly sided with the USA in favour of democracy and against Fascism in Europe.

The CIA coup in Guatemala, 1954

A telling example of blocked social reform took place in Guatemala. Ubico's long dictatorship ended in 1944 when Juan José Arévalo was elected, who as an intellectual and pursuer of a "spiritual socialism"[18] began to seek out a reform

---

[15]A point developed by J.Carrière in his April-May 1991 lectures on "Central America: The Dilemma of Revolutionary Transformation", given at CEDLA (Center for Latin American Research and Documentation), Amsterdam.

[16]The infamous *Matanza* (slaughter) of 1932 took place in the setting of the Great Depression and unemployment of coffee pickers. The price of export coffee dropped more than 50% after 1929, not recovering until the 1940s. Cf.Jorge Cáceres, *et al.*, *El Salvador: Una historia sin lecciones* (San José: FLACSO, 1988), p.119. In 1932 plans were laid for a protest uprising calling for a revolt among the military. Agustín Farabundo Martí, principal leader of the new Communist Party in El Salvador, was arrested January 22, 1932 but the rebellion went ahead that evening. A massacre by the army and civilian *vigilantes* took place systematically through out the country during the next weeks; estimates of the killing vary between 10,000 to 30,000. Martí, whose last shout was *Viva el socialismo!* was shot February 1, 1932. The later coalition of guerrilla groups, the Farabundo Martí Liberation Front (FMLN: *Frente Farabundo Martí para la Liberación Nacional*), takes its name from the fallen leader.

[17]Nuccio, *What's Wrong, Who's Right in Central America?*, p.24,

[18]Arévalo is quoted as saying: "...we are not materialist socialists. We do not believe that man is primarily stomach. We believe that man is above all else a will for dignity...", Dunkerley, *op.cit.*, p.138. Cf.also Hubert J.Miller, "Catholic Leaders and Spiritual Socialism during the Arévalo Administration in Guatemala, 1945-1951", ch. 5 in Ralph Lee Woodward, *ed.*, *Central*

programme. Arévalo's measures began to allow for worker organization; by cancelling the vagrancy law, peasant labour could at least in theory enter a free market of labour and hope for wage raises; further, the new obligation of leasing out uncultivated lands at no more than 5% of the harvest was a step toward transformation. When Jacobo Arbenz was next elected in 1950, a systematic programme was put in place for land reform which especially ran into problems when it sought to expropriate land from the United Fruit Company.[19] At the time of the Arbenz land reforms, 2% of the population in Guatemala controlled 74% of arable land, while 76% occupied only 9% of the land in subsistence plots. The agrarian reform law of 1952 was aimed at larger holdings which were under-cultivated. This affected the UFCO which is said to have held control of 550,000 acres with some 85% uncultivated. The Arbenz government proposed paying the company in government bonds for some 400,000 acres at a price according to the company's own tax declarations. While these changes were the first real reforms in Guatemala, some saw them as a turning to communism (this being the Cold War years when rhetoric was very rife). The Communist party had made some very limited gains at this point in Guatemala. The rhetoric and ensuing CIA-planned invasion were quite out of proportion to the supposed 'danger', aside from the basic question as to national sovereignty in the face of foreign aggression. In 1954 the CIA organized 'Operation Success', training a small army in Honduras and flying aerial bombings (from out of Nicaragua) over Guatemala City to scare the Arbenz regime into resigning, which it did. After this the political right had no doubt that the USA would always come to the aid of the oligarchy, while the political left began to conclude that there was no nonviolent road to social transfor-mation, since USA intervention could be counted on to protect the status quo in Latin America. Since this episode Guatemala has known no similar measures for reform and the army is the dominant political arbiter. Dunkerley remarks:

"'Operation Success' [the coup against the Arbenz government in 1954] was, of course, an almost exclusively US-directed campaign...The principal characteristics of the campaign have become familiar to later generations precisely because its success encouraged repetition in 1961, in the Bay of Pigs invasion of Cuba, and, from 1982, in the siege of Sandinista Nicaragua. ...there is a remarkable consistency in the rationale and methods employed, ranging from the interdiction of arms - real or imagined - from the Soviet bloc; funding of counter-revolutionary forces operating across borders; a concerted campaign of diplomatic isolation in both regional and global fora; condemna-tion of basic social reforms as Communist in character; economic boycott; manipulation of the relative liberty permitted to local media as well as use of clandestine broadcasts; aerial and maritime sabotage; assertion of an underlying Soviet 'imperialistic' conspiracy and mortal danger to the hemispheric order; and agitation of the religious question."[20]

America: Historical Perspectives on the Contemporary Crises (New York: Greenwood Press, 1988). Miller notes the inadequate distinction at this time - also insufficient, he points out, in the encyclicals of Leo XIII and Pius XI - between socialism and communism, so that the church did not support the reform movement as it could have.

[19]The history is recounted in detail in Stephen Kinzer and Stephen Schlesinger, *Bitter Fruit* (New York: Doubleday, 1981).

[20]Dunkerley, p.152.

As we enter the 1960s and '70s, we see economic growth in Central America, but also lost opportunities for political reform until the oil crisis of 1973 and a slide downhill into the regional crisis of the 1980s. At that point we hear of revolution in Nicaragua, unending civil war in El Salvador,[21] death squads, scorched earth and strategic hamlets in Guatemala.[22] Renewed Roman Catholic social thought becomes suspect of subversive tendencies.[23] From Medellín, 1968 and on to Puebla, 1979, we also hear the Roman Catholic bishops with a new voice in the middle of new repressions. Then into the 1980s the Christian Democrats make their debut in Central America (Duarte and Cerezo), yet without encountering the results their own ideals call for, leading to the common criticism that they are but a mask for the continuing military regimes. Liberation Theology in these years goes on developing and attracting attention.

4. The crisis of the 1980s

a) Nicaragua
For a whole decade, starting in 1979, Central America was a pressure cooker attracting the world's attention, especially because it became a high priority for the Reagan administration which saw Nicaragua as the first of a whole series of falling dominos. Indeed, the end of the forty-five years of the Somoza dynasty and the beginning of the decade of the Sandinista dominance of the revolution meant unheard of changes in Central America.

When the FSLN (*Frente Sandinista de Liberación Nacional*) marched into Managua in July 1979, no one knew what the next decade might bring. However, everyone was agreed that *Somocismo* must go. The perspective we present here is that the Sandinista revolution was:

i) nationalist (anti-imperialist);
ii) redistributionist (in a social-economic-political sense);
iii) pluralist (as to mixed economy, popular democracy and relative ideological freedom - the context of comparison being with Somocismo and with neighbouring countries;
iv) popular (in the interest of the people rather than specifically in the interests of one small sector of the nation).

These Sandinista values have not been without some basic tensions. One of the

---

[21]For example, Americas Watch Committee and The American Civil Liberties Union, *Report on Human Rights in El Salvador* (New York: Vintage, 1982). Marvin F.Gettleman, *et al., El Salvador: Central America in the New Cold War* (New York: Grove, 1981).

[22]cf.Jonathan L.Fried, *et al., Guatemala in Rebellion: Unfinished History* (New York: Grove Press, 1983), p.327-332 for a chronology on guerrilla struggle and army atrocities. In order to curb the guerrillas the army turned to the scorched earth strategy of burning down villages and massacring peasants. Also, Tom Barry & Deb Preusch, *Central America Fact Book* (New York: Grove, 1986), ch.11: "Guatemala".

[23]For example, Berryman, *Religious Roots*, p.101: "...in 1966 several peasants were jailed [in El Salvador] for having 'subversive literature' - which turned out to be copies of Pope John XXIII's encyclical *Pacem in Terris* distributed by Christian Democrats."

continuities between *Somocismo* and *Sandinismo* is that both have identified the party all too closely with the state.[24]

From Somocismo to Sandinismo

The final stages of *Somocismo* began rather apocalyptically with the earthquake in 1972 which tumbled the centre of Managua causing some 10,000 deaths, twice as many injured, and making some 300,000 homeless. The blatant government corruption of profiteering from international earthquake aid sent to Nicaragua, the speculation in land and reconstruction contracts which led to great profits for Somoza, pushed the country ever closer to revolution. The Somoza regime did not fall merely because of its anachronist attitudes but also because of the increase in political personalism (i.e. corruption and private profit by the oligarchy which made little distinction between *res publica* and its own private interests), and because increased military brutality was necessary to keep the system in place.[25] The Somoza system kept control through the PLN (*Partido Liberal Nacionalista*) which continued to win 'elections' through the mechanism of identity cards given to those who voted for the party. Only those with such a card could work in the public sector and any dealings with state agencies were negative or even antagonistic without this card. It may be noted that while in other Central American countries the National Guards often operate independently and wield power over the government, the Nicaragua National Guard was an extension of the Somoza dynasty.

The killing of one of the most important Somoza critics, newspaper editor Pedro Joaquín Chamorro of *La Prensa* (January 10, 1978) was a clear sign of the end. Among *La Prensa's* critique of the regime just before the assassination had been an article on the sale of Nicaraguan blood to the USA, suggesting that the dictatorial regime was quite willing to literally bleed its own people for some fast dollars. Some 50,000 demonstrated at the editor's funeral. On August 22 of the same year members of the Terceristas[26] captured the National Palace together with the entire congress and forced Somoza to make some concessions. In January 1979 there were demonstrations and strikes to mark the anniversary of the death of Chamorro. In February the Carter government suspended military aid to Nicaragua. By May, Mexico broke diplomatic relations and the OAS (Organization of American States) called for Somoza's resignation. May 30 the FSLN declared their "final offensive". In June there were general strikes. Through simultaneous attacks in various regions of the country by the FSLN the National Guard became too thinly stretched to hold

---

[24]Dunkerley, *Power*, p.269f.: "...Sandinismo...shares with Somocismo that peculiarly Nicaraguan tendency to elide the party with the state...agency and structure become infernally entwined."

[25]*Ibid.*, p.228-236: "The Peculiarities of the Somocista State".

[26]In 1975 the FSLN split into factions: 1) The *Tendencia Proletaria* which wanted to establish a Marxist-Leninist party and concentrate more on the urban working class; 2) the *Guerra Popular Prolongada* tendency which preferred a concentration on the rural campaign against the National Guard; and 3) the *Tendencia Tercerista (Insurrectional)* which emphasized multi-class alliances and the potential for insurrectionist politics on a wide scale. Cf.Peter Rosset & John Vandermeer, *The Nicaragua Reader: Documents of a Revolution under Fire* (New York: Grove Press, 1983), section 22: "The Historic Program of the FSLN".

back the revolution which became a fully popular uprising. On July 19, 1979 the National Guard, already disintegrated, surrendered and the FSLN forces occupied Managua. The success of the final offensive depended on a broad front of:

i)   sustained popular uprising and strikes;
ii)   the military tactics of the Sandinistas;
iii) a divided oligarchy;
iv)   wide-spread national and international recognition that the regime must go.

The war against Somoza cost some 50,000 lives. In the coming years the war against the *contras* would cost another 30,000 lives. Indeed, the immediate years after the revolution would be a struggle against tremendous odds, partly because of the country's bankruptcy and destroyed infrastructure, but also because of the economic boycott and *contra* assaults.

A decade of revolutionary reconstruction
   An assessment of the Sandinista decade can point to some troubling questions on ideological tendencies; the closing down from time to time of opposition voices; treatment of the Misquito Indians; economic policies which, though mixed,[27] did not produce the hoped for results while under great strain due to the *contra war* agitation; and military spending. It cannot be denied that the destabilization policies of the Reagan administration were of such magnitude as to keep the Sandinista Reconstruction Government under severe economic and political-military pressures, to the extent that the Washington policy never allowed the Sandinistas a fair chance. The positive elements of the Sandinista programme included: improvement

---

[27]According to tables found in Dunkerley, p.293:
Production by Property Sector (% GDP)
(APP = public sector: *Area de Propiedad Popular*)
(L/M = Large/Medium; S = Small)

	1977	1980	1982
Agriculture	(22)	(22)	(24)
APP	-	14	21
Private (L/M)	77	63	54
Private (S)	23	23	25
Manufacturing	(22)	(25)	(24)
APP	-	25	31
Private (L/M)	85	60	54
Private (S)	15	15	15
Construction/Mining	(9)	(7)	
APP	10	80	90
Private (L/M)	75	5	5
Private (S)	15	15	5
Commerce/Services	(42)	(36)	(40)
APP	10	25	38
Private (L/M)	60	25	12
Private (S)	30	50	50
Government	(5)	(10)	(9)
Total GDP			
APP	11	34	39
Private (L/M)	67	38	31
Private (S)	22	28	30

of literacy (from 60% to 88%);[28] healthcare improvement;[29] redistribution of considerable land to the poor; open forums allowing for critique. The Sandinistas aimed to unlink the Nicaraguan economy from over-dependence on foreign exchange and they hoped to achieve some basic food security for the population. While the goals of redistribution of opportunities and resources were clearly having effect, the long-term problems of a war economy, capital flight, hyperinflation[30] with an eroding away of the real minimum salaries[31] and war weariness finally brought the revolutionary momentum to a standstill.[32]

Popular democracy

The Sandinistas were concerned with achieving something that would go beyond 'Somocismo without Somoza'. That is, not just the Somoza dynasty had to be removed, but also the class structures. The revolution can be said not to have taken a one-class route, but rather held on to a more inter-class nationalism aimed at redistribution of national resources and popular democracy. There was a turning to popular mobilization and organizations.[33] The sweeping literacy and health crusades are typical of this turn to the grassroots. The mass organizations were a main channel for FSLN influence among the population. This caused ambiguity as to how far these were but a party front, and in how far they were more pluralist. While the goal of erasing grassroots poverty and maintaining considerable freedom for critique within the popular organizations leads to a positive evaluation, there were worried voices, also from the church hierarchy, which critiqued Sandinista policies on several issues, but especially on the ideological tone. Others, especially those associated with liberation theology, were enthusiastic about Sandinismo.

---

[28]Richard Fagen, *Forjando la Paz: El desafío de América Central* (San José: DEI, 1987), p.145:

Central America (1985)

	C.Rica	El Sal.	Guat.	Hond.	Nica.
Pop. (in mill.)	2.52	4.86	7.96	4.40	3.27
GDP pr.cap. US$	1,020	710	1,120	670	880
Infant mort.pr.thous.	20	70	67	81	84
Life expectation	73	57	59	62	60
Literacy (%)	90	67	56	60	88

[29]cf.David C.Halperin and Richard Garfield, "Development in Health Care in Nicaragua", p.340-346 in Rosset & Vandermeer, *The Nicaragua Reader*.

[30]cf.Torres-Rivas, *América Central Hacia el 2000*, p.306 for Central American statistics 1980-1988.

[31]cf.note 88 which shows the indice to move from 100 in 1980 to 44 in 1985.

[32]cf.Dunkerley, p.308ff. where he charts the huge economic costs of *contra* aggression and financial aggression to Nicaragua. The national debt he lists as follows:

Nicaraguan debt in comparative perspective
(per cent of GDP)

	1978	1979	1980	1981	1982	1983	1984	1985
NICARAGUA	51	74	86	99	123	143	170	196
HONDURAS	49	56	59	60	61	68	74	79
COSTA RICA	54	59	73	73	78	84	85	87
MEXICO	26	25	27	33	34	37	38	37
LATIN AMER.	30	31	33	37	39	43	44	44

[33]Richard Stahler-Sholk, "Building Democracy in Nicaragua", ch.4 in George A.Lopez & Michael Stohl, eds., *Liberalization and Redemocratization in Latin America* (New York: Greenwood Press, 1987).

Christians in the revolution

The evaluation of the relationship between a Christian identity and Sandinista politics has at times suffered from overwrought propaganda from both sides.[34] It has at the same time been pointed out that after a decade of Sandinismo, the number of Roman Catholic priests as well as the number of Protestant pastors has grown significantly in Nicaragua.[35] Critique has been levied against the censorship of *La Prensa*, on the treatment of the Miskito Indians, and the use of a declared 'state of siege' to maintain periods of censorship, including of *Radio Católica*. In defense it has been recalled that these actions were done during war years and are not without many parallels in Latin America and elsewhere. It is clear that sections of the churches and outspoken Christians have taken a role in the Nicaraguan revolution in a way wholly distinct from the Cuban revolution. Many leaders within the revolutionary reconstruction have pointed to their Christian motivation.[36] Among these is Ernesto Cardenal, widely known through his poetry, his recorded dialogues from the Christian base community of Solentiname, and his travels. In 1965 Cardenal, at the age of 40, was ordained a priest in Managua. During his Solentiname years (1965-77) Cardenal combined his art, his priestly service and his political consciousness in an experimental grassroots movement. Solentiname is a group of tiny islands in Lake Nicaragua. Cardenal and some friends originally intended to set up an artistic and mystic community. Only later did the political aspect become so dominant. The four volumes of *The Gospel in Solentiname* record dialogues of the mainly peasant members as they reflect on passages of the Gospels, applying these directly to their situation and the conflict in Nicaragua. The dialogues contain commentary which relies on a hermeneutical key of class consciousness and revolutionary renewal. By the mid 1970s Cardenal was actively supporting the Sandinistas and left behind his pacifist standpoint: "In Nicaragua, as in other parts of Latin America, nonviolent struggle is not possible." By October, 1977, the Solentiname commune had become Sandinista and the young people joined an attack against the National Guard. Some were killed in action, some went to prison and others escaped to Costa Rica. The buildings of Cardenal's community were destroyed except for the church which was turned into an army barracks. After the fall of the Somoza regime in July, 1979, Cardenal was named Minister of Culture of Nicaragua. In September of that year he reported to the press: "This is a Christian revolution. The people of Nicaragua are, in the great majority, Christian, and that is why the people carried out the revolution....The church never condemned recourse to weapons for a just cause. Pope Paul VI said that armed struggle and violence were legitimately moral in the case of evident and prolonged dictatorship - and ours was truly prolonged."

Critique remains on what may at times be seen as a rather close identification of Cristianismo and Sandinismo, just as the reactionary right often supported the

---

[34]For critique against the Sandinistas, see for example, Humberto Belli, *"Cristianismo y Sandinismo"* in Arturo Cruz y José Luis Velázquez, eds., *Nicaragua: Regresión en la Revolución* (San José: Libro Libre, 1986), p.189ff.

[35]cf.Fagen, *Forjando*, p.74.

[36]cf.Teófilo Cabestrero, *Revolutionaries for the Gospel: Testimonies of Fifteen Christians in the Nicaraguan Government*, trans.Philip Berryman (Maryknoll: Orbis, 1986).

contras in the name of the faith, as well. A rather embarrassing polarization for those seeking a Christian approach to political ethics.

Reagan geopolitics

Meanwhile, it is doubtful whether Washington understood the Central American situation. Or, more likely: the threat of Sandinista Nicaragua was not so much that it could directly harm the USA; rather, it was the example of a nation taking an independent course from the USA, which particularly caused the over-reaction.[37] The question of whether the Sandinistas were redirecting resources to the poor majority was largely forgotten in Washington. The Reagan case against Sandinista Nicaragua essentially dealt with four points:[38]

i)   Nicaraguan aid to the guerrillas in El Salvador;
ii) Nicaraguan military build-up;
iii) The ties to communist countries;
iv) Sandinista "totalitarian" ideology.

As for the first point, the supposed supply line via Nicaragua was never established. The second point is a half truth: while Nicaraguan army build-up was large (between 1983 and 1988 the troops were doubled to reach 70,000, compared with 15,400 in Honduras and 39,000 in El Salvador), this was done in the context of the *contra* war and, after the USA invasion of Grenada - October, 1983 - heightened expectations of an invasion of Nicaragua. The accusation of military build-up loses considerable weight in the face of the Washington-*contra* pact, not to forget the Washington support of the El Salvador army.[39] The third factor, ties to communist countries, must also be judged in the light of policies (including the economic boycott, i.e., ostracization by the Reagan government), which helped push Nicaragua in that direction. The fourth accusation, the "totalitarian" ideology of the Sandinistas, was not carefully judged during the simplistic ideological bipolarities which typified the Reagan approach; seen in the perspective of the long decades of the Somoza regime, the Sandinistas made several improvements on the former "authoritarianism" of that era, including steps toward 'popular democracy', as discussed above. Whatever the ideological inadequacies of the Sandinistas, the picture painted by the Reagan administration was often so far from the actual state of affairs that the USA government was soon accused of:

i)   clandestine operations (later revealed in the Iran-Contra affair);
ii) persistent distortion in its portrayal of the situation in Nicaragua;

---

[37]cf.Noam Chomsky, "U.S.Polity and Society: The Lessons of Nicaragua", in Thomas W.Walker, *ed.*, *Reagan Versus the Sandinistas: The Undeclared War on Nicaragua* (London: Westview, 1987), p.303.

[38]cf.Harold Molineu, *U.S.Policy Toward Latin America: From Regionalism to Globalism* (Oxford: Westview Press, 1990), p.195ff.

[39]Present troop levels are placed at: Honduras, 23,000; Nicaragua, 28,000; Guatemala, 46,000; and El Salvador, 56,000. cf.*Latin American Regional Reports: Mexico & Central America*, 5 Dec. 1991, p.6.

iii) abuse of human rights through the terrorist attacks by the *contras* on agricultural and educational workers;

iv) waging war without declaring war (condemned by the International Court in the Hague);

v) a kind of tunnel vision fixation toward liquidating the Sandinistas (which arises from a simplistic bipolar world-view of the Free West against Communism without telling the whole story of repressive regimes nestled as 'friendly dictators' in 'our own backyard');

vi) all the while forgetting the long history of USA-Somoza cooperation in Nicaragua;

vii) a good/evil dualism between capitalism and socialism which allowed the plight of the poor to be forgotten during the ideological name-calling.

The effects of sandinismo

While the Sandinista emphasis was on popular organizations rather than liberal democracy, they did in fact go by the rules and allow themselves to be voted out in the 1989 election (if only - as some would add - because the whole world was watching). The significance of this is high when one remembers the context, where the Somoza regime maintained its power for forty years in spite of elections. After they lost the elections the Sandinista party engaged in some serious self-critique, admitting they had become victims to a triumphant mentality which no longer accorded with the real situation, that they had made too many decisions from the top without input from the grass roots, that the people had grown weary of the military draft, the dragging war, the economic tumble, and that they had not fully made the transition from a guerrilla front to a democratic political party in a way that satisfied the voters.[40]

Concluding, we may presume the long-term effects of Sandinismo to be many, the more important of which include:

i) contributing to the end of Somocismo;

ii) a heightened nationalism in the face of dependency;

iii) significant attention to the poor in educational and health programmes;

iv) the opening up of a social movement which changed Nicaraguan party politics;

v) a new stimulation for and cooperation with sections of the church seeking an "option for the poor".[41]

b) El Salvador

The history of the crisis in El Salvador includes such characteristics as:

---

[40]cf.Paul Jeffrey, "Nicaragua: Sandinistas recognize errors", *Latin America Press*, Oct.4, 1990, p.5.

[41]Rosa María Pochet & Abelino Martínez, *Nicaragua, Iglesia: ¿Manipulación o Profecía?* (San José: DEI, 1987). Berryman, *Religious Roots of Rebellion*, ch.8: "Christians in Sandinista Nicaragua". Conor Cruise O'Brien, "God and Man in Nicaragua", ch.8 in Dermot Keogh, *ed.*, *Church and Politics in Latin America* (London: Macmillan, 1990).

i) Agroexport dependency, especially affected by falling coffee prices and high interest rates that increase foreign debts.

ii) Increased dispossession of subsistence lands among the rural population.

iii) Repeated election frauds.

iv) High unemployment.

v) A circle of right-wing and left-wing violence (which began to spiral after the 1977 election fraud and led the nation into prolonged civil war).

vi) Capital flight and brain drain.

vii) High financial and military support policies by the U.S.A. (By 1988 total USA support was more than $600 million a year).

From mid 1979 hundreds were dying violent deaths as death squad action increased and according to some estimates 14,000 died in 1980 during the escalating conflict, while 1981 added another 17,000 deaths.[42] The central problem for El Salvador during the 1980s and even into the 1990s has thus been the civil war; the political theme has often circled around the need and possibility for dialogue and national reconciliation. This has been continually complicated by the overtly high USA intervention which feared that El Salvador was the next in line of the "falling dominos".[43] The attack on the conscientizing church has been particularly strong, as especially recalled in the shooting of Archbishop Oscar Romero and similarly the killing of six Jesuit priests, including both the rector and vice-rector of the Central American University in San Salvador, in November, 1989.

Archbishop Oscar Romero

The life and death of Archbishop Oscar Arnulfo Romero is one more sign of the changing status of the Latin American Roman Catholic church. Ordained in 1942 in Rome, he returned to El Salvador where he devoted himself to his work as a priest, eventually to become a bishop in 1970. Of a genuine concern for spirituality, he was generally known to be basically status quo and conservative in his ideas on church authority.[44] But the build-up of the conflict between right and left and the unprecedented attack on the church in El Salvador was to unfold a drama as yet unresolved. Romero's appointment as Archbishop followed closely upon the "Monday Massacre" (Feb.28, 1977) in the plaza of San Salvador, where more than a hundred were killed and many more wounded and arrested.[45] Some days later Archbishop Romero's friend, Rutilio Grande, a worker priest among the poor, was murdered by a death squad. Other priests were picked up and tortured. In his radio speeches Oscar Romero rejected violence. Events worsened and the systematic killing of civilians increased. On February 17, 1980, Archbishop Romero requested President Jimmy Carter to stop the military aid to El Salvador. In his last radio sermon March 23, Oscar Romero said to the nation:

---

[42]Dunkerley, *Power*, p.384f.

[43]As Dunkerley, p.338, says, there is much evidence to encourage the view "that a Salvadorean revolution would have quickly followed that in Nicaragua were it not for US intervention".

[44]cf.Musto, *Catholic Peace* p.234.

[45]cf.Philip Berryman, *The Religious Roots of Rebellion*, p.117ff.

"...I would like to make a special call upon military men and specifically to the rank and file of the National Guard and police in the barracks. Brothers, you are part of our people. You are killing your own *campesino* (peasant) brothers and sisters. Above any order to kill that a man may give, the law of God must prevail: "Thou shalt not kill! ... I beg you, I implore you, I order you in the name of God: Stop the repression!"[46]

The following day, while saying Mass at the Carmelite hospital, he was shot.[47]

The decade of the 1980s was one of prolonged guerrilla struggle against an army receiving enough USA support to prevent the revolution from succeeding, while at the same time such support ensured the maintenance of the status quo. The judicial system has no autonomy before the army, which explains the gross violation of human rights which allows the army to torture and kill suspected subversives, members of their families, or out of frustration *campesinos* accused of harbouring guerrillas.[48]

Christian Democrats: José Napoleón Duarte

A hopeful moment came during the first phase of the Christian Democratic Party (PDC) under Duarte and the attempt he made at peace talks with leaders of the FMLN in October, 1984.[49] Yet the hoped for way out through the consolidation of the political centre under the Christian Democrats did not end the war nor lead to a sufficient level of democratization and economic reactivation.[50] After a couple of hopeful years, the Christian Democrats appeared to have been forced into an inactive stalemate with no way around the dominant forces which control the situation in El Salvador. A number of tensions and contradictions[51] have been pointed out for the Christian Democratic influence in El Salvador (and Guatemala):

i) There is a conflict between the Christian Democratic democratizing programme and repressive army practices which escape control.

ii) The land reform and other redistribution programmes are blocked by the dominant power bloc which does not make concessions.

---

[46]cf.Third World Guide, p.522.

[47]Both the judge appointed to investigate the death of Romero, as well as U.S.A. Embassy sources, pointed to a plan by General José Alberto Medrano (founder of the right-wing paramilitary death squad, ORDEN) and to Major Roberto D'Aubuisson, former leader of the National Republican Alliance party (ARENA). Cf.James R.Brockman, *The Word Remains: A Life of Oscar Romero* (Maryknoll: Orbis, 1982); *Archbishop Oscar Romero: Voice of the Voiceless, The Four Pastoral Letters and Other Statements* (Maryknoll: Orbis, 1985).

[48]cf.Charles Clements, *Witness to War: An American doctor in El Salvador* (New York: Bantam, 1984).

[49]José Napoleón Duarte, with Diana Page, *Duarte: My Story* (New York: Putnam's, 1986), ch.9: "Peace Talks".

[50]cf.Rafael Menjívar Larín, "El Salvador: problemas y perspectivas", in Torres-Rivas, *América Central Hacia el 2000*, p.213.

[51]Geske Dijkstra & Miguel Antonio Chorro, "La política de El Salvador (1984-1987): Florecimiento y ruina del PDC", in Mats Lundahl & Wim Pelupessy, *Crisis Económica en Centroamérica y el Caribe* (San José: DEI, 1989), p.175: "Las promesas electorales de José Napoleón Duarte, que básicamente consistieron en conseguir la paz y producir más justicia social, estuvieron en contradicción con los intereses de los grupos de los cuales dependían: la administración estadounidense e, internamente, la Fuerza Armada y la burguesía."

iii) The Christian Democratic intention of seeking a pacification process goes against the tendency of two of its allies: the Armed forces and Washington.[52]

iv) As a middle sector party, the Christian Democrats have no clear support base in a situation so polarized as to leave a vacuum at the centre.

v) The Duarte programme became stymied and ended up doing nothing; a clear case of "rule by abstention".[53]

vi) The Christian Democrats in Central America have achieved some partisan mobilization but not popular mobilization.

vii) They have not thoroughly challenged the dependent capitalist model.

viii) They have not made an adequate analysis of the contending forces of power.

ix) The resulting political opportunism contradicts their promises of transformation.

Lessons from El Salvador

Violent deaths are estimated as high as 80,000 for the decade of war in El Salvador; the number of emigrants and refugees have been calculated to be some 29% of the population (by 1989 the population totalled more than 5 million). When the number of dead due to the war are counted, along with those dedicated to military activity and those who have been displaced, then according to some statistics more than 2 million have abruptly been wrenched from the economically active population, or a staggering 41,9% of the total population.[54] The long war in El Salvador gives cause to rethink strategies for transformation:

i) USA foreign policy in the region must be fundamentally questioned. While the 1969 Nelson Rockefeller report to Congress suggested that the USA should look to the military as "the essential force of constructive social change" in Latin America, it is time for Washington to listen seriously to better informed sources.

ii) It must be admitted that the long-term internal political control which has excluded the left from the political arena (exclusionary military politics) has led to a spiral of violence.

iii) As for the Christian Democratic debut in Central America, there has been every difficulty in realizing their programme of a new alternative; beginning with talk of transformation, they soon had trouble escaping the impression of appearing to be a Yankee Puppet.

iv) The tactic of guerrilla war must likewise be practically and intrinsically called into question, since the final offensive of the FMLN proved impossible to achieve and has led to prolonged war; but also because it has helped channel many human and financial resources away from other strategies for change.

v) It has been rightly written from the Central American University in San

---

[52]*El Salvador: ¿Es La Democracia Cristiana un Partido de Centro?* (Mexico: Centro de Investigación y Acción Social, 1987), p.29.

[53]J.Carrière, Center for Latin American Research and Documentation, Amsterdam.

[54]Menjívar Larín, *Ibid.*, p.205f.

Salvador: "For some reason the war began, for some reason the war continues, and without resolving this reason, without resolving the causes and the means, this great problem of war violence will not end."[55]

c) Guatemala

Guatemala is the one country in Central America with a high percentage of indigenous people: the Maya Indians form half the population. Since the C.I.A. intervention of 1954 ending the reform period in Guatemala, military politics have provided a legacy of repression as not yet overcome. The future is uncertain.[56] In 1988 it was calculated that 85% of the children under five years old are affected by various grades of malnutrition. Due to a high birthrate some fifty thousand young people enter the work market every year, only to find that those from previous years also have no steady work. Some 35% of Guatemalans have turned to forms of Protestant Christianity - the highest percentage in Latin America. The most urgent social question is redistribution of wealth and welfare in its various forms: political influence, land, wages, education, healthcare.

Exclusionary politics

The tradition of exclusionary politics in Guatemala leads to a systematic elimination of the opposition and a cooperation between the military and the oligarchy in ensuring a cheap labour supply, through repression of trade unions, subsistence wages, and the lack of land which forces the poor to become migrants looking for day-labour and seasonal work. Thus many live on the margin of a money economy with no prospect of rising above the poverty of a hand to mouth existence. At the time that the Jacobo Arbenz government (1950-54) began land redistribution, 2% of the population controlled 74% of the arable land, as verified by the World Bank. Results of the 1954 coup (cf.I.3) include:

i) Guatemalan politics, at the time opening to reform movements and the political opposition, was turned back by foreign intervention;
ii) Since then there has been no open politics nor any land reform.
iii) Wider implications were drawn for Latin America: the democratic route to transformation will be blocked by the USA if it goes against their economic interests.
iv) Nationalization of property and political-economic decisions to alleviate poverty will be interpreted as a communistic threat by the USA.

The 1959 Cuba revolution inspired guerrilla movements in Latin America, also in Guatemala, leading to a decade of optimism by the violent left (1959-1968). The waves of guerrilla and state violence have peaked in ferocity in Guatemala during

---

[55]Universidad Centroamericana, *Revista ECA*, no.486-487, San Salvador, April-May, 1989: "Por algo empezó la guerra, por algo sigue la guerra y, sin resolver ese algo, sin resolver las causas y los medios no se va a terminar este gran problema de la violencia de la guerra...."

[56]cf.René Poitevin, "Guatemala: un futuro democrático incierto", in Torres-Rivas, *América Central Hacia el 2000*, p.193ff.

1966-68; 1970-73; and 1978-84.[57] The conflict has led to a high number of 'disappearances', and during the more violent period under Ríos Montt, starting in March 1982, there were systematic massacres, scorched earth tactics (burning of villages) and the formation of strategic hamlets (resettling the population to villages under military control where there is forced inscription into civil patrols and economic reliance upon the army's provision of supplies)[58]. The Ríos Montt government's counter-insurgency campaign "pacified" the Indian highlands through its "beans and bullets" (*frijoles y fusiles*) programme of channeling aid to government collaborators in strategic hamlets while terrorizing suspected guerrilla sympathizers with torture and death.[59] Thousands of refugees fled to southern Mexico. The indigenous peoples have thus especially suffered, caught between the guerrillas and the state army. Most of these Mayas are subsistence farmers and seasonal labourers, already exploited without the war, but even more so through the military conflict. The guerrilla struggle has failed in Guatemala and has been pushed back to the fringes.

Democratic facade

After the years of worst conflict there was a turn to politics of the centre and hope for democratization with the election of Christian Democrat Vinicio Cerezo, the first civilian president (1986-90) in sixteen years and only the second after 1954. The best Social Democratic leaders had already been assassinated, effectively removing the centre-left from influence. After Cerezo took office the political killings decreased for a time. But the Cerezo government achieved no transformations, tied as it was to - and pliable toward - the army. In fact, Cerezo could not really expect any transformation, promising as he did before his election not to undertake any agrarian reforms, not to call the army in question, nor to nationalize foreign companies (since, he said, that would cause capital flight).[60] Little wonder that this kind of democracy has been called a democratic facade. While following an entirely inadequate internal strategy, one positive point was Cerezo's push for the formation of a Central American Parliament and a regional neutralism which helped the Arias peace plan find acceptance. During the 1980s the Guatemalan army - right-wing, but also nationalist - refused cooperation with Reagan's regional strategy and did not participate in manoeuvres in Honduras. The last election (November 1990) brought to power another civilian president, Jorge Serrano Elias (the first elected Protestant president in Latin American) who has experience as negotiator with the guerrillas under the Cerezo government. He began to form a new social pact in the hope of making some reforms, but the structures are not

---

[57]Dunkerley, *Power*, p.430.

[58]*Ibid.*, p.496. He provides a list of the massacres at the peak period of March - July 1982.

[59]Stan Persky, *America, the Last Domino* (Vancouver: New Star Books, 1984), ch.6: "Born-Again Brutality". Roland Ebel, "Guatemala: The Politics of Unstable Stability", ch.23 in Howard J.Wiarda & Harvey F.Kline, *Latin American Politics and Development* (Boulder, Colorado: Westview Press, 1990). Beeson and Pearce, *A Vision of Hope*, p.248.

[60]Cerezo spoke of "the creation of a new order, the key to which will be the taking of power by the National Army and the Christian Democrats", *Central America Report*, Nov.21, 1986. However, for the armed forces in Central America to play a reforming role there must first be a purification and the re-educating to a new perspective.

open for any significant changes. Latest reports tell of increasing human rights abuses.[61] Even today only about 4% of the workers are unionized; the infant mortality rate for the indigenous population - at 134 per thousand - is twice as high as for the rest of the population; similarly the average life-span for the indigenous is much lower, at merely 45 years. Since the peasants have less and less land available it is not to be expected that social unrest will stop. Politics must be opened to a wider scale of representation. The systematic repression of progressive leaders guarantees the maintenance of an unjust status quo. The long evident conclusion that the "trickle-down" theory of socioeconomic development has not worked in Guatemala (nor elsewhere in the Isthmus) leads to the thesis that external development assistance and internal attempts at harmonization will have little impact on poverty so long as the economic and political elites maintain an exclusionary vision which marginalizes the poor.[62]

d) Honduras

The statistics for poverty in Honduras, like so many regional statistics, are not entirely clear but remain very disconcerting, being among the highest in the hemisphere, whether one measures the high infant mortality, the illiteracy of 40%, or the rural living conditions, where the majority of adobe housing still have a dirt floor and lack running water and electricity.[63] On occasion those who have immersed themselves in the poverty of the campesinos have swung to a revolutionary-socialist position, sometimes in the name of the Christian faith,[64] but there has been no major guerrilla movement. Unlike Guatemala, Honduras has no large indigenous population; unlike Nicaragua, it began no major push toward revolution-

---

[61]cf.*Latinamerica Press* vol.23, no.34 (sept.19,1991): "Guatemala's violent nightmare worsens: Despite peace talks, human rights deteriorate", p.1f.

[62]cf.Lars Schöultz, "Guatemala: Social Change and Political Conflict", in John Womack, *ed.*, *Trouble in Our Backyard* (New York: Grove, 1983), p.181. José Luis Chea, *Guatemala: La Cruz Fragmentada* (San José: DEI, 1988). Rodolfo Cardenal, "Radical Conservatism and the Challenge of the Gospel in Guatemala", p.205ff. in Keogh, *Church and Politics in Latin America*.

[63]General sources that report on world statistics (such as *Almanaque Mundial*) and even specific reports on Central America, such as María Eugenia Gallardo & José Roberto López, *Centroamérica: La Crisis en Cifras* (San José: FLACSO, 1986), p.192 may have an overly optimistic descending scale for infant mortality.

Infant mortality
(annual statistics per thousand live births)

	1965-70	70-75	75-80	80-85	95-2000
GUATEMALA	115	90	79	68	40
SALVADOR	n.d.	101	85	71	42
HONDURAS	n.d.	111	95	81	46
NICARAGUA	n.d.	109	96	84	51
COSTA RICA	60	67	29	20	16

In contrast to the above, in 1984 the Ministry of Health of the Government of Honduras placed infant mortality at 117 (per thousand). Cf.Lucila Funes de Torres, *Los Derechos Humanos en Honduras* (Tegucigalpa: Centro de Documentación de Honduras, 1984), p.22, and Julio Antonio Bueso, *El Subdesarrollo Hondureño* (Tegucigalpa: Editorial Universitaria, 1987), p.19. A recent article states that "almost 10 percent of Honduran children die before age 5", *Latinamerica Press*, March 14, 1991, p.7.

[64]For example, Padre J.Guadalupe Carney, *To be a Revolutionary: The explosive autobiography of an American priest, missing in Honduras* (San Francisco: Harper & Row, 1985).

ary change; unlike El Salvador, it is not highly populated, nor has it entered the spiral of violence of a long civil war; unlike Costa Rica, Honduras has not made the turn to terminating its army politics and promoting education and social democracy. Honduras is thus not to be confused with any of its neighbours.[65] It became infamous during the 1980s as the USA military base for President Reagan's regional anti-Nicaragua campaign. As the Honduran political analyst, Enrique Aguilar Paz, put it at a major conference on Honduras, there is a compiling problem of marginalization, political imposition, economic exploitation, corruption and silence, which taken all together spell out a situation of fear to transform.[66]

Honduras[67] has traditionally been thought of as the classic banana republic[68] where companies could dominate governments. For example, in 1950 the banana companies accounted for 91% of tax revenue from income and profits for Honduras.[69] Since then bananas have gradually given way to other products, such as coffee, beef, and the wood industry. If no longer fully a banana republic, it is likewise to be noted that the second qualification, 'republic', does not particularly connect well to the root meaning of *res publica,* whereby it is understood that politics is a public matter and not just a question of private law in the sense of personalistic *caudillismo* and *clientelismo* (cf.1.IV.1). Yet, for a number of reasons Honduras has traditionally remained less violent than El Salvador, Guatemala and Nicaragua. Among these reasons, are:

i)   Honduras is less densely populated and there was for a time more opportunity for land;
ii)   the foreign banana enclave kept the formation of the local oligarchy subdued; the dominant classes were sufficiently weak that it was possible to force them to make more social concessions than in some neighbouring countries;
iii)   the *campesinos* gained experience in waged labour and trade union organization after the strike of 1954;
iv)   while political party formation was traditional and new parties recognized but slowly, the syndicalist activity and peasant organization received attention;

---

[65]cf.Harvey K.Meyer, *Historical Dictionary of Honduras* (Metuchen, N.J.: Scarecrow Press, 1976). James D.Rudolph, *Honduras: a country study* (Washington: American University, 1984).
[66]Enrique Aguila Paz, "Democracia plena o pseudo democracia" in *Honduras: Realidad Nacional y Crisis Regional* (Tegucigalpa: CEDOH - *Centro de Documentación de Honduras,* 1986), p.61, where he arranges the five items according to an acrostic spelling 'miedo' (fear):
"M arginamiento social, que nos hunde en la Ignorancia.
I mposición política, que establece una verdadera Inquisición.
E xplotación económica, que nos ha causado tanta Indigencia.
D eshonestidad y corrupción, que genera una general Inmoralidad.
O lvido y silencio a los anteriores problemas, la triste Indiferencia."
[67]For an overview, Leticia Salomón, "Sistema Político, Fuerzas Armadas y Crisis Centroamericána", in Salomón, *ed.*, *Honduras: Panorama y Perspectivas* (Tegucigalpa: CEDOH, 1989), p.1-46. Rafael del Cid y Janet Shane, "Honduras en la antesala del 2000: desafios y opciones de una sociedad en crisis", Torres-Rivas, *coord.*, *América Central Hacia el 2000,* p.221-236. Roger Isaula, *Honduras: Crisis e Incertidumbre Nacional* (Tegucigalpa: Editores Unidos, 1988).
[68]cf.José Roberto López, *La Economía del Banano en Centroamérica* (San José: DEI, 1986).
[69]cf.Dunkerley, p.526.

v)   the governments have been less coercive and more willing to negotiate and sometimes open to reforms.

The longer pattern in Honduras has been one of mainly military government, interspersed with weak civilian government and continued coups.[70] There have at times been reformist military governments, as there have also been repressive governments whose head of state was civilian. The military reformist government of López Arellano in 1972-75 came up with a national plan for development (*Plan Nacional de Desarrollo*) and in those years pushed through significant agrarian reforms by redistributing land.[71] The same government made a significant increase in banana export taxation, moving it from twenty-five to fifty cents a crate (though this was suddenly lowered a few months later). At the time, Honduras had recently exiled thousands of El Salvadoran migrants from its territory and had also withdrawn from the Central American Common Market in which it lost out financially to its more industrialized neighbours. There was an upsurge in economic growth in Honduras during the second half of the 1970s. Meanwhile, in 1974, Hurricane Fifi, accompanied by major flooding, damaged the north coast where industry (San Pedro Sula) and banana plantations are located. Only the coffee crops, located in the mountains, remained unaffected. Among the well remembered incidents in these years was the conflict in Olancho[72] in June, 1975, when landlords persuaded the army garrison at Juticalpa to attack *campesinos*, who were staging protest marches to the capital, demanding land. On June 25 six campesinos were shot and some nine other bodies (including two priests) soon found buried in a well on an Olancho ranch, *Hacienda Los Horcones*, having first been tortured and then shot in a combined effort by agents of the military and local landlords to prevent 'subversives' from promoting the landtenure question.[73] In 1975 the López Arellano government fell when investigations into the suicide of the chairman of United Brands in New York, Eli Black, revealed that $1.25 million had been paid in Honduras as a bribe, thus explaining the reversal of the banana export tax. While the military government of López Arellano in the early 1970s instituted major land reform for a time, the civilian government of Roberto Suazo Córdova (1982-85) was actually dominated by the military to an extreme, thanks to the regional crisis that arose at the beginning of the 1980s when Honduras was drawn into Reagan-geopolitics. The militarization of Honduras during the 1980s was expedient to the Reagan understanding of things, since (i) the USA had lost a partner in the fall of

---

[70]The number of prime *jefes* functioning as presidents (under a variety of titles, often only for a few weeks in lieu of the president while a coup was being settled) totals 130 *jefes* during 167 years (starting the count in 1824). The average has been improving in our century to some 32 *jefes* during the past 91 years. A list of names starting in 1824 is given in Eduardo Sandoval, *Constitución de Honduras: Comentada con Sencillez* (Tegucigalpa: Industria Litografica Lempira, 1988), p.173-181.

[71]cf.Bueso, *El Subdesarrollo Hondureño*, p.93ff: "El Período del Proceso Reformista de las Fuerzas Armadas". Also, Dunkerley, *op.cit.*, p.552-557.

[72]cf.Gustavo Blanco & Jaime Valverde, *Honduras: Iglesia y Cambio Social* (San José: DEI, 1987), p.95ff. Also, Steven Volk with Anne Nelson, "Honduras: On the border of war", p.222 in Womack, *Trouble in our Backyard*.

[73]Blanco & Valverde, *op.cit.*, p.101.

the Somoza regime; (ii) Honduras has borders with Nicaragua, El Salavdor, and Guatemala; and (iii) Honduras was too dependent and lacking in national identity to protest loudly. Washington policies were assisted by the ideological bent of Colonel Gustavo Alvarez Martínez (later assassinated on the street in Tegucigalpa) who helped apply the extensive militarization to the country (the national security doctrine at this point gaining the upperhand), so that Honduras began to show significant decline in human rights, judged by the number of disappearances in the early 1980s.[74] Somewhat ironically, and no doubt also due to pressures from Washington, during the 1980s civilian presidents became the new norm for Central America, though during such troubled years that some are suspicious of the new fad being a new fraud. The election of the Azcona government in Honduras at the end of 1985 was the first time outside of Costa Rica that any of the other four countries had achieved a hand-over of government from one elected presidency to another.[75] After the removal of the *contras* and the reduction of the "low intensity conflict"[76] strategy in Central America, attention now turns to the neoliberal effects of the present governments (in Honduras, Rafael Callejas) and whether there are ways to transformation. A Honduran analyst[77] mentions the following causes for the economic crisis of the 1980s in Honduras:

The *external* causes have included:
i)   world recession;
ii)   lower prices for raw materials;
iii)   high bank interest on the international market.

Among the *internal* factors (some with external roots) are:
i)   the *latifundista* concentration of landownership;
ii)   excessive monopolization by transnational capital;
iii)   a development model which functions as an enclave of agroexport and ex-
       cludes the majority from participating in the gains;

---

[74]These remained low in comparison with some neighbouring countries: lists of *desaparecidos* are placed at 158 for the years 1980-85, and at 250 for the years 1980-88. For a detailed list of names and other information, cf.Bueso, *op.cit.*, ch.VII: "Los Derechos Humanos y los Refugiados". Also, Amnistia Internacional, *Honduras: Autoridad Civil - Poder Militar; Violaciones de los Derechos Humanos en la Década de 1980* (Madrid: EDAI, 1988).

[75]Dunkerley, *op.cit.*, p.581.

[76]Low intensity conflict involves a combination of strategic political, economic and military pressures on a situation. Thus in the case of Central America the Reagan administration used economic boycotts, support of mercenary forces, and large scale demonstrative military practice operations and preparation of new military bases to destabilize Nicaragua without actually declaring war and sending USA troops into Nicaragua. The low intensity military conflict doctrine allows for special forces to take rather high intensity actions against subversive movements. cf.Tom Barry, *El Conflicto de Baja Intensidad: Un Nuevo Campo de Batalla en Centroamérica* (Tegucigalpa: CEDOH, 1988). Víctor Meza, *et al.*, *Honduras-Estados Unidos: Subordinación y Crisis* (Tegucigalpa: CEDOH, 1988). Mark Rosenberg, *et al.*, *Honduras: Pieza clave de la política de Estados Unidos en Centroamérica* (Tegucigalpa: CEDOH, 1986). Raúl Vergara Meneses, *et al.*, *Centroamérica: La Guerra de Baja Intensidad* (San José: DEI, 1988). Gabriel Aguilera, *El Fusil y el Olivo: la cuestión militar en Centroamérica* (San José: DEI, 1989).

[77]Roger Isaula, *Honduras: Crisis e Incertidumbre Nacional*, p.36ff.

iv) insufficient diversification of products (due to lack of capital and extreme dependency on foreign markets);

v)   limited internal market and a holding back of industrial development.

Reports rather consistently point to the worsened plight of the poor, with the Roman Catholic and some other churches vocal on this point during the last years in Honduras.

e) Costa Rica

The ways in which Costa Rica traditionally *differs* from the other Central American countries we have been considering are several; the following points apply somewhat differently to each of the other four countries, as will be evident from our discussion until now. Of Costa Rica we may say:

i)   there is a spirit of political negotiation with no comparable state terror and disappearances;

ii)   there is a corresponding low level of social disorder;

iii) the elections have for a long time been the most fair and open;

iv)   there is an emphasis on public services and welfare (education, health, housing, nutrition);

v)   there is a high literacy rate;

vi)   there has also been a higher per capita GDP in Costa Rica;

vii) waged labour is more extensive than in the neighbouring countries;

viii) the security forces have received minimal expenditure (in 1985 less than 3% of the national budget whereas the regional average was some 25%).

When we ask *why* Costa Rica is different, the factors are similarly often listed as many, for example:

i)   the pre-Columbian patterns provided no mineral wealth nor indigenous labourers for the *conquistadores*;

ii)   thus the colonization pattern was less *señorial* and closer to the idea of homesteading;

iii) the temperate land produces well;

iv)   the disestablishment of the army and decisive turn to inclusionary politics with a social democratic welfare system since the coup of 1948;

v)   progressive education;

vi)   attention has been given to investment in manufacturing and economic modernization.

Few analysts would doubt that the turn to social democracy is the "key to [Costa Rica's] modern political economy"[78], or as also expressed: "the key concept has been inclusionary politics: the state has responded to popular pressures, protest and new demands, with negotiation" whereas the other countries of the region have

---

[78]Dunkerley, p.594.

been largely led by "exclusionary politics and an oligarchy syndrome leading to repressions".[79]

It must also be said that Costa Rica is not entirely different: there are many low incomes in Costa Rica that feel the economic pressures, too. Yet, it is clear that there has been a better distribution of social services (especially education and health care) which until the changes in Nicaragua found no comparison in the other countries. Costa Rica, via the Arias peace effort, led the way in democratizing regional politics in the face of systematic pressure from Washington. Costa Rica entered the 1980s as a continuing model of social democracy for Central America, but it was almost bankrupt. It underwent great pressures of economic dependency on the USA without falling into the militarization the Reagan administration wanted to see enforced there.[80] Costa Rica did not disintegrate during the violent decade of the 1980s but rather renewed its commitment to regional peace. The challenge of the 1990s is how to maintain its exemplary programme of social justice in the face of economic adjustments.[81]

II. DEVELOPMENT AND LIBERATION IN CENTRAL AMERICA

1. Uneven Development

An overview of economic development shows that the Central American economy grew considerably between 1950 - 1980.[82] However, after the 1973 'oil

---

[79]Jean Carrière in his lectures on Central America - CEDLA. Cf.Carlos José Gutiérrez, *El Pensamiento Político Costarricense: la Social Democracia*, vol.I and II (San José: Libro Libre, 1986). Also, Alfonso Carro, *ed.*, *El Pensamiento Social Demócrata: Antología* (San José: Editorial Costa Rica, 1986).

[80]cf.Frank J.Kendrick, "The Nonmilitary Neutrality of Costa Rica", p.241-259 in Woodward, *Central America: Historical Perspectives*.

[81]cf.further Francisco Barahona, *coord.*, *Costa Rica: Hacia el 2000, Desafíos y opciones* (Caracas: Nueva Sociedad, 1988). Edelberto Torres Rivas, *coord.*, *Costa Rica: Crisis y Desafíos* (San José: DEI, 1989). Jackie Roddick, *The Dance of the Millions: Latin America and the Debt Crisis* (Nottingham: Russell Press, 1988) ch.9: "Costa Rica".

[82]In this time period the population more than doubled while the production rose more than fourfold according to Dunkerley, ch.5 : "Uneven Development, 1950 - 1980", p.171f.: (GDP in millions of 1970 dollars).

	Pop.(thous.)	Urb.Pop.(%)	GDP ($ mill.)
Central America			
1950	8,082	16	1,955.1
1980	20,696	43	8,260.0
Costa Rica			
1950	801	26	257.3
1980	2,213	46	1,592.0
El Salvador			
1950	1,856	18	376.9
1980	4,797	44	1,526.0
Guatemala			
1950	3,006	14	767.1
1980	7,262	38	3,067.0
Honduras			
1950	1,369	10	320.2
1980	3,691	40	1,011.0
Nicaragua			
1950	1,050	19	233.6

149

shock' the economy was into problems which the rise in interest rates on foreign debts was soon to severely aggravate, while the region then became intertwined in political-military instability of the 1980s.[83] Meanwhile, in spite of the economic growth and improvement of some social indicators,[84] the inequitable distribution of income and land contribute to a growing potential for social unrest.[85] In the region as a whole it is claimed that the 76% of all 'farms' (i.e. family subsistence plots) which are left to the poor masses cover just 11% of the cultivated land.[86] Countless *campesino* families have access to but tiny peasant plots and must hire

1980	2,733	54	1,064.0

[83]For a detailed review of the years 1959 - 1985 see William Ascher y Ann Hubbard, *eds.*, *Recuperación y Desarrollo de Centroamérica* (San José: Tomás Saraví, 1989), p.156. For an overview since 1970 cf.Gallardo & López, *Centroamérica: La Crisis en Cifras*, p.48. For 1982-88 cf.Torres-Rivas, *America Central hacia el 2,000*, p.305. Cf.also Richard Fagen, *Forjando la Paz*, p.148.

Growth of GDP per capita

	70-80	1980	1981	1982	1983	1984	1985	1986	1987	1988
GUATEMALA	3.0	0.9	-2.0	-6.1	-5.4	-2.8	-3.3	-2.6	0.2	0.6
EL SALV.	0.2	-11.3	-9.6	-6.5	-0.3	1.3	0.5	-1.2	0.8	-0.8
HONDURAS	1.3	-0.9	-2.4	-5.4	-3.6	-1.2	-1.9	-0.9	0.9	-0.2
NICARAGUA	-2.4	-6.6	1.9	-4.0	1.2	-4.8	-7.3	3.9	-1.7	-12.1
COSTA RICA	2.7	-2.3	-4.8	-9.7	-0.3	4.8	-2.1	2.4	1.7	0.4

[84]Improvement is seen in life-span and in literacy. cf.Gallardo & López, *op.cit.*, p.191.

Life expectation at birth
(average years)

	1970	1975	1980	1985
GUATEMALA	50	54	56	59
EL SALVADOR	56	59	62	65
HONDURAS	51	54	57	60
NICARAGUA	52	54	54	60
COSTA RICA	65	68	71	73

Literacy (percent: 1970/1985)

	1970	1985
GUATEMALA	48	56
EL SALVADOR	60	67
HONDURAS	53	60
NICARAGUA	53	88
COSTA RICA	90	90

[85]Gallardo & Lopéz, *op.cit.* give the distribution of income as follows:
Structure of **Income Distribution** in 1980
(percentage of income received by each stratum)

	20% poorest	30% - mid.	30% + mid.	20% high
GUATEMALA	5.3	14.5	26.1	54.1
EL SALVADOR	2.0	10.0	22.0	66.0
HONDURAS	4.3	12.7	23.7	59.3
NICARAGUA	3.0	13.0	26.0	58.0
COSTA RICA	4.0	17.0	30.0	49.0

[86]cf.Dunkerley, p.179-200. Also Gustavo Arcia, "Evaluación del Desarrollo Rural en Centroamérica", ch.2 in Ascher & Hubbard, *op.cit.* Also Michael Redclift, "Land, Hunger, and Power: The Agrarian Crisis in Latin America" in Fernando Enrique Cardoso, *et al.*, *The Crisis of Development in Latin America* (Amsterdam: CEDLA, 1991), p.24: "The unequal distribution of land ownership in Latin America lies at the heart of the development crisis.... The most extreme examples are from Central America:...by 1980 2 per cent of the Salvadorian population owned 57 per cent of the national territory, and almost all the fertile land. In Costa Rica, 1982, 3 per cent of the population owned 54 per cent of the land... In Honduras...5 per cent owned 60 per cent of the land, while in Guatemala only 2 per cent of the farms occupied over 80 per cent of the land area."

themselves out under such abusive salary and seasonal (often migratory) working conditions that large portions of the population are undernourished. The mounting imbalance of land ownership is part of the effect of expansion by commercial farms which increasingly have eliminated the land left for the subsistence sector. This would not be such a major point if the subsistence sector could turn to new jobs in the manufacturing sector or elsewhere, but these are not available. The growth of the agroexport sector has not provided jobs corresponding to the land it dominates. While coffee has the advantage of requiring intense labour, the banana industry, for some decades receding in the region, has also become sufficiently mechanized to keep employment much lower than earlier. A serious problem has come through expansion of cattle ranching which has taken over large sections of agricultural land, endangering the already leached soil, and requiring but a tiny fraction of labour compared to several other sectors of agriculture. The expanding export beef industry for fast food chains has been called the "hamburgization of the forests".[87] Economic development has been very 'uneven development'. During the 1980s the real minimum salary took a sharp downward turn,[88] and unemployment ran rampant.[89] The growing population[90] can only contribute to the pressure cooker

---

[87]Ingemar Hedström, *Somos Parte de un Gran Equilibrio: La Crisis Ecológica en Centro-américa* (San José: DEI, 1988), ch. III.

[88]Torres-Rivas, *op.cit.*, p.311:

Central America: real minimum salaries: 1978-86
(Indicator: 1980 = 100)

	1978	1979	1980	1981	1982	1983	1984	1985	1986
COSTA RICA	96	99	100	90	86	99	104	112	118
SALVADOR	97	87	100	93	83	73	74	64	55
GUATEMALA	79	71	100	121	126	115	117	94	69
HONDURAS	102	108	100	105	105	96	92	90	86
NICARAGUA	126	119	100	92	78	60	67	44	-

[89]Along side the high unemployment, the subemployment through seasonal and day-labour work causes large sections of the population to have no guarantee of even a minimum salary. The following is based on Gallardo & López, *op.cit.*, p.189:

Open Unemployment
(percentage of Economically Active Population)

	1970	1979	1980	1981	1982	1983	1984	1985
GUATEMALA	-	-	3	3	5	8	11	12
SALVADOR	10	7	16	25	30	30	30	-
HONDURAS	-	-	15	18	21	23	24	-
NICARAGUA	-	-	18	11	20	15	16	-
COSTA RICA	4	5	6	9	10	8	7	7

Subemployment
(percentage of EAP, estimates)

	1970	1980	1985
GUATEMALA	54	43	45
SALVADOR	45	55	-
HONDURAS	-	64	-
NICARAGUA	-	49	22
COSTA RICA	31	26	-

[90]Torres-Rivas, *op.cit.*, p.76:

Population of Central America
(Pop.in thousands plus density per.km.2)

	1985	D	2000	D	2025	D
COSTA RICA	2,642	51	3,711	71	5,250	111
SALVADOR	4,768	227	6,739	320	11,299	538
GUATEMALA	7,963	73	12,222	117	21,668	199
HONDURAS	4,383	39	6,846	61	11,510	103

effect unless a way is found to make more equitable use of that wonderful re-source: the minds and hands of the people.[91]

2. U.S.A. and the falling dominos

The perceived problem of the falling dominos is not unrelated to USA foreign policy in Central America. This policy has been characterized by features, as:

i)   Cooperation with the oligarchies (often indicating, even if unintentionally, a preference for friendly dictators than for governments which want to change the status quo).

ii)   A "gunboat and dollar" tactic (militarization and economic boycotts have too often replaced negotiations).

iii) A framework of East-West conflict (it is also North-South).

iv)   An emphasis on political divisions (either democracy or totalitarianism) but not on economic divisions (wealthy elite and impoverished masses).

v)   During the 1980s a double standard in evaluating progress and human rights in Nicaragua and El Salvador.

vi)   Unilateral influence in financing and trade systems.

vii) An isolation from world approval (as for example President Reagan's dismissal of the decisions of the World Court in the Hague).

The United States of America intervention in Central America has been very high. After a policy of sending the Marines to Central America during the first decades of the present century, a new strategy was attempted through an alliance with the local ruling elites and the training and support of the local military. The policy preferred "friendly dictators" to popular nationalist revolution which would be uncertain toward USA interests and liable to fall into the hands of communist ideologues. The Cold War years of a bi-polar world heightened the Manifest

---

NICARAGUA   3,272   25   5,261   40   9,219   70

[91]Barry & Preusch, *The Central America Fact Book*, p.131: "Five factors contribute to this recent economic stagnation [after 1978]: 1) falling commodity prices, 2) absence of strong economic growth in the developed nations, 3) deepening debt and rising interest rates, 4) increasing political crisis, and 5) contraction of the regional market.

Economic Trends in Central America

* Inequities in income and land ownership worsen.
* Majority of work force becomes unemployed or underemployed.
* National income and average personal income sink to levels of 10 to 20 years ago.
* Elites block necessary reforms in land tenure, taxation, and labor laws.
* Continuing instability in commodity prices combines with shrinking markets to prevent economic recovery.
* Intraregional trade drops even further.
* Capital flight dries up domestic capital.
* Austerity programs imposed by IMF, World Bank, and Washington squeeze the poor and spark civil unrest in cities.
* Debt crisis escalates.
* Consensus builds that external debt is unpayable and related austerity programs are impossible to bear.
* United States pours in economic assistance in a desperate attempt to prevent governments and economies from collapsing.
* Foreign and elite interests cling to worn-out development strategies that make countries more dependent on foreign governments, corporations, and markets."

Destiny idea, now called 'defending democracy and the Free West'. There was also considerable face-saving at stake in the controlling attitude of USA foreign policy toward Central America. If Washington was unable to guard the direction of things in her "back patio", she would appear weak, indeed. The result, however, has led to increased anti-USA attitudes. Some of the best chances for reform came after the Second World War, but only Costa Rica managed to ride well on this crest of change. Ironically, even as perestroika was just around the corner in the USSR, the 1980s Reagan policy toward Central America had not advanced beyond "Operation Success", 1954. In Central America "the archaic ruling class have survived beyond their natural life-span, strengthened by injections of USA military and economic help."[92]

We see during the 1980s how simplistic views triumphed in USA foreign policy toward the region until Central America itself finally came up with a solution to the Washington-Managua scenario. It took considerable "engineering of consent"[93] to keep up the aid for the *contras*. One of the main levers used to move Congress time and again to approve funding was the theory of "falling dominos". Along with "low intensity warfare" there has been "low intensity democracy". The picture presented by President Reagan, and others, had a way of double speaking.[94]

The question of aid

When we turn to the question of aid, it has been argued that aid is often more detrimental than helpful.[95] The basic thesis is that much foreign aid actually works against the interests of the poor for numerous reasons, such as:

i)   foreign aid tends to stabilize the status quo and take the focus off true

---

[92]J.Carrière, *op. cit.*

[93]By engineering of consent we think of all the efforts that go into scientifically studying ways of becoming "experts in legitimization", manipulation of public opinion, the use of the mass media and political theatrics to move people to support ideas and programmes. Cf.Noam Chomsky, *Intellectuals and the State/De intellectuelen en de staat* (Baarn: Wereldvenster, 1978).

[94]Consider some phrases from his address to the joint session of Congress (April 27, 1983), reprinted in Leiken and Rubin, *Central America Crisis Reader*, p.548-554; comments in brackets ours:
"New national elections will be held this year [in El Salvador] and they will be open to all political parties." ['All' does not include social democratic thinkers whose party formation had been hindered, nor union leaders and other leaders of popular organization who have been murdered.]
"We should not -and we will not - protect the Nicaraguan government from the anger of its own people. But we should, through diplomacy, offer an alternative." [The core of that 'diplomacy' was the hiring of the *contras*.]
"All our neighbors [in Central America] ask of us is assistance in training and arms to protect themselves while they build a better, freer life...." [Does the 'better life' coincide with unprecedented levels of militarization and national debts?]
On the double speak tactics see Stan Persky, *America, The Last Domino*, p.237. The history of misrepresentation is persistent. For example, at the time of the 1954 coup in Guatemala, Vice President Richard Nixon declared that the coup was "the first instance where a Communist government has been replaced by a free one. ...The whole world is watching to see which does the better job." [The Guatemalan government was not 'Communist'; the 'free one' proved to be very unfree. The 'whole world' has seen the result: the ensuing human rights record has been among the worst in the Western hemisphere.]

[95]The points are summarized from Tom Barry & Deb Preusch, *The Soft War: The Uses and Abuses of U.S. Economic Aid in Central America* (New York: Grove Press, 1988).

153

        reforms and a priority of self-sustaining development;

ii)   the majority of foreign aid reaches those in control first and only reaches the poor through a trickle-down system;

iii)   aid is often self-interestedly tied to USA business opportunities with considerable aid money spent on USA goods;

iv)   when aid concessions go hand in hand with agreements on prohibiting restrictions on foreign business and investment, then the multinationals have opportunity to drive local firms out of business, operate without due taxation, and drain the country of *unprocessed* agricultural commodities and cheap natural resources, encouraging the agroexport model (which mainly benefits the large landowners: agroexport crops hold the best land while the majority of *campesinos* scratch their malnourished living from subsistence plots);

v)   the more aid "given", the more strings attached, that is: the more dependency on USA foreign policy; thus in the 1980s the quid pro quo meant acceptance of USA-sponsored military build-up;

vi)   conditions for aid often relate to IMF austerity programs which de-emphasize public-sector spending and demand a cut-back in government social service spending, thus hurting the poor the most;

vii) aid money without sufficient analysis of the problems and accountability of spending becomes a pattern of throwing money at problems without addressing the root causes; the results include waste, corruption and dependency;

viii) since the bottom 40 percent of the populous are peasants locked into poverty, with no social mobility nor choices for occupational activity, ideals about free market progress are irrelevant to them; meanwhile, the private-sector bias in aid policy helps the business class more than the poor;

ix)   some funded projects are seen as highly detrimental to the poor, as for example, the growth of the export beef industry which demands huge areas of land, leaving the rural poor with ever less.

Stagnation, marginality and denationalization

Thus many argue that aid and international loans must be seen within a process of denationalization which reinforces the process of stagnation and marginality. The circular causation process[96] can be described as:

i)   colonial-formed elites are socially dysfunctional;

ii)   coercive repression is used against rising popular movements;

iii)   the inherent stagnation and the repression render the status quo equilibrium increasingly dependent on external conditions;

iv)   agrarian exports economy (with lack of industrialization) leads to deficits in balance of payments;

v)   the deficits are compensated by foreign loans;

vi)   the loans aggravate the inherent disequilibrium, increasing the indebtedness.

The question: why dominos fall

---

[96]cf.Helio Jaguaribe, *Political Development: A General Theory and a Latin American Case Study* (New York: Harper & Row, 1973), p.474, from which we have summarized the points.

Rather than reacting out of fear for falling dominos, the question as to why dominos fall must be adequately addressed. Some would argue that they should fall; that is: fall away from the "oligarchic syndrome", from "dependent capitalism" and the "democratic facade" model and find new structures for political-economic justice as well as economic growth. According to a recent analysis: "Central America today is being plagued by the perception of those outside the region that things are improving, after a decade of civil war, proxy invasions, ballooning foreign debts and nose-diving economies. ...[A] new phase has begun in the 150-year-old U.S. foreign policy cycle of neglect, alarm and intervention."[97]

3. Regional unity: from the peace plan to economic development

Looking back on history we see that Central America is a failed federation. Not only because of military rivalry but also because of the failure to sustain their common market and the late arrival of the Central American parliament, opened October 1991.[98] However, there can be no doubt that regional unity was the key in negotiating peace at the end of the 1980s and will be a key for progress in the 1990s.

The Central American summit meetings on a "Procedure to Establish a Firm and Lasting Peace in Central America" went through a number of stages, finally achieving the end of the *contra* war through regional negotiations. The process for negotiating peace was attempted for years by the Contadora Group[99], namely Mexico, Venezuela, Panama and Colombia, four nations on the border of the Central American dispute who first met on the Panamanian Island of Contadora, January, 1983, to begin forming a peace plan after other separate proposals by Mexico and Venezuela had failed.[100] Later sections of the steps toward peace are referred to as the Peace Plan of President Arias,[101] who received the Nobel Award for Peace (1987) for his initiative and on-going persistence in finding regional unity. The regional process of negotiating peace through a series of presidential summit meetings often goes by the name of the agreement of "Esquipulas II" (the first major summit meeting in which the points for achieving peace were outlined and signed by the presidents of all five nations).[102] The European

---

[97]Matthew Creelman, "Central America slips off the geopolitical map", *Latinamerica Press* vol.23, no.18: May 16, 1991, p.3.

[98]cf.R.Barahona, *La Comunidad y el Parlamento Centroamericanos* (San José: FLACSO, 1989).

[99]See the "document of objectives" adopted by the Contadora group presented to the secretary general of the United Nations on October 6, 1983, by the foreign secretary of Mexico, Bernardo Sepulveda, reprinted in Falcoff & Royal, *The Continuing Crisis*, appendix B, p.489-491. For the same and the later revised drafts, cf.Robert S.Leiken & Barry Rubin, *eds.*, *The Central American Crisis Reader* (New York: Summit Books, 1987). For longer history, cf.Luis Méndez Asensio, *Contadora: Las Cuentas de la Diplomacia* (Mexico: Plaza y Janés, 1987). Also of related interest, Liisa North, *Medidas para la Paz en América Central* (San José: FLACSO/Instituto Canadiense por la Paz, 1988).

[100]cf.section III: Chronology, for a list of some of the events in the regional crisis and steps toward peace.

[101]cf.Guido Fernández, *El Desafío de la Paz en Centroamérica* (San José: Editorial Costa Rica, 1989).

[102]The major presidential summit meetings after years of Contadora meetings and then the announcement of the Arias peace plan were: (1) Esquipulus II: "Procedure to Establish a Firm

155

Community was active in encouraging the Central American peace plan.[103]

4. Inadequacy of one dimensional analyses

It is evident that development and liberation are multidimensional problems. Theories have variously included factors such as culture, colonialism, institutional inertia, economic systems, dualist society problems, world economy, and numerous other ways of formulating the problem of underdevelopment and dependency. We shall present four sets of factors, not unrelated, under the categories a) Culture b) Colonial history (dualist society); c) International division of labour (agroexport model); d) Neocolonial pressures (USA interventionism).

a. Culture

There are those who say that the problem of underdevelopment is primarily a lack of modernization of culture (cf.ch.1.III.1): while the indigenous culture was pretechnical and noninnovative, tied to the rhythms of rain and sun, and essentially nonacquisitive,[104] the conquering culture was more *señorial* than developmental. The cultural argument says that if only there was more education, technology, capital investment, initiative and change orientation in Latin America, things would be different. The cultural pattern holding back progress has been based on patron-client relationships rather than on functional merit. While the cultural analysis has its place,[105] it must not be separated from the historical process in Latin America which includes imposition of dependency and a specific form of insertion into the world economy.

b. Colonial history

It is true that the colonial history in Central America was not modernizing, as the statistics for literacy and other factors show. There was in much of the region a reluctance to share power, so that the result was the maintenance of an antiquated feudal-style dualist society. Without the emergence of the middle sectors, democracy cannot function. When challenged by the emancipating desires of the masses,

---

and Enduring Peace in Central America" (Guatemala, August 1987); (2) San José (Alajuela): "Common Declaration of the Central American Presidents" (Costa Rica, January 1988); (3) Sapoá: "Agreement for a Definite Cease Fire" (Nicaragua, March 1988); (4) Costa del Sol: "Common Declaration of the Central American Presidents" (La Paz, El Salvador, February 1989); (5) Tela: "Agreement of Tela" (Honduras, August 1989). For a copy of the agreements of each meeting and commentaries, cf.Victor Hugo Tinoco, *Conflicto y Paz: El Proceso Negociador Centroamericano* (Mexico: Editorial Mestiza, 1989). Also, Latin American Faculty of Social Sciences (FLASCO), *Second White Paper: Esquipulus II: On Advances Achieved in the Process of Fulfilling the Peace Accord for Central America* (Costa Rica: University for Peace, 1988).

[103]Alfredo Guerra-Borges, *Hechos, Experiencias y Opciones de la Integración Económica Centroamericana* (San José: FLACSO, 1987).

[104]cf.Lyle N.McAlister, *Spain & Portugal in the New World: 1492-1700* (Oxford: Oxford University Press, 1984), p.87.

[105]cf.W.Raymond Duncan, *Latin American Politics: A Developmental Approach* (New York: Praeger Publishers, 1976), ch.6: "Attitudes and Values". Piero Gheddo, *Why is the Third World Poor?* (Maryknoll: Orbis, 1973). Gunnar Myrdal, *La Pobreza de las Naciones* (Barcelona: Ariel, 1974). Ingolf Vogeler & Anthony R.de Souza, *Dialectics of Third World Development* (New Jersey: Allanheld and Osmun, 1980).

this dualist and nonmodernizing social pattern (led by dysfunctional elites), often turns to military repression rather than consensus politics. It is exclusionary towards popular movements.[106] The lack of entrepreneurial advancement was not experienced by the elites as a hindrance where there was so much cheap labour available.

c. International division of labour

Central America began its integration into the world economy under the mercantilist system of Spain and later in the 19th century through the coffee boom and then the banana enclaves. This agroexport model has given the region none of the advantages of other alternatives, such as the model followed by some newly industrialized nations. Since the poor masses in Central America are not the consumers of the export products, it is in the interest of the ruling classes to maintain the cheap labour. Little consideration has been given to higher paid labour and a domestic market for manufacturing. This form of insertion into the world economy tends to insure continued dependency.

d. Intervention

After the 1898 USA-Spanish war, the era of USA investment and intervention began in Central America, with the arrival of the banana companies and the marines (cf.section III: Chronology). This was the time in which the USA was emerging as an imperial power under the vision of Manifest Destiny and unilateral domination of the Americas. After World War II the domination by the USA in Central American affairs was largely in name of the containment of communism, which led to support of reactionary dictators ("authoritarianism is better than totalitarianism"), who while holding back social legislation made generous concessions to USA companies and military interests. The extremely high level of intervention we reviewed in regard to Nicaragua and El Salvador leads to the thesis that USA support helps keep the archaic system in place.

5. Central America and political-ethical theory

a. Regional goals

Our analysis of Central America leads to the following kinds of goals for the region:
i)   Recognition of the need for major *structural* changes is urgent.
ii)   Resolving of the *guerrilla conflict* by negotiation and genuine steps toward eliminating the conditions which give rise to guerrilla movements.
iii) Reversal of the *descending economic spiral*.
iv)   A *new style of leadership* is urgent, geared to justice and efficiency.
v)   *Educating the populace* and provision of vocational training programmes.
vi)   Continued development of *regional unity* and economic integration, with a stronger voice (through the new Central American Parliament and a strength-

---

[106]Daniel Camacho & Rafael Menjívar, *Movimientos Populares en Centroamérica* (San José: FLACSO, 1985).

ened common market) toward USA or other foreign powers.

vii) Continued exploration of contacts with the European Economic Community as well as "south-south" relationships.[107]

b. Christian Democracy

May we expect help from Christian Democracy for Central America? Our study leads primarily to a case of disappointed expectations with little reason for renewed expectations at present. The reasons are several (ch.2.III.3; ch.3.II.5). Christian Democracy in Central America has been a fainter echo of the élan reached by Frei in Chile (which also ended in disappointment). Among the essential reasons for failure of achieving lasting reforms is an inadequate method for moving from theory ('common good') to practice (especially popular distributive justice) under the contending pressures of oligarchic traditions and foreign pressures. Political reforms failed in El Salvador (I.b) and were not even promised in Guatemala (I.c). We conclude that the Christian Democrats have step by step allowed their political-ethical vision to become accommodated to the democratic-facade situation in these two Central American countries.

This does not exclude that a reexamination of their own roots in the light of the desperate situation of Central America's poor could help renew their reforming impact. For there is sufficient critique of social structures in, for example, Frei's *America Latina: Opción y Esperanza*, to call the Christian Democrats to give prime attention to the question of poverty. However, given the sliding off in another direction, namely toward a pragmatic politics which brings no changes to the lot of the poor, we expect the contribution by the Christian Democrats to continue to disappoint those hoping for a more just society in several parts of Central America. While the Christian Democrats may be the 'lesser evil' in a given situation, they do not, at present, merit the title of being the 'hopeful option'.

c. Liberation Theology

Some liberation theologians are to be counted among Central America's martyrs, and others are on the long list of those who have been persecuted and tortured because of the 'social question'. An outspoken 'option for the poor' is often answered with repressions. May we expect help from Liberation Theology for Central America? There can be no doubt that various impulses usually associated with Liberation Theology (though not thereby belonging solely to this movement) have had important effects in drawing attention to the social question and stimulating a move toward providing a space for reflection and change. Such impulses include working among the poor, socio-political analysis, changes in seminary and university education, influence in CELAM, a new way of reading the Bible, expectations of a different role for the church. The influence of publications has been strong, even though such publications are viewed as dangerous (and even forbidden) reading by many in authority. We judge that the full impact of such *concientización* is yet to come in several parts of Central America.

---

[107]cf.also the points drawn together in Gordon Spykman, *et al.*, *Let My People Live: Faith and Struggle in Central America* (Grand Rapids: Eerdmans, 1988), p.99.

There has also been a strong reaction against Liberation Theology. Many fear what they see as the use of a reductionist hermeneutic and, more to the point of the present study, what they suppose to be a revolutionary ethics which is likely to promote violence. We have not found Liberation Theology - and we largely view it here through the writings of Gutiérrez - praising violence. What it does do is attempt to be a 'voice for the voiceless', reminding all who hear that the poor are hungry, uneducated, unemployed; and that this is a structural question of oppression (not merely a problem of underdevelopment). The answer then, must involve liberation (and not merely more development along the two-track system of poor and rich). We hold this to be an important contribution of Liberation Theology to Central America. Without this 'voice for the voiceless' - most notably raised and repeatedly silenced in El Salvador, the awareness would be less.

Our critique has included stating that Liberation Theology tends to be strong in appeals for implementation of human rights and distributive justice, and correctly so, but it is weak in both comparative political-ideological analysis and in including some animation toward better production. It is strong on analyzing the roots of poverty, but weak on analyzing the roots of wealth. That much wealth comes from oppression is certainly very true in Central America as our review of exclusionary politics in this chapter shows. However, part of the need in Central America is also the problem of generating wealth. There is the question of underdevelopment. When Liberation Theology goes beyond a negative analysis of technology and capital and includes a more comparative critique, its contribution might be more effective.

d. A democratic spirit?

We could say that Central America must seek a democratic spirit, if that word had not already "fallen into emptiness" (Roberto Sosa). Meanwhile, there is no value-free interregnum during which we may contemplate a blank drawing-board; there is thus no easy road to a new *concertación* worthy of being so named. Into the 1990s in Central America there has been a swing away from the popular push of the 1980s and a new dominance by neoliberal governments. It is typical of the neoliberal policies to emphasize economic growth and deemphasize the distributionist elements of development; short-term sacrifices (such as polarization of income distribution and postponement of alleviation of social miseries) are seen as temporarily necessary in order to gain in the long run. The question is: just how long will that be?

What do we learn from all this for our theme of development and liberation? The following points:

1) Development, while an internal question of national affairs, is also much more.
2) The high dependency of Central America illustrates the problem of national liberation in the face of colonial and neocolonial forces.
3) The reaction to the crisis by the Christian Democrats in Central America has not been adequate for transforming the tradition of exclusionary politics.
4) The reaction to the crisis by Liberation Theology has sharpened the under-

159

standing of economic and political domination,[108] correctly wanting to begin where the need is greatest, but lacks an economic analysis of development.

5) The role of inclusionary or exclusionary politics is a key for transformation.
6) The crisis of the 1980s in Central America and the ensuing public debate on USA foreign policy has led to many being more informed on the problem of economic and military dependency in the region.
7) Our study of Central America reenforces the thesis that the need for development and liberation are two interrelating aspects of the problem of structural poverty.

Transition to chapter six

In this chapter we have seen in some detail the many pushes and pulls that make political ethics both so volatile and volcanic in Central America. We also saw how the various countries have much in common and many differences. One must conclude that both development and liberation are high priorities for the region. Development should not be confused with any given developmentalist model. The question of development rightly leads to the question of liberation. By liberation we understand the freeing from domination and oppression. This factor is as much a ground for development as development also is for liberation. The two are aspects of the one reality. In our last chapter we shall draw our final conclusions which also function as a challenge for continued investigation.

A p p e n d i x

III. CENTRAL AMERICA CHRONOLOGY

Most of our listings here will refer to the five core countries of Central America, with but occasional asides to note something of a wider context. One of the main lines we trace in this chronology shows the overbearing USA interventionism in Central America. Since the data is plentiful we shall have to be content here with samples that indicate so much more.[109]

1821 Sept.15 Guatemala and other Central American provinces declare independence from Spain.
1823 Monroe Doctrine (European powers must not intervene in Americas).
1824 Costa Rica, Guatemala, Honduras, Nicaragua, and El Salvador form Central American Federation, with capital in Guatemala City.
1838 Political conflict between federation provinces and capital: Central American Congress allows provinces to leave federation.
1847 Guatemala declares itself a "republic" (independent country) and other Central American

---

[108]cf.Jon Sobrino, *Resurrección de la verdadera Iglesia: Los Pobres, lugar teológico de la eclesiología* (Santander: Sal Terrae, 1984).

[109]We have gathered the data from numerous sources. For day by day reporting between 1979 and 1986, see Torres & Coraggio, *Transición y Crisis en Nicaragua*, p.135-248. Much of the material after 1988 has been drawn from *Latinamerica Press*, published in Lima, Peru, and from *Latin American Regional Reports*, published by *Latin American Newsletters*, London.

provinces follow suit, thus closing the possibility of reunion as a federation of provinces of one nation.

1848 Mexico loses half its territory in USA-Mexican war.

1850 During next five years the Trans-Panama railway is built; much of Central American commerce moves from the Caribbean to the Pacific ports.

1860 Filibuster William Walker executed at Trujillo.

1895 Major efforts during next four years to restore Central American Federation fail.

1898 Spanish-American war. USA troops in Cuba.

1901 USA acquires Puerto Rico. United Fruit Company (UFCO) becomes first transnational corporation in Guatemala.

1903 Panama separates from Colombia (whose Senate refused USA permission to build a canal).

1904 Panama monetary system based on US dollar.

1905 USA marines land in Honduras for first of five times in next 20 years.

1908 USA troops land in Panama for first of four times within next decade.

1910 Foundation of Pan-American Union (becomes OAS in 1948).

1912 USA troops begin 20 year repeated occupation of Nicaragua.

1914 Panama Canal opens. USA troops in Haiti for next 20 years.

1916 USA Marines occupy Dominican Republic for next 8 years.

1917 USA Marines occupy Cuba for next 5 years.

1926 For next eight years Augusto Sandino leads opposition against USA Marines in Nicaragua.

1931 Dictator Maximiliano Hernández Martínez takes power in El Salvador. USA lends support to dictator Jorge Ubico in Guatemala and Carías Andino in Honduras.

1932 Economic crisis years lead to more repression and *la matanza* massacre of 10,000 to 30,000 in peasant revolt (Pipi Indians) in El Salvador (USA warships stand by during these weeks).

1933 President Franklin Roosevelt announces 'Good Neighbour Policy' for Latin America without armed USA intervention: beginning of 'national security doctrine' whereby USA sets up National Guard in Nicaragua (commander Somoza Garcia is 'a son-of-a-bitch but *ours*', says Roosevelt). USA Marines withdraw from Nicaragua.

1934 Sandino betrayed and killed by members of Nicaraguan National Guard. Guard chief Anastasio Somoza Garcia dominates Nicaragua until 1956.

1944 Dictator Ubico resigns under pressure of violence and protests in Guatemala. World Bank and International Monetary Fund set up by industrial nations.

1945 Begin reform decade in Guatemala: Juan José Arévalo elected president; envisions "spiritual socialism".

1948 Organization of American States (OAS) founded. José Figueres and his army/party of National Liberation quickly oust fraudulent conservative government in Costa Rica: beginning of social democratic reforms. Army banned in Costa Rica.

1949 USA Army School of the Americas founded in Panama (later known in some circles as 'School of the Dictators' and 'School of the Coups').

1951 Reform-minded Jacobo Arbenz wins election in Guatemala.

1952 Fulgencia Batista seizes power in Cuba and begins repressive dictatorship.

1953 Arbenz government confiscates 400,000 acres uncultivated land from United Fruit Co. for redistribution. USA fears communist infiltration in Guatemala.

1954 CIA plans and finances a coup in Guatemala; Arbenz ousted; Colonel Carlos Castillo Armas installed by CIA; land reform reversed. In Honduras first major strike by banana workers leads to recognition of unions; banana company responds to wage raise by large reduction in the number of employees.

1956 Castro and companions arrive from Mexico in Cuba to begin guerrilla struggle. Anastasio Somoza assassinated in Nicaragua. His sons Luis and Anastasio, jr., continue domination until 1979.

1957   Carlos Castillo assassinated in Guatemala. President Eisenhower establishes Office of Public Safety (OPS) to train Latin American police.

1958   Rockefeller begins USA Inter-American Council to promote private sector development in Latin America.

1959   Cuban Revolution against Batista: Fidel Castro.

1960   Formation of Central American Common Market. Panama Canal zone becomes centre for USA counterinsurgency training.

1961   Failed USA "Bay of Pigs" invasion of Cuba. President Kennedy creates Alliance for Progress to promote Latin American development. AID (USA Agency for International Development) is established. FSLN (*Frente Sandinista de Liberación Nacional*: Sandinista National Liberation Front) founded.

1962   Cuba missile crisis solved through compromise: Soviet Union agrees to remove the weapons; USA promises not to invade the island.

1966   During next three years USA Special Forces in cooperation with Guatemala army counterinsurgency campaigns together with right wing paramilitary squads said to lead to the death of some 8,000.

1968   General Omar Herrera Torrijos takes power in Panama.

1969   Border skirmish between Honduras and El Salvador. Collapse of Central American Common Market.

1971   Beginning of guerrilla movements in El Salvador.

1972   Earthquake devastates Managua. Opportunist corruption by Anastasio Somoza Debayle of international relief aid and land and housing speculation increases opposition to his dictatorship.

1975   United Brands pays $1.25 million bribe to lower banana tax in Honduras, saving $7.5 million in taxes.

1980   Literacy campaign in Nicaragua said to raise literacy from 50% to 87%. University education free of charge in Nicaragua.

Jan   'Spanish Embassy' killing of 39 who protest army repressions in Guatemala.

Feb   Archbishop Oscar Romero of El Salvador writes President Carter requesting that the USA stop military aid to El Salvador because of severe military abuses.

Mar   Oscar Romero shot while saying mass. A week later USA approves $5.7 million in military aid to El Salvador.

Apr   In El Salvador various popular organizations unite to form FDR (*Frente Democrático Revolucionario*: Revolutionary Democratic Front).

May   Rio Sumpul massacre of 600 Salvadoran peasants by Salvadoran and Honduran armies.

Jun   27 trade union leaders taken captive in Guatemala City

Nov   In El Salvador the FMLN (*Frente Farabundo Martí para la Liberación Nacional*: Farabundo Martí National Liberation Front) unites 5 guerrilla organizations.

Dec   José Napoleón Duarte elected president of the Government Junta in El Salvador. Four USA churchwomen raped and killed by Salvadoran army; USA stops military aid. *Socorro Juridico*, the legal aid office of the Archdiocese of San Salvador placed the estimate of deaths due to political violence at 10,000 for the year 1980, 8,000 it is said, killed by government forces.

1981   Three year civilian death count reaches 35,000 in El Salvador. Nicaragua conducts health campaign reducing infant mortality, it is said, by 40%.

Jan   FMLN calls for "final offensive" in El Salvador. USA resume military aid to El Salvador. Newly installed President Reagan by-passes Congress to provide more military aid. Archbishop Rivera y Damas of El Salvador, with backing of Duarte, the Pope, European Social and Christian Democrats, visits Washington to urge negotiations about El Salvador. Washington rejects offer.

Feb   Guatemalan army kills some 1500 Indian *campesinos* in the province of Chimaltenango.

Mar USA suspends aid to Nicaragua, charges that Cuban arms pass through Nicaragua to El Salvador.

Jul President Torrijos of Panama killed in suspicious plane crash.

Sep Belize gains independence from Great Britain. In Guatemala thousands more killed in past months, including USA priest Stanley Rother.[110]

Nov USA authorizes $19 million to destabilize Nicaragua. Roberto Suazo Córdova elected first civilian president in Honduras in more than two decades.

Dec In Atlacatl USA-trained Salvadoran brigade said to murder 1,000 civilians during search-and-destroy missions. *Socorro Juridico* of the Archdiocese in San Salvador places political deaths in El Salvador for 1981 at 12,500.

1982

Jan Reagan proposes Caribbean Basin Initiative (CBI) economic and military aid plan. Administration uses $20 million from CIA funds for *contras* (Nicaraguan contrarevolutionaries).

Feb Four guerrilla groups form *Unidad Revolucionaria Nacional* Guatemalteca (Guatemalan National Revolutionary Unity). President López Portillo of Mexico proposes peace plan of negotiations for Nicaragua and El Salvador.

Apr "Ocean Venture" USA military practice operation involving 45,000 soldiers, 60 boats and 350 planes.[111]

May Luis Alberto Monge elected president in Costa Rica.

Jun General Efraín Ríos Montt declares himself president and commander-in-chief of Guatemala and initiates the "beans and bullets" campaign.

Aug United Nations reports 287,000 refugees in Mexico and Central America. World Council of Churches reports Guatemalan government responsible for 9,000 deaths in last 5 months. USA ignores more negotiation urged by Pope John Paul II; López Portillo of Mexico; Herrera Campins of Venezuela; and FMLN in El Salvador.

Sep Mexico and Venezuela propose steps toward peace in Central America.

Nov More than a hundred congressional representatives sign a letter asking Reagan to respond positively to the Mexico Venezuela proposal.

1983

Jan Mexico, Venezuela, Colombia and Panama form Contadora Group for negotiations of peace for Central America.

Mar Pope John Paul II's homiley in Managua interrupted by a section of the crowd calling for peace in Central America.

Apr WHO and UNICEF declare Nicaragua a country providing a "model in health". Nicaraguan Bishops Conference denounces the mixing of Christianity with a partisan politics under the name of Iglesia popular.

May Reagan calls *contras* "freedom fighters". USA confirms the establishment of a new base for military training at Puerto Castilla in Honduras. This leads to much controversy in the country.

Jul Presidents of the Contadora nations issue a ten point programme for peace. Daniel Ortega responds with six point programme. Reagan announces six months of military naval exercises along both coasts of Nicaragua.

Aug "Big Pine II" massive military training for a half year in Honduras including bombing practices near San Lorenzo at the border of Nicaragua and El Salvador. Coup in Guatemala against Ríos Montt.

---

[110]cf.Henri J.M.Nouwen, *Love in a Fearful Land: A Guatemalan Story* (Notre Dame: Ave Maria Press, 1985).

[111]For detailed summary of military practice campaigns cf.Julio Antonio Bueso, *El Subdesarrollo Hondureño*, p.358ff.

Oct   *News Week* affirms that the CIA have a budget of $80 million for the Contra war. USA invasion of Grenada heightens tensions, especially for Nicaragua which expects a similar invasion soon.

1984

USA military aid to Honduras increases 20 times from 1980 level.

Mar   CIA helps *contras* mine Nicaraguan harbours breaking international law; USA undemocratically dismisses value of Hague World Court. In Honduras head of the Arms Forces, General Gustavo Álvarez, removed. Critique of his pro *contra* policies and ignoring of human rights is widespread.

Apr   Military practice "Ocean Venture '84" reported to involve 30,000 soldiers and 350 USA boats.

May   José Napoleón Duarte elected in El Salvador.

Jul   After 5 years the Sandinistas have redistributed land to some 45,000 poor families.

Aug   The Vatican insists that the priests Fernando Cardenal (Minister of Education), Ernesto Cardenal (Minister of Culture) and Miguel D'Escoto (Foreign Minister) renounce their government positions in Nicaragua.

Sep   Nicaragua agrees to Contadora peace plan; USA does not accept.

Oct   Duarte holds peace talks with FMLN/FDR. No lasting outcome.

Nov   Daniel Ortega elected in Nicaragua. Ronald Reagan reelected in the USA.

1985

May   USA trade embargo on Nicaragua.

Jun   Congress approves $27 million in 'humanitarian' aid to the *contras*.

Aug   Private right-wing organizations' aid to *contras* said to almost equal USA government aid.

Oct   Daniel Ortega announces the need for the USA to dialogue on peace and says the *contra* war has cost 11,000 deaths, 5,000 wounded, the destruction of 321 schools and 50 health centres. European Parliament voices strong criticism of USA *contra* policy. USA Catholic Bishops Conference calls for the end of financing the *contra* war.

Nov   European Economic Community provides $35 million aid for the five Central American countries.

Dec   José Azcona Hoyo (Liberal Party) president in Honduras. Christian Democrat Marco Vinicio Cerezo Arévalo wins election in Guatemala and expresses to the international community the idea of constituting a regional Central American Parliament.

1986

Feb   Oscar Arias (*Partido de Liberación Nacional*) elected in Costa Rica. Jimmy Carter and committee visit Managua and declare their support of Contadora efforts for peace. Dictator Duvalier abandons Haiti on a USA Air Force plane. Reagan solicits $100 million from the Congress for the *contras*.

May   Esquipulus I: Summit meeting of Central American presidents: Oscar Arias Sanchez (Costa Rica), José Napoleón Duarte (El Salvador), Vinicio Cerezo Arévalo (Guatemala), José Azcona Hoyo (Honduras) and Daniel Ortega Saavedra (Nicaragua) in Esquipulus, Guatemala. Reagan administration renews economic embargo against Nicaragua. The Minister of Foreign Trade of Nicaragua informs that the year old embargo has caused 14% recession in Nicaragua's commerce.

Jun   Central American vice-presidents meet in Guatemala to agree on the formation of a Preparatory Committee of the Central American Parliament. USA House of Representatives approves $110 million for the *Contras*. The International Court of Justice in the Hague emits its verdict on the case presented in April by Nicaragua, denouncing USA aggression toward Nicaragua.

Dec   Agrarian reform in Nicaragua said to have redistributed 2,8 million *manzanas (1 manzana* = 1.6 acres) helping 100 thousand *campesinos* during the seven years of revolutionary reconstruction.

164

Chronology

1987

Aug   "Esquipulus II". Major summit meeting in Guatemala whereby the points for regional peace are signed by all five presidents of Central America.

Oct   Second meeting of the Preparatory Committee of the Central American Parliament; a Parliamentary Constitution[112] is approved and later signed by all countries.

Nov   Nicaragua agrees to talk with *contra* forces. Daniel Ortega requests Cardinal Miguel Obando y Bravo to act as mediator. USA Congress submits report on the Iran-Contra case suggesting infringement of the Constitution.

Dec   President Oscar Arias receives Nobel Award for Peace.

1988

Jan   San José (Declaration of Alajuela) Central America summit meeting; the five presidents issue a joint declaration to fulfil Esquipulus II. In El Salvador Archbishop Arturo Rivera y Damas calls for an end to the death squads. In Nicaragua some 10,000 hold a demonstration on the tenth anniversary of the assassination of Pedro Joaquín Chamorro, demanding that Esquipulus II be fulfilled. Maintaining and equipping the army now costs Nicaragua 50% of the national budget.

Mar   Guatemalan bishops publish a pastoral letter, "A Cry for Land", calling for agrarian reform. In El Salvador right wing party ARENA (*Alianza Republicana Nacionalista*) wins a majority of seats in the parliament.

1989

Feb   "Costa del Sol" (La Paz), Central America summit meeting in el Salvador.

Aug   "Tela Agreement" at Central America summit meeting, Honduras.

Oct   Violence and torture on the increase in Guatemala according to Catholic bishops, with more than 110 political assassinations since July. Similar reports of escalation of arrests, disappearances and torture in El Salvador where $90 million in aid was approved by the USA Senate without any conditions on human rights attached. Reports on Honduras say that 50% of the 4.3 million population are illiterate; 70% live in terrible housing conditions and 25% do not have access to even minimal health care; 40% of the population suffer some degree of malnutrition; one third has no steady employment.

Nov   Salvador Army makes strongest attack on the churches since the late 1970s, symbolized in the November 16 murder of six Jesuit priests (called 'communists' by the army) at the Central American University (UCA), including Rector Ignacio Ellacuria and Vice-Rector Martín Baró during escalation of FMLN offensive and military bombings to rout guerrillas. In Honduras Raphael Leonardo Callejas wins elections.

Dec   USA military invasion of Panama to capture Gen.Manuel Antonio Noriega, reportedly leaving at least 5,000 dead. For Guatemala the total of killed and 'disappeared' during past ten years is placed at 40,000 and for El Salvador, 70,000. UNICEF reports that infant mortality in Nicaragua has decreased by 50% during the last ten years (from 128 to 62/thousand).According to UNICEF Latin America begins the 1990s with more than 200 million people living in poverty. Of every 100 persons that begin primary school 54 do not finish.

1990

Jan   Cristiani's government charges eight soldiers, including a colonel, with November's murder of the six Jesuit priests. In Nicaragua Cardinal Obando y Bravo urges the population not to vote for the FSLN in coming election. Sandinistas say that the *contras* are responsible for more than 30,000 dead in eight years of war.

Feb   In Nicaragua Violeta Barios de Chamorro (*Unidad Nacional Opositora* party) wins election and Sandinistas are voted out of power, though with strong minority, after ten years of revolutionary reconstruction.

---

[112]A copy of the Constitution is found in Barahona, *La Comunidad*, p.47-58.

May   The newly inaugurated president of Costa Rica, Rafael Calderón (*Unidad Social Cristiana* party) faces problem of maintaining Costa Rica's social democracy in the face of huge foreign debts.

Jun   First Central American economic summit meeting amid controversy over suggestions from Mexico that a free trade zone be created between Canada, the United States, Mexico and Central America. A Central American Economic Action Plan hopes to integrate the region as a block within the world economy. Under pressures from the International Monetary Fund, economic adjustments are cutting government spending and privatizing state enterprises. The European Economic Community announces that it will increase aid to the region by 60 percent over the next four years. Ceremony ending the 9-year-old *contra* war.

Jul   Central America dominated now by neoliberal governments which are in turn choked by unpayable external debts left over from a decade of war, capital flight and falling prices for agroexport.

Sep   In various countries indigenous groups question the coming "celebration" of 500 years of European discovery-oppression of the indigenous in Latin America. In Nicaragua the Sandinistas review their loss at the polls, engage in self-critique and dialogue on the best way to prepare the party for the future.

Oct   Despite 90% increase in the cost of living during the last four years in Guatemala, coffee pickers' wages have not risen. Costa Rica's forests are reported to be disappearing faster than any others at the rate of 6.9% annually.

Dec   Reports on army massacre of fifteen campesino peasants at Santiago Atitlán in Guatemala. It is also said that only 4% of Guatemala's labour force is unionized: between 1981-85 134 union leaders were killed or disappeared. Even when the government decreed a wage bonus for workers to compensate inflation a year ago, only 17% of the firms complied. A year after the USA invasion of Panama reports on the number who died remain secret: while the U.S. Southern Command says 300, human rights groups say up to 5,000.

1991

Jan   Critics see George Bush's "Initiative for the Americas" as implementing World Bank and International Monetary Fund-imposed adjustment plans benefitting only the large transnational companies and increasing the transfer of capital from the periphery to the centre (up North). In Guatemala the new President Jorge Serrano Elias promises to hold talks with the guerrilla movement. It is said that some 4,000 were assassinated in political conflict during Cerezo's administration and that during the last 30 years some 100,000 have died because of civil war and paramilitary actions in Guatemala.

Feb   In Haiti the first democratically elected president takes office five years after the fall of the 29-year Duvalier family dictatorship. The Rev.Jean-Bertrand Aristide who is known for his work with the poor grassroots church and who has declared he will not receive his presidential salary amid such poverty of the people promises to transform the country.

Mar   According to official statistics in Guatemala, the mortality rate for indigenous infants is 134 per thousand, or twice as high as for the non-indigenous population. The average life-span for the indigenous is 45 years. Guatemala government and URNG (*Unidad Revolucionaria Nacional Guatemalteca*) hold talks in Oslo on an agenda which includes themes of: democratization of society, human rights, the role of the army, agrarian reform, constitutional and electoral reforms.

Apr   During ll years of civil war in El Salvador it is reported that more than 75,000, mainly civilians, have been killed. During the present year a cholera pandemic is spreading through Latin America, hitting the urban and rural poor the hardest because of contaminated water supply.

May   Andean Pact members sign the Caracas Act, in which Bolivia, Colombia, Ecuador, Peru and Venezuela agree to eliminate intraregional tariffs in 1992 and form a common market by 1995. In Central America the III Summit of Congress and Legislative Assembly Presidents from C.A. and Panama met to analyze the role of the new Central American Parliament. In Costa Rica the Central American Human Rights Commission calls for "a Central America without armies". At San José VII (the series began in Costa Rica in 1984) the European Community agreed that Central America should have greater access to European markets. In Guatemala human rights are regressing; president Serrano announces a commission to investigate the disappearances.

Jun   In El Salvador a USA military advisor testifies to prior knowledge of the assassination plans leading to the Nov.16 killing of six Jesuit priests. Critics fear that the tri-nation pact being planned for a North American Common Market (between Canada, the USA and Mexico: from the 'Yukon to the Yucatán') will be a new stepping stone for U.S. entrepreneurs into Latin America, whereby economic expansionism will thoroughly overrun the ecosystem of Latin America.

Jul   Leonardo Boff, Rio de Janeiro, says that the 500th anniversary of Columbus' arrival should be a time to recognize the great destruction caused by colonization and that the industrial nations should now accordingly forgive Latin America's external debt. "Between 1987 and 1990 almost 70 journalists were killed in Latin America."[113]

Sep   A law suit is filed in New York by a human rights group against former General Héctor Gramajo accused of directing massive human rights abuses under the Ríos Montt regime during the 1982 slaughter of thousands in the Guatemalan *altiplano* province of Huehuetenango. In Haiti a military coup overthrows president Jean Bernard Aristide.

Oct   CELAM IV held at Santo Domingo. Nicaragua drops claim in the World Court of Justice against the USA for violating international law and costing Nicaragua billions during the Sandinista years. The International Monetary Fund begins new loans to Nicaragua. USA writes off 88% of Nicaraguan and 50% of Honduran bilateral debt.

Dec   President Cristiani states that the civil war has cost 75,000 lives during the past twelve years in El Salvador. A Peace plan is arranged through departing UN secretary-general Pérez de Cuéllar. According to Hermán Delgado, director of Central America's intergovernmental nutrition institute (San José), economic adjustment programmes continue to affect the region's poor adversely.

---

[113]*Latinamerica Press* (vol.23, no.28) July 25, 1991.

CHAPTER SIX

CONCLUSIONS: *VERITAS OMNIA VINCIT*

"hay un muerto flotando en este río
y hay otro muerto más flotando aquí"

Oscar Hahn[1]

"there's a dead body floating in this river
and there's another one floating here"

"The experience of God and witness to a just life becomes ever clearer in Latin America because structural injustice is there given explicit or implicit theological sanction. The presently prevailing structures - a capitalism of dependence and national security, whatever their forms - function as real deities with divine characteristics and their own cult. They are deities because they claim attributes that belong to God alone: ultimacy, definitiveness, and inviolability. They have their own cult because they demand the daily sacrifice of the masses and the violent sacrifice of any who resist them."

Jon Sobrino[2]

Introduction

After the foregoing chapters it becomes apparent that it is inadequate to turn any political-ethical theory into a salvific apriority separated from the historical situation. The virtues and vices of Latin America's currents of oligarchic feudalism, liberal-capitalism, socialism, popular movements and military regimes must continue to be examined, as also the impact of international relations, in the light of the need for transformation, specifically toward the eradication of poverty. We now draw together some conclusions (which relate in a diversified way to such a large continent) via various aspects of the grid we have applied to our mapping of political ethics and transformation in Latin America. We stated earlier (ch.1:III.4: *Theory and complex reality*) that we do not pretend to solve the development/liberation debate. We shall, however, underscore some of the features we learned from this symposium.

1. Colonial Christianity

Colonial Christianity, which was an expression of a cultural era, is best understood as characterized by 'ontological' rather than 'functional' attitudes (cf.ch.2.I-.2). We mean, thus, a way of thinking which remains abstract rather than empirical, typified by a hierarchical teaching on being (ontology) and a rigid social pattern whereby a person's position is more important than functional effectiveness. The negative characteristics which accompany this static pattern do not therefore imply that functionalism is without its own problems. It is, however, necessary to admit that the colonial Christianity which arrived with Columbus was not dynami-

---

[1]Oscar Hahn, "Un Ahogado Pensativo a veces Desciende" in Julio Ortega, *ed.*, *Antología de la Poesía Hispanoamericana Actual* (Mexico: Siglo Veintiuno, 1987), p.372.

[2]Jon Sobrino, *The True Church and the Poor* (London: SCM Press, 1985), p.166.

cally renewing. Colonial Christianity, in its dominant effect (with notable exceptions), did not contain the kind of ethical orientation prepared to break through the conquistorial attitude and the feudal (señorial) stasis; it did not think in terms of educating the people to read and think for themselves; it had little sympathy for developing the material side of life; it's nature-grace dualism contributed to what has been called a long absence of interest in technological advance. The 'ceremonial' (in the sociological sense of 'tradition maintaining') orientation of much of Latin American culture has not been open to the spreading of power and the learning of functional (instead of clientelist and authoritarian) management skills. In a word, the values which accompanied colonial Christianization were not modernizing. This meant that in Latin America, political ethics were for centuries more entrenched in a paternalistic (Frei) charity approach rather than directed to advancements in structural changes. Christian values were interpreted as requiring acceptance of poverty rather than as dynamically challenging injustices.

2. Dualist society...and insertion into the world economy

That the colonial conquest was an immense act of creating *dependency* is clear enough. It was also deeply exclusionary of egalitarian values and, not unrelated, of economic and political progress.[3] The viewpoint on Latin America as a dualist society runs as follows: While in Western Europe after the Renaissance the strong social stratification gradually became mellowed by the emerging bourgeoisie which formed a balance between the nobles and the peasants, this social change did not reach the Iberian peninsula, which maintained an aristocratic and bureaucratic society.[4] This was transplanted to Latin America, where the colonial conquest made immense tracks of land and cheap labour available, which guaranteed a long life to the dysfunctional elitist tradition. The aims of the elites have not been compatible with the empowering of the poor masses. One of the few points on which Frei, Gutiérrez and Novak agree, is the fundamental bifurcation and downward spiral resulting from the dualist society. It remains an important starting point for analyzing possibilities of transformation.

The dualist tradition, rightly regarded by many as a basic problem, has further been seen to have been aggravated by the agroexport use of land and the dependency pattern of insertion of the former colonies into the world economy. Problems of the agroexport system include:

---

[3]cf.Arthur F. McGovern, "Dependency Theory, Marxist Analysis, and Liberation Theology", in Marc H.Ellis & Otto Maduro (Maryknoll: Orbis, 1989), p.277: "The same colonial heritage, however, points to other factors that help to explain why Latin America failed to follow the path of industrial development - and agricultural development - that ocurred in Northern Europe and the United States. The Spanish brought with them a disdain for manual work, and Spanish mercantilist policies prevented Latin America from producing manufactured goods for itself and from open trading with other nations. ...This structure of concentrated ownership deprived the great masses of the population access to their own land and trades. One could characterize this legacy in Marxist terms as lack of control over the means of production; but one could also describe it in terms of the absence of any real experience of free enterprise."

[4]cf.Helio Jaguaribe, *Political Development: A General Theory and a Latin American Case Study* (New York: Harper & Row, 1973), ch.21: "The Dualistic Society".

i)   investment and profits are often tied more to foreign companies than to local entrepreneurs;

ii)   the agroexport system takes land away from the local *campesinos*;

iii) since the products go to foreign markets, there is no incentive to raise local wages to increase local buying power;

iv)   the concentration on primary products for export does not keep pace with the rising costs of imported manufactured products;

v)   the decision-making concerning use of land and foreign loans remains in the hands of the oligarchies who benefit from the system;

vi)   the trickle-down advantages to the marginalized masses is outweighed by the disadvantages (for example nationals debts) passed on to them.

3. Modernization

According to the "modernization" perspective, massive and structural poverty are due to a lack of development, i.e., to a lack of rationalization of society and technology which can eradicate poverty. Should poverty continue, or even increase in some sectors of the world, then according to this view some basic ingredients are missing, especially the secret of generating wealth through high production methods, capital accumulation and wise reinvestment, along with incentives to improve the work ethic and reduce population growth. The modernization perspective has also been called the institutionalist perspective, for it claims that the key to development is especially related to the effectiveness of a country's institutions. In parts of Latin America, 'institutionalized' patterns include:[5]

i)   extreme concentration of landownership;

ii)   authoritarian politics;

iii) deficiencies in the educational system;

iv)   technological lag; capital flight;

v)   inadequate taxation;

vi)   monopoly power of transnational corporations.

The problem of "institutional inertia" is so great that such factors will have to be included in any other approach.

However, a questioning of the modernization paradigm in Latin America, which has been voiced strongly since the 1960s, still continues because of the following kinds of signs of crisis based on statistics between 1980-1987:[6]

i)   export volume grew by 50%;

ii)   real wages fell by 20%;

iii) terms of trade deteriorated by 22%;

iv)   despite pressures from social forces, government operational expenditures have been reduced;

---

[5]cf.James L.Dietz & James H.Street, *Latin America's Economic Development: Institutionalist and Structuralist Perspectives* (London: Lynne Rienner Publishers, 1987), p.43.

[6]E.V.K.Fitzgerald, "Latin America in the World Economy", in Fernando Enrique Cardoso, *et al.*, *The Crisis of Development in Latin America* (Amsterdam: CEDLA, 1991), p.8ff.

v)   debt service and capital flight have financed economic growth in the north, not in the south;

vi) 'roll over' debts have become unpayable;

vii) restrictive conditions on new loans hurts the poor the most;

viii) the state in Latin America has become too weak (dependent) to fulfil its calling of promoting distributive justice;

If one accepts some expressions of development theory, then the assumption is that humankind is moving from impoverishment to riches, and can continue to do so with the right mix of investment, production, innovative technology and democratic culture. Other views question the progress character of economic growth, which, it is said, must not be taken to be a sufficient definition of development. Critique on the belief in modernization suggests that attempts at economic growth in Latin America - under the present conditions of insertion into the global economy - brings new inadequacies, alienations and dominations (for example, loss of land and community for the *campesinos*, unemployment, urban slums, a new monopoly by the multinationals, increased debts with higher interests). While it is to be admitted that "development is a long, difficult, arduous, wrenching process,"[7] a fundamental question is whether the poor nations can 'modernize' under the weight of present dependency on the dominant centres. Thus the critique on modernization also asks whether the limits to the earth's resources and the corresponding stewardship this implies, does not also demand that we seriously review the great gap between the rich and the poor nations, and implement structural changes for steps toward more equality. Not only must an ever-increasing consumption pattern be questioned in Western society, but also the unilateral economic-political pressures. Economic success is not the only virtue to be taken into account. In the colonial and neocolonial path to riches there are great vices: military conquest, slave labour, underpaid peasantry, and, for example, the current ecological exploitation (the selling of tropical forests to obtain dollars to meet debt payments). It is, however, not necessarily modernization of Latin American development, as such, that is to be questioned, but rather certain models of modernization which have not been sufficient to alleviate the problems of poverty and dependency. The modernization model has largely been one of primary goods export while the need is to pursue expansion of labour-intensive manufactured exports.[8]

The strengths of some modernization analyses are found in attention to internal factors which impede development. Both the development and the liberation perspective can agree that the rural - and increasingly urban - poor must be freed from their bondage. We have noticed throughout this study that there are cultural roots which help explain the sources of poverty. Progress is not a mechanistic concept; it involves lifeviews, values, human relationships, political ordering. In

---

[7]Howard J.Wiarda and Harvey F.Kline, *Latin American Politics and Development* (Boulder, Colorado: Westview Press, 1990), p.586.

[8]Carlos Fortin, "Rise and Decline of Industrialization in Latin America", in Fernando Enrique Cardoso, *et al., The Crisis of Development.*

the case of Latin America, the internal factors impeding progress (for example, the lack of universal education and better distribution, but also of production) are tied to external factors introduced since the conquest. The 'dualist' society withholds cultural development from a large segment of the population. Until there is a transformation of values toward more equality and spreading of progress, that is, a transformation from exclusionary to inclusionary political ethics, there is little hope for development and for liberation from poverty, despite the pouring in of foreign investment, aid, and loans (which in fact are always offset by the centrifugal draining of capital, natural, and human resources). Without a transformation in the most basic concepts of justice in society, the aid and loans remain largely within the oligarchic enclaves and rather than helping the poor, put them literally in debt.

In our view the confrontation of poverty in Latin America must take into account modernization analysis, and at the same time go beyond this by including themes often overlooked by modernization analysis. One such theme is the question of dependency.

4.Dependency

The dependency perspective, which often goes by the name of the 'world system' approach, sees massive and structural poverty in many parts of the globe as due to colonial dominance which later turned into neocolonial dominance, whereby these regions of the world provide a global proletariat for the industrial (capitalist and socialist) nations. As for Latin America, it is said that the poor are so numerous because the local elites in collaboration with foreign markets and foreign political dominance, are manipulating national resources while maintaining a dualist society. During the 1980s the drastic foreign debt crisis provided considerable fuel for the conflagration already signalled by the structuralist dependency focus. There is much to be said for the idea that Latin America moved from *un*development to *under*development, especially through the colonial-neocolonial insertion into the global economy.

We saw that Gutiérrez, in his *Teología de la Liberación*, included the dependency perspective as an integral part of his theorizing on the need for liberation. We also saw that Frei, in his *América Latina: Opción y Esperanza*, refers to the fact of dependency, but sees this more as a *result* rather than a *cause* of underdevelopment. The cause of continued dependency after independence from Iberian control, involves, according to Frei, internal feudal patterns and a lack of regional organization.

In our opinion the modernization and the dependency perspectives are not mutually exclusive unless pressed in an inordinately reductionist manner. However, the tendency to disavow the term 'modernization' by dependency analysts, and the term 'dependency' by modernization analysts, does indicate a degree of reductionism on both sides. Said succinctly: whatever the dependency perspective's flaws,[9]

---

[9]cf.Jorge Larrain, *Theories of Development: Capitalism, Colonialism and Dependency* (Cambridge: Polity Press, 1989). Cf.also John Sheahan, *Patterns of Development in Latin America: Poverty, Repression, and Economic Strategy* (New Jersey: Princton University Press, 1987).

to hunt them down does not take away from the flaws of the development position (for a comparison see ch.1.III.4), which has too easily assumed that the whole world can join the economic growth model and enjoy steady improvement. We noted that there is one feature which the modernization (underdevelopment) and the liberation (dependency) perspectives have in common, and that is that they see the local elites as a vital link in maintaining dependency and in failing to foment national development.[10]

While from the dependency perspective we may learn of the long shadow of colonial and neocolonial domination which has helped impose foreign control and debt peonage on Latin America, from the modernization perspective we may learn that many of the poverty factors have been internally imposed by local decision making. The immediate answer as to why the poor are so numerous comes down to such concrete problems as the increasing landlessness of the *campesinos* and high unemployment/subemployment of unskilled labour, which is underpaid. This state of affairs relates, in turn, to numerous other factors, such as a lack of educational opportunities, of infrastructure and technology, and of political decision-making in the popular interest.

While Eduardo Frei was right in calling for regional cooperation in order to confront foreign power blocks, Gustavo Gutiérrez was right in focussing on the power of the poor, since without conscientization and solidarity toward liberation, the dominant forces that maintain the injustices of the repressive status quo will not of themselves voluntarily transform the system. However, there is little hope for transition from dependency when "the rich countries need the entire world in order to continue their own economic expansion".[11]

5. Social Encyclicals

The Social Encyclicals, the Christian Democratic movement in Latin America, and Liberation Theology have one basic factor in common: they desire to relate the Christian faith to political praxis. They are not content to view the two in disjunction. How the relationship is to be envisioned, varies. While the encyclicals maintain that the Christian faith should lead to concern about and improvement in the area of justice in society, the orientation has changed along with the historical conditions. There is a transition from primarily speaking of social cooperation to a more outspoken search for a solidarity position with the poor, though both factors are of central concern in the encyclicals. What further remains constant is the critique toward two positions, namely, an overwrought socialism and an overwrought economic liberalism. In my estimation, the refusal to identify completely

---

[10]McGovern, *Liberation Theology and Its Critics*, p.169 mentions several factors which contribute to the underdevelopment/dependency problem in Latin America: "...a pattern of property ownership with land concentrated in the hands of a few and the vast majority left propertyless; a Spanish culture imposed on an indigenous Indian people creating a rigid class stratification; a political system that kept power in the hands of the landowning oligarchy or the military; an economy geared for external markets to the neglect of both agricultural and industrial products to meet domestic needs; a consequent dependency on foreign markets and foreign investors, often supported in this century by U.S. political-military interventions."

[11]Bob Goudzwaard, *Capitalism and Progress: A Diagnosis of Western Society* (Toronto: Wedge, 1978), p.123.

with either liberalism or socialism is an advantage. We have further shown that within the critique by the encyclicals of these two positions, there has been a renewed appreciation for certain qualities of both. There has also been a move from micro to macro structural analysis. That change is due to a continued orientation to the global situation. The encyclicals have been relevant enough to inspire the imagination and also receive critique from various sides of the political spectrum. Part of that critique is that they "hang in the air" (according to Novak, who would like to see the virtues of democratic capitalism acknowledged), and that they do not sufficiently expose the "idolatry of private property" (according to Hinkelammert, who would like to see the connection between western capitalism and Third World debt peonage more specifically denounced). In our opinion it can be defended that as ethical reflection by the church, the more recent encyclicals do fulfil relatively well the purpose of stimulating analysis of, and a search toward solutions for, poverty. That is, while aiming at a balanced position, there are sufficiently sharp statements to preclude the acceptance of what they themselves point out to be glaring injustices. It must be granted that the contribution from Latin America, as for example through CELAM II (Medellín 1968), and the many expressions of Liberation Theology, gave the Vatican reason to sharpen the moral questioning of poverty.

6. Christian Democracy

When we consider the Christian Democratic movement, we see that it began in Latin America, as in the case of Eduardo Frei, with considerable critique of the injustices and with promises of true reforms which would reach down to some of the root problems, such as landtenure and illiteracy. But the élan of the movement did not hold. It has spoken strongly on Latin American repressive violence from the right and counterviolence from the left and even taken some practical steps toward implementing a politics of compromise rather than conflict, as when José Napoleon Duarte held talks with the FMLN and when Vinicio Cerrezo launched the idea of a Central American Parliament. However, there are a number of critical tensions (cf.ch.3.II.5 and ch.5.I.4.b "Christian Democrats") which do not make Christian Democracy a specially hopeful option for transformation. When in power in Central America the Christian Democrats have not in practice favoured conse-quent reform measures; their effect has been that of providing a facade for oligarchic-military politics (cf.ch.5.II.5.b).

In our opinion fair judgment would say that while Christian Democracy has within its political theory the making of a contribution toward transformation, there is an ambivalence within the movement which continues to call their effectiveness into question. When they push reforms through they lose the support of the right (as Frei in Chile); when they avoid reforms, they are no longer taking their own political ethics seriously. There is, in fact, a high tension between the two aspects of the announced *Revolución en libertad*, so that the left finds the movement not really revolutionary, and the right finds it endangering the freedom of private ownership (understood oligarchically) when it does seek transformation. The result is that the movement easily settles for a pragmatic politics which leaves behind the promised transformation. The Christian Democrats could do better through closer coalitions with those most interested in social legislation that will be helpful to the marginalized. When not appearing to remain true to their own ideals, or when not effective in implementing their reform programmes, they will continue to be seen as no better than other *'reformismos'*. If Christian Democracy is serious about its Christian perspective, we may expect that it will be open to dialogue with changing political theologies, including Liberation Theology. While we have seen the rise and fall of the Christian Democratic parties in Latin America, it would be over-hasty to conclude that the era of their influence is past. The deeper question is whether they can move beyond the tenuous image of holding up a democratic facade and can actually carry out significant transformation. This seems doubtful. In our opinion the Christian Democrats have not dealt thoroughly with their own identity and for that reason have increasingly moved from a popular (siding with the marginalized poor) position to a pragmatic one (achieving electoral success here and there, but not achieving transformation).

7. Liberation Theology

Liberation Theology has its own distinctive contributions. Just as Christian Democracy opens up some space in the centre of practical politics (sometimes centre-right and sometimes centre-left), so Liberation Theology opens up space in the area of theoretical paradigms and basic grassroots movements to allow a strong anticapitalist voice which turns to a democratic-popular social concern favouring the marginalized masses (making an "option for the poor"). Our study of Gustavo Gutiérrez shows that he thought it important to combine his "new way of doing theology" with "dependency theory", though he did not do so wholly uncritically and indeed later relativized this approach considerably (cf.ch.4.II.5.a, "Expanding the view"). We do find that a manner of speaking which tends to divorce *modernization* and *liberation* has led Liberation Theology to appear at times to jump over the development question. However, it must be remembered that Liberation Theology does not mean to deny the need for development, but rather questions "developmentalism" and "modernization" or the model of "dependent capitalism", which is seen to hold Latin America in a peripheral status of debt peonage to the wealthier centres of the global economy. When it comes to development, Liberation Theology intends to contribute to the quest for endogenous development. As an expression of a Christian political ethic, Liberation Theology, may be characterized as:

i) Emphasizing prophetic critique of the situation in Latin America and in the world economy;

ii) pointing out the domination and oppression which has led the Latin American elites to impose a 'culture of silence' (*'cultura del silencio'*)[12] on the indigenous and the poor, allowing them no political voice nor economic share;

iii) more convinced of the need for a confrontation orientation rather than a harmony model of political change;

iv) distinctively in favour of working with the base and changing things through

---

[12]Enrique Dussel, *Filosofía Etica de la Liberación* (Buenos Aires: Aurora, 1987), part I: p.153.

the power of the poor;

v)   having an anticapitalist stance;

vi)   favouring a popular approach, earlier called 'socialism' by Gutiérrez, but not
      fully defined, except that it must be democratic (in the 'popular' rather than
      'liberal' sense) and an option for the poor, in contrast to the present model
      which is seen as 'dependent capitalism'.

As with any other current of thought and action, so, too, with Liberation Theology:
its strengths tend also to include some weaknesses which are not unrelated. An
emphasis on some aspects of transformation has left lacunae toward other aspects,
as for example:

i)   A too easy acceptance of the dilemma of either underdevelopment or depen-
      dency as causing poverty and either modernization or liberation as being the
      answer. It does not seem that the dependency theory, which was a central
      thesis in Gutiérrez' *Teología de la Liberación* (1971), is as entirely adequate
      to explain the poverty and oppression, as he at first assumed.[13] The problem
      is more multidimensional. However, as we saw (ch.4.II.4), Gutiérrez is
      willing to relativize this central thesis.

ii)   Theology of Liberation seems flawed in its political ethics by a lack of
      critical appreciation of the liberal, capitalist and technical contribution to
      development. Strong on social justice, Liberation Theology is weak on
      analyzing the relationship between productive efficiency and better distribu-
      tion.

This critique should not, however, distract us from recognizing that Liberation
Theology has rightly pointed to the idolatrizing[14] of the profit motive (as viewed
from the periphery) as a cause of oppression and poverty. Liberation Theology has
given an undeniable impetus to transformation in Latin America. All analyses of
Latin America and ideological perspectives bring their own risks. While some may
suppose that after the demise of communism, Liberation Theology, too, will
whither away, it rather seems that we continue to need a careful evaluation of the
"magic of the market" and its effects in the Third World. As long as there is
"structural poverty" under repressive regimes in parts of Latin America, Liberation

---

[13]cf.John R.Pottenger, *The Political Theory of Liberation Theology: Toward a Reconvergence
of Social Values and Social Science* (New York: State University Press, 1989), p.109: "Yet
even though dependency theory may be useful for liberation theologians to explain the skewed
economic relationship between First and Third World countries, it may not be comprehensively
adequate to explain all impoverished conditions inside the Third World." Cf.also David
Lehmann, *Democracy and Development in Latin America: Economics, Politics and Religion in
the Postwar Period* (Cambridge: Polity Press, 1990).

[14]This remains an important aspect of the debate in our time. Similarly, Goudzwaard, *op.cit.*,
p.152: "...we are reminded of Keynes' comments about the worship of modern gods: 'Avarice
and usury and precaution must be our gods for a little longer still. For only they can lead us
out of the tunnel of economic necessity into daylight.' Undoubtedly Keynes' observation
contains a large measure of irony. But...we might well be confronted with a situation parallel to
that of idol worship in primitive cultures. ...as soon as the 'gods' have led us out of the dark
tunnel of economic necessity into daylight we can discard them...but will the gods in turn let us
loose?"

Theology is not likely to disappear. We can expect on-going paradigm shifting and perhaps a new way of doing theology, even within Liberation Theology. The new way Gutiérrez originally called for included a better contextualization. There is no reason that this could not include a more comparative approach to economic ideologies and the relating of themes of development and liberation.

We must further credit Liberation Theology with maintaining a dialectical tension between faith and society and between oppression and liberation. As paradigms of progress change we must not assume that Liberation Theology is fatefully tied to the perceived lacunae we have mentioned. The fact that poverty continues demands new attempts at conceptual clarity for both the themes of development and liberation. Liberation Theology has performed an important service in opening up more political debate and bringing the plight of the poor to centre stage. Its continued strength, which may not be ignored, is the call for a moral commitment to the poor. Liberation Theology is needed as a "voice of the voiceless". Its perpetual contribution is to challenge the priorities of status quo ethics, a status quo which is often maintained through cruel repression in parts of Latin America. (cf.further ch.5.II.5.c)

8. Central America

Our study of Central America brings to light some extreme aspects of underdevelopment and dependency. The region attracted a flurry of analysis during the 1980s. In spite of the overextended rhetoric which surrounded some of the analysis, one of the important results was a new awareness of the strong dialectic between repression and revolutionary change in the region. The 'falling domino' theory turned out to be an entirely inadequate way of (mis)speaking about the change from Somocismo to Sandinismo. The 1980s Central American crisis eventually produced some steps toward regional cooperation (regional autonomy instead of dependency in decision-making) which may continue to help answer the need for both development and liberation.

We learn from the Contadora and Arias Peace Plan that persistence in regional cooperation can change the historical course, even when going against U.S.A. pressures.[15] In fact, this kind of success encouraged the meeting of a Latin American debtors' cartel in December, 1987, to demand changes in the debt crisis.[16] The choice is between changes toward more dependency or more autonomy.[17] It cannot be overstressed that regional agreements and regional bargaining rather than unilateral approaches will remain a key to change in Latin America. If it is true, as both Frei and Novak say, that economic growth can be achieved by integrating the marginalized into the national economy, then means must be sought to realize this and to persuade the dysfunctional elites that this is to the advantage

---

[15]cf.Richard J.Bloomfield & Gregory F.Treverton, *eds.*, *Alternative To Intervention: A New U.S.-Latin American Security Relationship* (London: Lynne Rienner Publishers, 1990). Harold Molineu, *U.S. Policy Toward Latin America: From Regionalism to Globalism* (Oxford: Westview Press, 1990).

[16]Jackie Roddick, *The Dance of the Millions: Latin America and the Debt Crisis* (Nottingham: Bertrand Russell Press, 1988), p.234.

[17]Helio Jaguaribe, *Political Development*, p.476.

of the 'common good'.

9. The common good

The concept of the common good points to the basic task of the state to maintain justice and harmony in society. It is a favourite concept in the encyclicals and in the vocabulary of the Christian Democratic movement and may take on a sharp appeal for the transformation of society. However, it has two drawbacks: i) the appealing to this concept easily remains too abstract; and, ii) it can be used to gloss over distortions of social-economic justice in order to give harmonization the priority. The argument then becomes that change is dangerous to the 'common good'. Because of this fall of good concepts into misuse, Liberation Theology has preferred to speak of the preferential option for the poor, specifically to point out that an analysis and strategy (praxis) which does not begin with the situation of the marginalized poor, cannot properly understand the roots of the problem, nor how to prioritize an answer. Like the concepts of 'democracy' and 'God', so the 'common good' has also "fallen into emptiness" (Roberto Sosa) in Latin America. However, exactly because the 'common good' is an important term in the Latin American tradition, it is important to be explicit about the vital consequences this has for justice in society. The connecting of the 'common good' to the principle of 'solidarity' (defending the weakest sectors of society) in *Centesimus Annus* (cf.ch.2-.VIII.3) encourages such explicitness. The concept can be worthily used to encourage pursuit of consensus politics and also lends itself for the plea to not exclude the most needy from sharing in human rights and distributive justice. It has been promoted as a way of paying attention to the lack of international government, as when Pope John XXIII says in *Pacem in Terris*, pointing to the need of a new world order: "...at this historical moment the present system of organization and the way its principle of authority operates on a world basis no longer corresponds to the objective requirements of the universal common good."[18]

Indeed, we saw that the same encyclical connects the norm of the common good to the priority of giving "more attention to the less fortunate members of the community, since they are less able to defend their rights and to assert their legitimate claims" (cf.ch.2.II.4). It would seem appropriate to admit, with Gutiér-rez, that the concept of the 'common good' has often become mistakenly unde-manding. As a result an adequate response, in our opinion, must both revitalize the concept, and go beyond it with new emphases, such as the 'option for the poor'.

10. Option for the poor.

This, too, can be interpreted in various ways within the debate as to whether distributive justice means to each according to their need, their work, their rank, their results (etc.).[19] That is, in moving from wider norms (such as the 'common good' and 'an option for the poor') to concrete actions (such as in political programmes, through the *comunidades de base* movement, and various forms of *concientización*), one needs to pass through the filters of mediating analyses and

---

[18]*Pacem in Terris*, par.135.

[19]cf.Agnes Heller, *Beyond Justice* (Oxford: Basil Blackwell, 1987).

strategies. The mediating strategies are the arena of a great debate. For example, when, on the one hand, we hear Gustavo Gutiérrez say that the source of woes is capitalism, while, on the other hand, we hear Michael Novak say that the source of woes is a lack of capitalism, then fundamental analysis of the region must be considered, as well as terminological clarity. In this case, part of the contradiction is resolved by clarifying that Gutiérrez is especially speaking of internal oligarchic and external foreign capitalism. And when Novak speaks of capitalism, he is thinking of 'democratic capitalism', which includes social legislation and a cultural ethos which limits the negative undertow of the profit motive.[20] But Novak glosses over the fact that while such is possible within a nation, it is largely missing in international relationships. Regardless, the point is that Gutiérrez and Novak each have a considerably different definition of capitalism in mind. For that reason the partners in the debate between the development position and the liberation position has sometimes spoken passed each other.

Dependency and debts

It has been said that international relationships are led by interests little short of "economic anarchy"[21] in which economics are viewed as global war.[22] We may expect political ethics to ask about the norms for the ordering of these relationships. Some assume that the basic economic norm is that of economic growth; however, even more basic is economic stewardship, which has been argued to be part of the contribution of Christian ethics.[23] Are we primarily consumers or caretakers? Structural poverty is only to be eradicated by structural changes. Development, has, however, turned into developmentalism (*desarrollismo*), which we saw means that development has stayed among the national elites and foreign enclaves leaving the poor majorities not merely excluded from gains, but actually pushed further into poverty by landlessness and spiraling national debts. The loans and aid funding often seem to have a price (economic, political and social) so high that they do not relate well to development and liberation. The loaning of more funds for the payment of past loans continues the debt crisis.[24] With the floating interest rate the new loans in the early 1980s caused even greater problems. The debt peonage, long applied by the oligarchies to the *campesino* peasants, has in turn been applied by the richer nations to the poorer, so that 'dependent capitalism' has become especial-

---

[20]cf.also Peter L.Berger, *The Capitalist Revolution: Fifty Propositions About Prosperity, Equality, and Liberty* (New York: Basic Books, 1986). On p.218 he makes the remarkable statement that if we are looking for a preferential option for the poor, then "there can be no question that capitalism, as against any empirically available alternatives, is the indicated choice."

[21]Pierre Bigo, *The Church and Third World Revolution* (Maryknoll: Orbis, 1977), p.256ff.

[22]Herman Verbeek, *Economie als Wereldoorlog* (Kampen: Kok, 1991).

[23]Bod Goudzwaard & John van Baars, "Norms For the International Economic Order", in *Justice in the International Economic Order* (Grand Rapids: Board of Publications of the Christian Reformed Church, 1980), p.223ff.

[24]cf.Gary W.Wynia, *The Politics of Latin American Development* (Cambridge: University Press, 1985), p.97f. Also, Jackie Roddick, *The Dance of the Millions*, p.35ff: "Between 1978 and 1984, Latin America's total interest payments increased by 360 percent." Cf.also Franz J.Hinkelammert, *La Deuda Externa de América Latina: El Automatismo de la Deuda* (San José: DEI, 1989).

179

ly a debt peonage system. However, we may not conclude that there is only a one-dimensional explication for massive poverty in Latin America: while increase in the interest rates was a major factor in this debt peonage, there are also factors involving the role of the debtor countries, such as fiscal policies whereby government spending outruns the limited possibility of raising taxes on the economic elites.[25] Even granted the domestic problems of limited markets and tendency to rely excessively on external loans, external forces such as petroleum prices, adverse terms for trade, and high interest rates severely aggravated the situation, so that it is presently said that Latin America "is suffering its worst depression since the 1930s".[26]

Dysfunctional elites

We saw that both the modernization and the liberation perspective agree on one factor: that the local elites have been dysfunctional in promoting the common good. The dependency and the underdevelopment approaches do not have to disagree on the fact that external capital has promoted a continuation of 'colonial structures' and re-entrenched the interests of the oligarchy, so that internal exploitation has accompanied the pressures of the international system.[27] A necessary priority would seem to be the turning to a political consensus ethic which tempers the tendency of oligarchism and the economic anarchy of *bellum omnium contra omnes*. To work toward the common good also presupposes that the dominant elites and those in power understand that national improvements and the eradicating of poverty are very much in their own interest as well: for, when the social question is not solved, there is a build up toward social unrest, the results of which can be endless civil war. Of course, too much "reliance upon the human capacity for transcendence over self-interest"[28] leads to nothing but the status quo. That is the

---

[25]Jeffrey D.Sachs, *ed.*, *Developing Country Debt and the World Economy* (Chicago: University of Chicago Press; National Bureau of Economic Research), ch.1. Cf.further Sue Branford and Bernardo Kucinski, *The Debt Squads: The US, the Banks and Latin America* (London: Zed Books, 1988). Stephany Griffith-Jones, *ed.*, *Managing World Debt* (New York: St.Martin's Press, 1988).

[26]Abraham F.Lowenthal, *Partners in Conflict: The United States and Latin America in the 1990s* (London: John Hopkins, 1990), p.189: "The statistics on Latin America's distress are stark. ...Rates of unemployment and underemployment remain high in many countries, upwards of 40 percent in some. Hardships caused by unemployment and low wages have been compounded by deep cuts in public expenditures for health, housing, education, and social security. Malnutrition is worsening in some nations.... For eight years the total flow of funds to Latin America from loans and investments has been substantially less than interest payments and the profit remittances of foreign companies. ...About one-quarter of Latin America's savings were drained each year for interest payments, sharply reducing the funds available for investment. Capital flight [is] on a massive scale...." Cf.also Kevin J.Middlebrook and Carlos Rico, *eds.*, *The United States and Latin America in the 1980s: Contending Perspectives on a Decade of Crisis* (Pittsburgh: University of Pittsburgh, 1988).

[27]Theotonio Dos Santos, *Imperialismo y Dependencia* (Mexico: Ediciones Era, 1978), p.302f: "...este capital se invertía en la modernización de la vieja estructura colonial exportadora y, por tanto, se aliaba a los factores que mantenían el atraso de estos países. Es decir, no se trataba de una inversión capitalista general, sino de la inversión imperialista en un país dependiente. Este capital venía a reforzar los intereses de la oligarquía comercial exportadora.... En los países subdesarrollados hay, por tanto, un sistema de explotación interno que se liga al sistema internacional."

[28]Reinhold Niebuhr, *The Children of Light and the Children of Darkness* (New York:

weakness of reformist expectations. There must be an empowering of the poor. But since the marginalized masses do not have the means for organization and success-ful impingement for change, the repressive regimes do not first of all run into problems from them, but rather the decisive factor often hinges on the disaffected subelite who have the social mobility and preparation necessary to provide new awareness and leadership. This new awareness is called forth through normative criteria (as, for example, moral principles), as well as through the factual pressures of stagnation, marginalization and denationalization, which can lead to structural analysis and a renewal of political ethics.

If the 'common good' means pursuing the 'greatest good for the greatest number', then the idea of 'a preferential option for the poor' is essential in a situation where the poor are marginalized from the most basic goods, such as food, shelter, education and employment.

The poor: empowering the grassroots

The statistics are presently not encouraging for many parts of Latin America. When we say high debt peonage, adverse terms of trade, and capital flight, we are really also saying: the painful fact is that many are underfed, underschooled, and underemployed. When the economy falls, infant deaths, street children, tensions and crime rise. This situation must be struggled with on many levels, both personal and structural, including debt servicing (and debt "forgiving", suggested as a suitable remembrance 500 years after Columbus), and the improvement of trade and democratic strengthening.

The fact continues that the marginalized are often actively oppressed in parts of Latin America, limiting the role of social actors. The current talk of 'transition to democracy' must not hide the fact that the strengthening of formal democracy under foreign pressures, as in Central America, unfortunately in practice does not exclude continued suppression of social movements most relevant to the daily needs of the poor. While theories about the consciousness of the poor are often idealized, the poor being of many mind-sets, it remains important that the grassroots move-ment can play a significant role in opening up democratic space and stimulating the discourse on civil rights.[29] The *movimiento de base* has hope of gradually empow-ering the poor and transforming the institutions of society which have continued the exclusionary style of power and wealth. Obviously there must be a raising of the wages of the poor.[30] In so far as much analysis in Latin America has had the tendency to recognize "class conflict (rather than, say science or education or reform) as a principal mechanism of social change",[31] there must be continued

---

Scribner's, 1972), p.39.

[29]David Lehmann, *Democracy and Development*, p.154.

[30]It is interesting to hear Adam Smith, *An Inquiry into the Nature and Causes of the Wealth of the Nations* (*eds.*, R.H.Campbell & A.S.Skinner: Oxford University Press, 1979), vol.1, p.99: "The liberal reward of labour...increases the industry of the common people. The wages of labour are the encouragement of industry, which, like every other human quality, improves in proportion to the encouragement it receives. ...Where wages are high, accordingly, we shall always find the workmen more active, diligent, and expeditious, than where they are low...."

[31]Harvey Cox, *Religion in the Secular City: Toward a Postmodern Theology* (New York: Simon & Schuster, 1984), p.157.

questioning of the best way to empower the poor. While transformation which leads to such empowering might be thought to go against vested interests, consciousness raising could be most effective when it shows that it is in the interest of all to seek justice and a better functioning society, whereby the goal is not merely wealth, but also well-being.

The social debt

While we do not conclude that the only source of poverty in the poorer countries is the dominance by the wealthy countries, we do believe that this crucial theme must be dealt with, and not only from an altruistic perspective, but from the perspective of the many interests and claims of nations comprising the one world community. To the degree that northern wealth in conjunction with the 'dysfunctional elites' takes advantage of and maintains the weak economic position of Latin America's debt peonage, to that degree there is culpability in the human cost which is passed on to the poorest. The present economic neoliberalization which characterizes changes taking place in Latin America, involves, it is rightly said, some premature euphoria[32] while the impoverished are excluded from improvements. It is not enough to look for signs of an increased GDP in Latin America. Economic growth, vitally important, is not a sufficient indicator as long as the region continues under the present model of dependency and a status quo which mixes the growing barrios of impoverishment with enclaves of consumerism, missing the mark, since this approach does not address the situation of the marginalized masses. Latin America must pay attention to the market; but that is not the only compass available. Freedom for the market must be accompanied by freedom for labour (to organize). There is an urgent situation when the concentration on the market and the solving of the debt crisis simultaneously implies a systematic exclusion of real human needs. This is the present situation in Latin America.[33]

The Christian ethics we have traced in the recent Encyclicals, in the Christian Democratic movement and in Liberation Theology, have one very important feature in common: they see the question of overcoming poverty as something more than a question of benevolence and aid. The social question is the question of the rights of the poor, intrinsically as persons, and also as members of communities, national as well as of the world community. Any hopeful option must build on that intrinsic

---

[32]*Latin American Newsletters* (London), "Economy & Business", Oct. 1991.

[33]As Fernando Enrique Cardoso says in Cardoso, *et al.*, *The Crisis of Development*, p.142: "Without doubt we have economic problems; solvable economic problems. But we have social problems which are much more difficult to face than we believed." Cf.also Samuel Blixen, Uruguayan journalist, on "Social debt to people rises in Latin America", *Latinamerica Press* vol.24, no.2 (Jan.23, 1992): "In one sense, the economic adjustments dictated by the international lending organizations have had unprecedented results: Latin America has never before been so politically and economically homogeneous. For the first time in history almost all of Latin America's governments have adopted a similar economic model, selling off state-owned industries, looking for ways to swap parts of their debt and applying budget cuts. The neoliberal policies, however, have yet to produce the results that many governments are expecting. ...Levels of absolute poverty have increased throughout the region, according to UN statistics. Unemployment has increased. ...The consequences of the fiscal policies have been devastating. Essential services such as health care, education and housing have had their budgets slashed. ...The misery belts that surround most Latin American cities continue to grow. The desperate situation of the most marginalized members of society has gotten worse...."

perspective.

11. Toward a hopeful option (*veritas omnia vincit*: truth conquers all things)

It will be evident from the multidimensional characteristics of structural poverty that there is no single answer to the social question in Latin America. There are various interests contending for attention: efficient production, income security and social welfare, educational opportunity, use of national and international resources, the regulation of multinational corporations, and for so many in Latin America, the ending of marginalization and repression. If one says 'development', then one must also say 'liberation'; if one says 'democracy', then one must also say '*concientización*'; if one says 'regional autonomy', then one must also speak of the 'global system'; if one says 'production', then one must also speak of 'distribution'. Narrow concepts of national interest frequently impede openness toward just international relationships. Reports during the last months continue to state that economic adjustment programmes imposed by international creditors are increasing the poverty of the already poor. The traditional development approach is as yet far from helping the poor majority. Rather than following patterns of "showcase modernity", Latin Americans would do well to creatively seek a development-liberation strategy whose first priority is to meet the basic needs of its populous via an endogenous model for transformation.

It is apparent that whatever analyses and strategies are applied, more is needed than merely following future possibilities of the same system, as if what is, is inevitable. Since conflicts of interest are both real and even inevitable, it is in the long-term interest of all to go beyond the partial truths of group-interest and self-interest, to an understanding of the moral basis of the other's claim. What rings true in both Frei's *América Latina: Opción y Esperanza* and in Gutiérrez' *Teología de la Liberación*, is that both have told a portion of the truth about on-going structural repressions, about misplaced priorities, and have spoken in their own way about making a new option. They do not deny that God and democracy have fallen into emptiness in Latin America; rather, given the reality of this disennobling, they yet inspire us to listen to the gospel of love and justice and to search for a new praxis of the same. Such truth telling[34] has the great merit of opening up debate on hopeful options and comprises a new way of doing political ethics in Latin America.

---

[34]In a letter to his Franciscan superiors in May, 1991, Leonardo Boff writes: "Possibly the scarcest resource in the church today is truth. There is a fear of the truth, of experience...and there is a fear of the God of life, of the poor, the humiliated and persecuted who no longer accept domination of any sort, who have found the church to be their ally and defender." cf.*Latinamerica Press*, vol.24, no.3: jan.30, 1992.

Bibliography
selected

Aguilera, Gabriel
1989   *El Fusil y Olivo: la Cuestión Militar en Centroamérica*. San José: DEI - Departmento Ecuménico de Investigaciones.

Americas Watch Committee and The American Civil Liberties Union
1982   *Report on Human Rights in El Salvador*. New York: Vintage.

Amnistia Internacional
1988   *Honduras: Autoridad Civil - Poder Militar; Violaciones de los Derechos Humanos en la Década de 1980*. Madrid: EDAI.

Antoine, Charles, *ed.*,
1985   *Christ in a Poncho: Adolfo Pérez Esquival and Nonviolent Struggles in Latin America*. Maryknoll: Orbis.

Antoncich, Ricardo
1987   *Christians in the Face of Injustice: A Latin American reading of Catholic Social Teaching*. Maryknoll: Orbis.

Antoncich, Ricardo & José Miguel Munárriz.
1987   *La Doctrina Social de la Iglesia*. Madrid: Paulinas.

Archetti, Eduardo P., Paul Cammack & Bryan Roberts
1987   *Latin America: Sociology of 'Developing Societies'*. London: Macmillan.

Arnaudo, F.
1975   *Las Principales Tesis Marxistas*. Buenos Aires: Pleamar.

Arroyo, Gonzalo
1974   *Golpe de Estado en Chile*. Salamanca: Sígueme.

Ascher, William & Ann Hubbard, *eds.*,
1989   *Recuperación y Desarrollo de Centroamérica*. San José: Tomás Saraví.

Assmann, Hugo, Enrique Dussel, *et al.*
1973   *Hacia una Filosofía de la Liberación Latinoamericana*. Buenos Aires: Bonum.

Assmann, Hugo, *ed.*,
1981   *El Juego de los Reformismos frente a la Revolución en Centroamérica*. San José: DEI.

Barahona, Francisco, *coord.*,
1988   *Costa Rica: Hacia el 2000, Desafíos y opciones*. Caracas: Nueva Sociedad.

Barahona, R.
1989   *La Comunidad y el Parlamento Centroamericanos*. San José: FLACSO.

Barry, Tom
1988   *El Conflicto de Baja Intensidad: Un Nuevo Campo de Batalla en Centroamérica*. Tegucigalpa: CEDOH - Centro de Documentación de Honduras.

Barry, Tom & Deb Preusch
1986   *Central America Fact Book*. New York: Grove Press.
1988   *The Soft War: Uses/Abuses of U.S. Economic Aid in C.America*. N.York: Grove Press.

Beeson, Trevor & Jenny Pearce
1984   *A Vision of Hope: The Churches and Change in Latin America*. London: Fount.

Belaunde, César H.
1982   *Doctrina Económico-Social: De León XIII a Juan Pablo II*. Buenos Aires: Clarentiana.

Bennàssar, Bartomeu
1986   *Moral para una Sociedad en Crisis: desafíos*. Salamanca: Sígueme.

Berger, Peter L.
1974   *Pyramids of Sacrifice: Political Ethics and Social Change*. New York: Basic Books.
1986   *The Capitalist Revolution: Fifty Propositions about Prosperity, Equality, and Liberty*. New York: Basic Books.

Berryman, Philip
1984   *Religious Roots of Rebellion: Christians in the C.American Revolutions*. London: SCM.
1987   *Liberation Theology: Essential Facts*. New York: Pantheon.

Bibliography

Bestard Comas, Joan
1984   *Mundo de Hoy y Fe Cristiana: Cambio Sociocultural.* Madrid: Narcea.

Betto, Frei
1985   *Fidel y la Religión: Conversaciones con Frei Betto.* Habana: Consejo de Estado.

Bieler, Andre
1961   *L'Humanisme Social de Calvin.* Geneva: Labor et Fides.

Bigo, Pierre
1977   *The Church and Third World Revolution.* Maryknoll: Orbis.

Blanco, Gustavo & Jaime Valverde
1987   *Honduras: Iglesia y Cambio Social.* San José: DEI.

Blomström, Magnus & Björn Hettne
1984   *Development Theory in Transition: The Dependency Debate and Beyond: Third World Responses.* London: Zed Books.

Bloomfield, Richard J. & Gregory F.Treverton, eds.,
1990   *Alternative to Intervention: A New U.S.-Latin American Security Relationship.* London: Lynne Rienner.

Boff, Clodovis
1980   *Teología de lo Político: sus mediaciones.* Salamanca: Sígueme.
1987   *Theology and Praxis: Epistemological Foundations.* Maryknoll: Orbis.

Boff, Clodovis & Leonardo Boff
1984   *Salvation and Liberation.* Maryknoll: Orbis.
1989   *Como Hacer Teología de la Liberación.* Bogotá: Paulinas.

Boff, Clodovis, Enrique Dussel, Pablo Richard, et al.,
1978   *The Church at the Crossroads: Christians in Latin America from Medellín to Puebla (1968-1978).* Rome: IDOC - International Documentation and Communication Centre.

Boff, Leonardo
1978   *Teología del Cautiverio y de la Liberación.* Madrid: Paulinas.
1981   *Jesucristo y la Liberación del Hombre.* Madrid: Ediciones Cristiandad.
1982   *Way of the Cross - Way of Justice.* Maryknoll: Orbis.
1985   *Church, Charisma and Power: Liberation Theology and the Institutional Church.* London: SCM.
1986   *Ecclesiogenesis: The Base Communities Reinvent the Church.* Maryknoll: Orbis.
1986   *Desde el Lugar del Pobre.* Bogotá: Paulinas.

Branford, Sue & Bernardo Kucinski
1988   *The Debt Squads: The US, the Banks and Latin America.* London: Zed Books.

Brockman, James R.
1982   *The Word Remains: A Life of Oscar Romero.* Maryknoll: Orbis.

Bueso, Julio Antonio
1987   *El Subdesarrollo Hondureño.* Tegucigalpa: Editorial Universitaria.

Cabestrero, Teófilo,
1983   *Ministros de Dios, Ministros del Pueblo: Ernesto Cardenal, Fernando Cardenal, Miguel D'Escoto.* Managua: Ministerio de Cultura.
1986   *Revolutionairies for the Gospel: Testimonies of Fifteen Christians in the Nicaraguan Government.* Maryknoll: Orbis.

Cáceres, Jorge, R.Guidos Béjar & R.Menjívar Larín
1988   *El Salvador: Una historia sin lecciones.* San José: FLACSO - Facultad Latinoamericana de Ciencias Sociales.

Caldera, Rafael
1986   *Especificidad de la Democracia Cristiana.* San José: Libro Libre.

Calvani, V.
1976   *The World of the Maya.* Barcelona: Minerva.

Camacho, Daniel & Rafael Menjívar
1985   *Movimientos Populares en Centroamérica.* San José: FLACSO.

Bibliography

Cantor, Norman F. & Michael S.Wertman, *eds.*,
1967   *Medieval Society 400-1450*. New York: Crowell.
Cardoso, Fernando Enrique, *ed.*,
1991   *The Crisis of Development in Latin America*. Amsterdam: CEDLA.
Cardoso, Fernando Enrique & Enzo Faletto
1969   *Dependencia y Desarrollo en América Latina*. Mexico: Siglo Veintiuno, reprint 1987.
CELAM Conference of Latin American Bishops
1968   *Documentos de Medellín*
1978   *Los Obíspos Latinoamericanos entre Medellín y Puebla: Documentos Episcopales 1968-1978*. San Salvador: Universidad Centroamericana.
1979   *Puebla: III Conferencia General del Episcopado Latinoamericano: "La Evangelización en el Presente y en el Futuro de América Latina"*. Mexico: Libería Parroquial.
1982   *Fe Cristiana y Compromiso Social: una reflexión sobre América Latina a la luz de la doctrina social de la iglesia*. Chimbote, México: CELAM -Depart. de Acción Social.
1984   *Desafíos a la Doctrina Social de la Iglesia en América Latina: Cinco años después de Puebla*. Mexico: CELAM, Instituto Mexicano de Doctrina Social Cristiana.
Chace, James
1984   *Endless War: How We Got Involved in Central America and What Can Be Done*. New York: Vintage.
Chase, Alfonso, *ed.*,
1985   *Las Armas de la Luz: Antología de poesía contemporánea de la América Central*. San José: DEI.
Chavez, Alcides Harnández, *coord.*,
1988   *Deuda Externa y Crisis en América Latina*. Tegucigalpa: Guaymuras.
Chea, José Luis
1988   *Guatemala: La Cruz Fragmentada*. San José: DEI.
Chomsky, Noam
1986   *Turning the tide: The U.S. and Latin America*. Montreal: Black Rose.
Chomsky, Noam & Edward S.Herman
1979   *The Washington Connection and Third World Fascism*. Montreal: Blackrose.
Chonchol, Jacques & Julio Silva Solar
1985   *Socialismo Cristiano - La Sociedad Comunitaria*. San José: Nueva Década.
Chopp, Rebecca S.
1986   *Praxis of Suffering: Interpret. of Liberation and Political Theologies*. Maryknoll: Orbis.
Christophe, Paul
1989   *La Historia de la Pobreza*. Estella: Verbo Divino.
CINAS - Centro de Investigación y Acción Social
1987   *El Salvador: ¿Es la Democracia Cristiana un Partido de Centro? Mexico: CINAS*.
Cleary, Edward L.
1985   *Crisis and Change: The Church in Latin America Today*. Maryknoll: Orbis.
Clements, Charles
1984   *Witness to War: An American doctor in El Salvador*. New York: Bantam.
Clissold, Stephen
1966   *Latin America: A Cultural Outline*. New York: Harper & Row.
Comblin, José
1979   *The Church and the National Security State*. Maryknoll: Orbis.
Compton, Roberto
1984   *La Teología de la Liberación: Una guía introductoria*. El Paso: Casa Bautista.
Conrad, Robert Edgar
1990   *Sandino: The Testimony of a Nicaraguan Patriot, 1921-1934*. Princeton University Press.
Conway, David
1987   *A Farewell to Marx: An Outline and Appraisal of his theories*. London: Penguin.

186

Bibliography

Concilium
1980   (10): "Christelijke Ethiek en Economie: het Noord-Zuid-conflict."
1984   (2): "The Ethics of Liberation - The Liberation of Ethics."
1984   (6): "Volk Van God Temidden Van De Armen."
1986   (5): "Theologie van de Derde Wereld: Kiezen voor de Armen: Een uitdaging voor rijke landen."
1987   (5): "De Kerk en de Christen-Democratie."
1990   (6): "1492-1992: De Stem van de Slachtoffers."
Cotler, Julio & Richard R.Fagen, eds.,
1974   Latin America - United States: The Changing Political Realities. Stanford Univer. Press.
Cox, Harvey
1984   Religion in the Secular City: Toward a Postmodern Theology. N.Y.: Simon & Schuster.
Crow, John A.
1980   The Epic of Latin America. Berkeley: University of California Press.
Cruz, Arturo & José Luis Velázquez, eds.,
1986   Nicaragua: Regresión en la Revolución. San José: Libro Libre.
Curran, Charles E.
1985   Directions in Catholic Social Ethics. Indiana: University of Notre Dame.
D'Antonio, William V. & Frederick B.Pike
1967   Religión, Revolución y Reforma: Transformación en Latinoamérica. Barcelona: Herder.
Davis, Nathaniel
1985   The Last Two Years of Salvador Allende. London.
De Barros, Marcelo & José Luis Caravias
1988   Teología de la Tierra. Madrid: Paulinas.
De La Torre
1982   Cristianos en la Sociedad Política. Madrid: Narcea.
De Lange, H.M. & H.Spee,
1985   "Kerkelijk spreken over vragen van makro-ekonomie", Tijdschrift voor Theologie vol.25.
De Renedo, Benedicto Tapia
1976   Hélder Câmara: Proclamas a la Juventud. Salamanca: Sígueme.
De Santa Ana, Julio, ed.,
1979   Towards a Church of the Poor: The Work of an Ecumenical Group. Geneva: WCC.
De Valk, J.M.M., ed.,
1989   Vernieuwing van het Christelijk Sociaal Denken. Baarn: Ambo.
De Vos, Peter, et al.
1980   Earthkeeping: Christian Stewardship of Natural Resources. Grand Rapids: Eerdmans.
De Vylder, Stefan
1976   Allende's Chile: Political Economy of the Rise and Fall of the Unidad Popular. London.
Deiros, Pablo Alberto
1986   Los Evangélicos y el Poder Político en América Latina. Grand Rapids: Eerdmans.
Dietz, James L. & James H.Street
1987   Latin America's Economic Development: Institutionalist and Structuralist Perspectives. London: Lynne Rienner Publishers.
Di Tella, Torcuato
1990   Latin American Politics: A Theoretical Framework. Austin: University of Texas.
Dooyeweerd, Herman
1979   Roots of Western Culture: Pagan, Secular, and Christian Options. Toronto: Wedge.
Dorr, Donald
1984   Option for the Poor: A Hundred Years of Vatican Social Teaching. Maryknoll: Orbis.
Dos Santos, Theotonio
1978   Imperialismo y Dependencia. Mexico: Era.
Draper, Thomas, ed.
1981   Democracy and Dictatorship in Latin America. New York: H.W.Wilson.

Duarte, José Napoleón, with Diana Page
1986   *Duarte: My Story.* New York: Putnam's.
Duchrow, Ulrich
1986   *Weltwirtschaft Heute: Eine Welt für bekennende Kirche?* Munich: Kaiser Verlag.
Duchrow, Ulrich & Gerhard Liedke
1989   *Shalom: Biblical Perspectives on Creation, Justice and Peace.* Geneva: WCC.
Duff, Ernest & John McCamant
1976   *Violence and Repression in Latin America.* New York: Macmillan.
Duncan, W.Raymond
1976   *Latin American Politics: A Developmental Approach.* New York: Praeger Publishers.
Dunkerley, James
1988   *Power in the Isthmus: A Political History of Modern Central America.* London: Verso.
Dunn, Oliver & James E.Kelley
1989   *The Diario of Christopher Columbus's First Voyage to America 1492-1493, Abstracted by Fray Bartolomé De Las Casas.* London: University of Oklahoma Press.
Duque, José
1983   *La Tradición Protestante en la Teología Latinoamericana.* San José: DEI.
Dussel, Enrique
1983   *Historia de la Iglesia en América Latina: Coloniaje y Liberación 1492/1983.* Madrid: Mundo Negro-Esquila Misional.
1986   *Etica Comunitaria.* Madrid: Paulinas.
1987   *Filosofía Ética de la Liberación.* Buenos Aires: Aurora.
Eagleson, John & Philip Scharper, *eds.*,
1979   *Puebla and Beyond: Documentation and Commentary.* Maryknoll: Orbis.
Ellis, Marc H. & Otto Maduro
1989   *The Future of Liberation Theology: Essays in Honor of G.Gutiérrez.* Maryknoll: Orbis.
Elwood, Douglas J.
1985   *Faith Encounters Ideology: Christian Discernment.* Quezon City: New Day.
Emmerij, Louis & Enrique Iglesias
1991   *Restoring Financial Flows to Latin America.* Paris: Organization for Economic Co-operation and Development: Inter-American Development Bank.
Escobar, Samuel
1987   *La Fe Evangélica y las Teologías de la Liberación.* El Paso: Casa Bautista.
Fagen, Richard
1987   *Forjando la Paz: El desafío de América Central.* San José: DEI.
Falcoff, Mark & Robert Royal, *eds.*,
1987   *The Continuing Crisis: U.S. Policy in C.America.* London: U.S.A. Public Policy Center.
Ferm, Deane William
1986   *Third World Liberation Theologies: An Introductory Survey.* Maryknoll: Orbis.
Fernández, Guido
1989   *El Desafío de la Paz en Centroamérica.* San José: Editorial Costa Rica.
Fierro, Alfredo
1974   *El Evangelio Beligerante: Introd. crítica a las teologías políticas.* Estella: Verbo Divino.
Fischer, Ernst
1970   *Marx in His Own Words.* London: Penguin Books.
Floristán, Casiano, *ed.*,
1971   *Comunidades de Base.* Madrid: Marova.
Fogarty, Michael
1957   *Christian Democracy in Western Europe 1820-1953.* London: Routlege & Kegan Paul.
Fonseca, Gautama
n.d.   *Integración Económica: El Caso Centroamericano.* Tegucigalpa: Lithopress.
Frank, André Gunder
1969   *Latin America: Underdevelopment or Revolution: Essays on the Development of Under-*

development. New York: Monthly Review Press.
Frankena, William K.
1963   *Ethics*. Englewood Cliffs, N.J.: Prentice-Hall.
Frei Montalva, Eduardo
1951   *Sentido y Forma de una Política*. Santiago: Editorial del Pacífico.
1967   *América Latina tiene un Destino*. Santiago de Chile: Editor Zig-Zag.
1970   "Perspectivas y Riesgos - Construcción de una Nueva Sociedad". Santiago: U. Católica.
1977   *América Latina: Opción y Esperanza*. Barcelona: Pomaire.
1978   *The Hopeful Option*. Maryknoll: Orbis.
Freire, Pablo
1970   *Pedagogía del Oprimido*. Mexico: Siglo Veintiuno.
Fried, Jonathan L., *et al.*,
1983   *Guatemala in Rebellion: Unfinished History*. New York: Grove Press.
Friede, Juan & Benjamin Keen
1971   *Bartolomé de Las Casas in History*. Northern Illinois University Press.
Funes de Torres, Lucila
1984   *Los derechos Humanos en Honduras*. Tegucigalpa: CEDOH.
Galeano, Eduardo
1971   *Las Venas Abiertas de América Latina*. Mexico: Siglo Veintiuno.
Gallardo, Helio
1989   *Actores y Procesos Políticos Latinoamericanos*. San José: DEI.
Gallardo, María Eugenia & José Roberto López
1986   *Centroamérica: La Crisis en Cifras*. San José: FLACSO.
Garaudy, Roger, *et al.*,
1966   *Christentum und Marxismus - Heute*. Wien: Europa Verlag.
Garrett, William R.
1988   "Liberation Theology and Dependency theory", in Rubenstein & Roth, *eds.*, *The Politics of Latin American Liberation Theology: The Challenge to U.S. Policy*. Washington: Institute for Values in Public Policy.
George, Susan
1985   *How the Other Half Dies: The Real Reasons for World Hunger*. New York: Penguin.
Gettleman, Marvin F., *et al.*,
1981   *El Salvador: Central America in the New Cold War*. New York: Grove Press.
Gheddo, Piero
1973   *Why is the Third World Poor?* Maryknoll: Orbis.
Gibellini, Rosino, *ed.*,
1977   *La Nueva Frontera de la Teología en América Latina*. Salamanca: Sígueme.
Girardi, Giulio
1988   *La Conquista de América: ¿con qué derecho?* San José: DEI.
Gnuse, Robert
1987   *Comunidad y Propiedad en la tradición Bíblica*. Estella: Verbo Divino.
Gottwald, Norman K., *ed.*,
1984   *The Bible and Liberation: Political and Social Hermeneutics*. Maryknoll: Orbis.
Goudzwaard, Bob
1978   *Capitalism and Progress: A Diagnosis of Western Society*. Toronto: Wedge.
Goudzwaard, B. *et al.*,
1980   *Justice in the International Economic Order*. Grand Rapids: Board of Publications of the Christian Reformed Church.
Goudzwaard, B. & H.M.de Lange,
1986   *Genoeg van te Veel - Genoeg van te Weinig: Wissels omzetten in de economie*. Baarn: Ten Have.
Goudzwaard, Bob & Henk Koetsier,
1989   *ABC van de Economie: De Dans om het Gouden Kalf*. Kampen: Kok.

189

Bibliography

Graham, Gordon
1986   *Politics in its Place: A Study of Six Ideologies*. Oxford: Clarendom Press.
Gremillion, Joseph
1975   *The Gospel of Peace and Justice: Catholic Teaching since Pope John*. Maryknoll: Orbis.
Griffith-Jones, Stephany, *ed.*,
1988   *Managing World Debt*. New York: St.Martin's Press.
Guerra-Borges, Alfredo
1987   *Hechos, Experiencias, Opciones - Integración Económica Centroamericana*. San José: FLACSO.
Gunnemann, Jon P.
1979   *The Moral Meaning of Revolution*. New Haven, Yale University Press.
Gustafson, James M.
1978   *Protestant and Roman Catholic Ethics: Prospects for Rapprochement*. Univ. of Chicago.
1981   *Theology and Ethics*. Oxford: Blackwell.
Gutiérrez, Carlos José
1986   *El Pensamiento Político Costarricense: la Social Democracia*. San José: Libro Libre.
Gutiérrez, Gustavo
1971   *Teología de la Liberación: Perspectivas*. Lima: CEP. *Id.*, 9th.ed. Salamanca: Sígueme.
1973   *"Apuntes para una Teología de la Liberación"*, in Gutiérrez, R.Alves & H.Assmann, *Religión, Instrumento de Liberación?* Madrid: Marova.
1977   *"Praxis de liberación y fe cristiana"* in Rosino Gibellini, *ed.*, *La Nueva Frontera de la Teología en América Latina*. Salamanca: Sígueme.
1977   *Freedom and Salvation: A Political Problem*, in Gutiérrez & Shaull, *Liberation and Change*. Atlanta: John Knox Press.
1979   *La Fuerza Histórica de los Pobres*. Lima: CEP.
1983   *We Drink from Our Own Wells: The Spiritual Journey of a People*. London: SCM.
Gutiérrez, Gustavo, L.Boff, P.Richard, J.Ratzinger, *et al.*,
1985   *Teología de la Liberación: Documentos sobre una polémica*. San José: DEI.
Hamilton, Michael P., *ed.*,
1986   *American Character and Foreign Policy*. Grand Rapids: Eerdmans.
Hedström, Ingemar
1988   *Somos Parte de un Gran Equilibrio: Crisis Ecológica en Centroamérica*. San José: DEI.
Heilbroner, Rober L.
1980   *The Worldly Philosophers: the great economic thinkers*. New York: Simon & Schuster.
1980   *The Making of Economic Society*. Englewood cliffs: Prentice-Hall.
Held, Virginia
1984   *Rights and Goods: Justifying Social Action*. New York: Free Press, Macmillan.
Hennelly, Alfred T., *ed.*,
1990   *Liberation Theology: A Documentary History*. Maryknoll: Orbis.
Hess, J.Daniel
1980   *From the Other's Point of View*. Kitchener, Ontario: Herald Press.
Hernandez Chavez, Alcides
1988   *Deuda Externa Y Crisis en América Latina*. Tegucigalpa: Guaymuras.
Hinkelammert, Franz J.
1981   *Las Armas Ideológicas de la Muerte*. San José: DEI.
1989   *La deuda Externa de América Latina: el automatismo de la deuda*. San José: DEI.
Hinkelammert, Franz J., *et al.*,
1988   *El Pensamiento Social de Juan Pablo II: Documentos y Comentarios*. San José: DEI.
Höfte, Bernard
1990   *Bekering en Bevrijding: De betekenis van de Latijnsamerikaanse theologie van de bevrijding voor een praktisch-theologische basistheorie*. Hilversum: Gooi & Sticht.
Hollenbach, David
1988   *Justice, Peace, & Human Rights: American Catholic Social Ethics in a Pluralistic*

context. New York: Crossroad.

Houtart, François, *ed.*,
1969   *Camilo Torres, Revolutie: Christelijke Opdracht*. Utrecht: Bruna.

Huizinga, J.
1954   *The Waning of the Middle Ages*. New York: Doubleday.

Iribarren, Jesús & José Luis Gutiérrez Garcia, *eds.*,
1986   *Nueve Grandes Mensajes - las encíclicas papales* . Madrid: Autores Cristianos.

Irving, R.E.M.
1978   *The Christian Democratic Parties of Western Europe*. Edinburgh: Allen & Unwin.

Isaula, Roger
1988   *Honduras: Crisis e Incertidumbre Nacional*. Tegucigalpa: Editores Unidos.

Jaguaribe, Helio
1973   *Political Development: General Theory; Lat. Amer. Case Study*. N.York: Harper & Row.

Keogh, Dermot, *ed.*,
1990   *Church and Politics in Latin America*. London: Macmillan.

Kinzer, Stephen & Stephen Schlesinger
1981   *Bitter Fruit*. New York: Double Day.

Kirk, J.Andrew
1979   *Liberation Theology: An Evangelical View*. Basingstoke: Morgan & Scott.
1980   *Theology Encounters Revolution*. Downers Grove, Illinois: Intervarsity Press.

Klarén, Peter F. & Thomas J.Bossert
1986   *Promise of Development: Theories of Change in Latin America*. Boulder: Westview.

Kouwenhoven, A.
1964   *Vrijheid en Gelijkheid*. Kampen: Kok.
1989   *De Dynamiek van het Christelijk Sociaal Denken*. Nijkerk: Callenbach.

Kryzanek, Michael J.
1990   *U.S.-Latin American Relations*. New York: Praeger.

Kruijer, G.J.
1983   *Bevrijdingswetenschap: Een partijdige visie op de Derde Wereld*. Meppel: Boom.

Lambert, Jacques
1978   *América Latina: Estructuras Sociales e Instituciones Políticas*. Mexico: Ariel.

Langley, Lester D.
1985   *Central America - the Real Stakes*. New York: Crown.

Larrain, Jorge
1989   *Theories of Development: Capitalism, Colonialism and Dependency*. Cambridge: Polity.

Lehmann, David
1990   *Democracy and Development in Latin America: Economics, Politics and Religion in the Postwar Period*. Cambridge: Polity Press.

Leiken, Robert S. & Barry Rubin, *eds.*,
1987   *The Central American Crisis Reader*. New York: Summit Books.

Leonard, Thomas M.
1985   *Central America and United States Policies, 1820s-1980s*. Claremont: Regina Books.

Lernoux, Penny
1982   *Cry of the People: The Struggle for Human Rights in Latin America - The Catholic Church in Conflict with U.S.Policy*. New York: Penguin.

Levine, Daniel H., *ed.*,
1986   *Religion and Political Conflict in Latin America*. London: University of North Carolina.
1990   "From Church and State to Religion and Politics and Back Again", in *Social Compass: Journal of the Internat. Federation of Institutes for Socio-Religious Research*, vol.37 (3).

Lopez, George A. & Michael Stohl, *eds.*,
1987   *Liberalization and Redemocratization in Latin America*. New York: Greenwood Press.

López, José Roberto
1986   *La Economía del Banano en Centroamérica*. San José: DEI.

Bibliography

Love, Joseph L.
1990   "The Origins of Dependency Analysis", *Journal of Latin American Studies* - Feb.1990.
Lowenthal, Abraham F.
1990   *Partners in Conflict: U.S. and Latin America in the 1990s.* London: John Hopkins Press.
Lowenthal, Abraham F. & J.Samuel Fitch, *eds.*,
1986   *Armies & Politics in Latin America.* New York: Holmes & Meier.
Macpherson, C.B.
1987   *The Rise and Fall of Economic Justice and Other Essays.* Oxford: University Press.
Manenschijn, G.
1982   *Eigenbelang en Christelijke Ethiek: rechtvaardigheid in een door belangen bepaalde samenleving.* Baarn: Ten Have.
1984   *Burgerlijke Ongehoorzaamheid: over grenzen aan politieke gehoorzaamheid in een demokratische rechts- en verzorgingsstaat.* Baarn: Ten Have.
1987   *Geldzucht de Wortel van Alle Kwaad? Economie tussen Moralisme en Amoraliteit.* Baarn: Ten Have.
1989   *Mogelijkheid en Noodzakelijkheid van een Christelijke Ethiek.* Kampen: Kok.
Marcuse, Herbert
1968   *Negations: Essays in Critical Theory.* Boston: Beacon Press.
1968   *Reason and Revolution* Boston: Beacon Press.
1968   *One-Dimensional Man.* Boston: Beacon Press.
Maritain, Jacques
1947   *Christianity and Democracy.* New York: Scribners.
1949   *Man and the State.* University of Chicago Press.
1966   *Humanismo Integral.* Buenos Aires: Carlos Lohlé.
Martín-Baró & Jon Sobrino
1985   *Archbishop Oscar Romero: Voice of the Voicless, The four Pastoral Letters and Other Statements.* Maryknoll: Orbis.
Martínez de Arróyabe, S. & C.Soria
1973   *Cristianismo y Nueva Sociedad.* Salamanca: Sígueme.
Martner, Gonzalo, *coord.*,
1986   *América Latina Hacia el 2000: Opciones y estrategias.* Caracas: Nueva Sociedad.
1987   *El Desafío Latinoamericano: Potencial a desarrollar.* Caracas: Nueva Sociedad.
McAfee Brown, Robert
1987   *Religion and Violence.* Philadelphia: Westminster Press.
McAlister, Lyle N.
1984   *Spain & Portugal in the New World: 1492-1700.* Oxford University Press.
McCann, D.P.
1981   *Christian Realism and Liberation Theology.* Maryknoll: Orbis.
McGovern, Arthur F.
1981   *Marxism: An American Christian Perspective.* Maryknoll: Orbis.
1989   *Liberation Theology and its Critics.* Maryknoll: Orbis.
Medcalf, John, *trans.*,
1985   *Vamos Caminando: A Peruvian Catechism.* Pastoral Team, Bambamarca. London: SCM.
Meléndez, Guillermo, *ed.*,
1984   *¡Queremos la Paz!: Documentos de organizaciones y grupos cristianos sobre la paz en Centroamérica.* San José: DEI.
Méndez Asensio, Luis
1987   *Contadora: Las Cuentas de la Diplomacia.* Mexico: Plaza y Janés.
Meza, Víctor
1981   *Política y Sociedad en Honduras.* Tegucigalpa: Guaymuras.
Meza, Víctor, *et al.*,
1988   *Honduras-Estados Unidos: Subordinación y Crisis.* Tegucigalpa: CEDOH.
Middlebrook, Kevin J. & Carlos Rico

192

Bibliography

1988   *The United States and Latin America in the 1980s: Decade of Crisis*. Pittsburgh Univ.

Míguez Bonino, José
1975   *Doing Theology in a Revolutionary Situation*. Philadelphia: Fortress Press.
1983   *Toward a Christian Political Ethics*. London: SCM.

Miranda, José
1982   *Marx and the Bible: A Critique of the Philosophy of Oppression*. Maryknoll: Orbis.

Molineu, Harold
1990   *U.S. Policy Toward Latin America: From Regionalism to Globalism*. Boulder: Westview.

Montenegro, W.
1984   *Introducción a las Doctrinas Político-económicas*. Mexico: CREA.

Moreno, Francisco José & Barbara Mitrani
1971   *Conflict and Violence in Latin American Politics*. New York: Thomas Crowell.

Munck, Ronaldo
1984   *Politics and Dependency in the Third World: The Case of Latin America*. London: Zed.
1989   *Latin America: The Transition to Democracy*. London: Zed Books.

Muñoz, Heraldo
1981   *From Dependency to Development: Strategies to Overcome Underdevelopment and In-equality*. Boulder, Colorado: Westview Press.

Musto, Jorge
1976   *Apuntes sobre Teología de Liberación*. Antigua, Guatemala: Popol Vuh.

Musto, Ronald G.
1986   *The Catholic Peace Tradition*. Maryknoll: Orbis.

Myers, Kenneth A., ed.,
1988   *Aspiring to Freedom: Commentaries on John Paul II's Encyclical 'The Social Concerns of the Church'*. Grand Rapids: Eerdmans.

Myrdal, Gunnar
1970   *The Challenge of World Poverty*. New York: Random House.

Neal, Marie Augusta
1987   *The Just Demands of the Poor: Essays in Socio-theology*. New York: Paulist Press.

Neuhaus, Richard John, ed.,
1988   *Preferential Option for the Poor*. Grand Rapids: Eerdmans.

Newfarmer, Richard
1984   *From Gunboats to Diplomacy: U.S. Policies for Lat. America*. London: J.Hopkins Univ.

Nida, Eugene
1974   *Understanding Latin Americans*. Pasadena: William Carey Library.

Niebuhr, H.Richard
1951   *Christ and Culture*. New York: Harper & Row.

Niebuhr, Reinhold
1952   *The Irony of American History*. New York: Scribner's.
1964   *The Nature and Destiny of Man: A Christian Interpretation*. New York: Scribner's.
1972   *The Children of Light and the Children of Darkness*. New York: Scribner's.

North, Liisa
1988   *Medidas para la Paz en América Central*. San José: FLACSO.

Nouwen, Henri J.M.
1985   *Love in a Fearful Land: A Guatemalan Story*. Notre Dame: Ave Maria Press.

Novak, Michael, ed.,
1980   *Democracy and Mediating Structures: A Theological Inquiry*. Washington, AEI.

Novak, Michael
1982   *The Spirit of Democratic Capitalism*. New York: Touchstone.
1986   *Will It Liberate? Questions About Liberation Theology*. New York: Paulist Press.

Nuccio, Richard A.
1986   *What's Wrong, Who's Right in Central America? A Citizen's Guide*. New York: Roosevelt Center for American Policy Studies.

Nuñez, Emilio A.
1986   *Teología de la Liberación*. San José: Editorial Caribe.
Nuñez, Emilio & William Taylor
1989   *Crisis in Latin America*. Chicago: Moody.
O'Brien, *ed.*,
1976   *Allende's Chile*. New York.
Ortega, Julio
1987   *Antología de la Poesía Hispanoamericana Actual*. Mexico: Siglo Veintiuno.
Peces-Barba Martínez, Gregorio
1972   *Persona, Sociedad, Estado: Pensamiento Social y Político de Maritain*. Madrid: Edicusa.
Persky, Stan
1984   *America, the Last Domino*. Vancouver: New Star Books.
Pochet, Rosa María & Abelino Martínez
1987   *Nicaragua, Iglesia: ¿Manipulación o Profecía?* San José: DEI.
Poelman, N.
1982   *Panorama der Ideologieën*. Baarn: Nelissen.
Prida Barrios, Antonio
1982   *Cristianismo: Compromiso Social*. Mexico: Librería Parroquial.
Pottenger, John R.
1989   *The Political Theory of Liberation Theology: Social Values*. New York: State University.
Rasmussen, Douglas & James Sterba
1987   *The Catholic Bishops and the Economy*. London: Social Philosophy and Policy Center.
Reinders, Johannes Sjoerd
1988   *Violence, Victims and Rights: A reappraisal of the argument from institutionalized violence with reference to Latin American liberation theology*. Amsterdam: Free Univ.
Richard, Pablo
1976   *Cristianos por el Socialismo: Historia y documentación*. Salamanca: Sígueme.
1985   *Raices de la Teología Latinoamericana*. San José: DEI.
1990   "The Church of the poor in the 1990s", *Lat.Amer. Press*, (Oct.25, 1990: vol.22, no.39).
Rivera Urrutia, Eugenio
1986   *Centroamérica: Política Económica y Crisis*. San José: DEI.
Roddick, Jackie
1988   *The Dance of the Millions: Latin America - the Debt Crisis*. Nottingham: Russel Press.
Rojas Bolaños, Manuel
1989   *Costa Rica: La Democracia Inconclusa*. San José: DEI.
Rojas Aravena, Francisco ed.,
1982   *Centroamérica: condiciones para su integración*. San José: FLACSO.
Rosenberg, Mark B.
1985   *Democracia en Centroamérica?* San José: CAPEL.
Rosenberg, Mark B., *et al.*,
1986   *Honduras: Realidad Nacional y Crisis Regional*. Tegucigalpa: CEDOH.
1986   *Honduras: Pieza Clave - Estados Unidos en Centroamérica*. Tegucigalpa: CEDOH.
Rosset, Peter & John Vandermeer
1983   *The Nicaraguan Reader: Documents of a Revolution under Fire*. N.York: Grove Press.
Rossi, Ernst E. & Jack C.Plano
1980   *The Latin American Political Dictionary*. Oxford: Clio Press.
Rostow, W.W.
1960   *The Stages of Economic Growth*. Cambridge University Press.
Rubenstein, Richard L. & John K.Roth, *eds.*,
1988   *The Politics of Latin American Liberation Theology: The challenge to U.S. Public Policy*. Washington Institute for Values in Public Policy.
Rudolph, James D.
1984   *Honduras: a country study*. Washington: American University.

Bibliography

Sachs, Jeffrey D., *ed.*,
1989   *Developing Country Debt and the World Economy*. Chicago: University of Chicago.
Salomón, Leticia, *ed.*,
1989   *Honduras: Panorama y Perspectivas*. Tegucigalpa: CEDOH.
Samuel, Vinay and Chris Sugden, *eds.*,
1987   *The Church in Response to Human Need*. Grand Rapids: Eerdmans.
Schumacher, E.F.
1974   *Small is Beautiful: A study in economics as if people mattered*. London: Sphere Books.
Schori, Pierre
1982   *El Desafío Europeo en Centroamérica*. San José: EDUCA.
Segundo, Juan Luis
1975   *Liberación de la Teología*. Buenos Aires: Carlos Lohlé.
1982   *El Hombre de Hoy ante Jesús de Nazaret: Fe e Ideología*. Madrid: Cristiandad.
1985   *Teología de la Liberación: Respuesta al Cardenal Ratzinger*. Madrid: Cristiandad.
Sheahan, John
1987   *Patterns of Development in Latin America: Poverty, Repression, and Economic Strategy*.
New Jersey: Princeton University.
Simon, Arthur
1975   *Bread for the World*. New York: Paulist Press.
Sklair, Leslie
1991   *Sociology of the global System*. London: Simon & Schuster.
Smith, Adam, *eds*.R.H.Campbell & A.S.Skinner
1976   *An Inquiry into the Nature and Causes of the Wealth of Nations*. Oxford: Univ. Press.
Sobrino, Jon
1976   *Cristología desde América Latina*. Mexico: Centro de Reflexión Teológica.
1984   *Resurrección de la Verdadera Iglesia: Los pobres, lugar teológico de la eclesiología*.
Santander: Sal Terrae.
Sosa, Roberto
1984   *Los Pobres*. Tegucigalpa: Guaymuras.
1985   *Secreto Militar*. Tegucigalpa: Guaymuras.
Spykman, Gordan, *et al.*,
1988   *Let My Poeple Live: Faith and Struggle in Central America*. Grand Rapids: Eerdmans.
Srisang, Koson
1983   *Perspectives in Political Ethics: An Ecumenical Enquiry*. Geneva: WCC, 1983.
Stackhouse, Max L.
1984   *Creeds, Society and Human Rights: A Study in Three Cultures*. Grand Rapids: Eerdmans.
Strain, Charles R., *ed.*,
1989   *Prophetic Visions and Economic Realities: Protestants, Jews and Catholics Confront the
Bishops' Letter on the Economy*. Grand Rapids: Eerdmans.
Swomley, John M.
1972   *Liberation Ethics*. New York: Macmillan.
Tamayo-Acosta, Juan José
1989   *Para Comprender La Teología de la Liberación*. Estella: Verbo Divino.
Tannenbaum, Frank
1962   *Ten Keys to Latin America*. New York: Vintage.
Thais, Eva
1985   *Catedrales y Espejos*. Tegucigalpa: Guaymuras.
Third World Guide
1986   Editoro Terceiro Mundo: Rio de Janeiro.
Timossi, Gerardo
1989   *Centroamérica, Deuda Externa y Ajuste Estructural: Las transformaciones económicas de
la crisis*. San José: DEI.
Tinoco, Victor Hugo

195

1989   *Conflicto y Paz: El Proceso Negociador Centroamericano*. Mexico: Editorial Mestiza.
Todaro, Michael P.
1977   *Economic Development in the Third World: An introduction to the problems and policies in a global perspective*. New York: Longman.
Tomassini, Luciano
1988   *Introducción a la Teoría de las Relaciones Internacionales*. San José: FLASCO.
Torres, Rosa María & José Luis Coraggio
1987   *Transición y Crisis en Nicaragua*. San José: DEI.
Torres, Sergio & John Eagleson, *eds.*,
1982   *The Challenge of Basic Christian Communities*. Maryknoll: Orbis.
Torres-Rivas, Edelberto
1989   *Interpretación del Desarrollo Social Centroamericano*. San José: FLACSO.
1987   *Centroamérica: La Democracia Posible*. San José: EDUCA.
Torres-Rivas, Edelberto, *coord.*,
1989   *América Central Hacia el 2000*. Caracas: Nueva Sociedad.
1989   *Costa Rica: Crisis y Desafíos*. San José: DEI.
Turner, Bryan S., *ed.*,
1990   *Theories of Modernity and Postmodernity*. London: Sage.
Vago, Steven
1989   *Social Change*. London: Prentice Hall.
Van Der Putten, Jan
1981   *Latijns-Amerika, politiek: gebeurtenissen in 25 landen*. Amsterdam: Van Gennep.
Van Erkelens, Herbert, *red.*,
1989   *Economie als Afgod?* Kampen: Kok.
Van Leeuwen, Arend Th.
1964   *Christianity in World History*. London: Edinburgh House.
1970   *Development through Revolution*. New York: Scribner's.
Van Meerssche, P.
1981   *De Noord-Zuid Confrontatie en de Nieuwe Internationale Economische Orde*. Hague: Martinus Nijhoff.
Van Nieuwenhove, Jacques
1991 *Bronnen van Bevrijding: Varianten in de Theologie van Gustavo Gutiérrez*. Kampen: Kok.
Van Nieuwenhove, Jacques, *ed.*,
1980   *Bevrijding en Christelijk Geloof in Latijns-Amerika en in Nederland*. Baarn: Ambo.
Van Nieuwenhove, Jacques & Georges Casalis, *eds.*,
1981   *Symposium: 'The Future of Europe: A Challenge to Theology - Dialogue with Third World Theologians/Dialogue avec des Theologiens du Tiers Monde*. Zeist: Woudschoten.
Van Nieuwenhove, Jacques & Berma Klein Goldewijk, *eds.*,
1991   *Popular Religion, Liberation and Contextual Theology*. Kampen: Kok.
Van Peursen, C.A.
1975   *Cultuur in Stroomversnelling*. Amsterdam: Elsevier.
Van Putten, Jan
1985   *Politieke Stromingen*. Utrecht: Aula.
Vatican Documents
1891 - *Rerum Novarum* (Leo XIII)
1931 - *Quadragesimo Anno* (Pius XI)
1961 - *Mater et Magistra* (John XXIII)
1963 - *Pacem in Terris* (John XXIII)
1964 - *Ecclesiam Suam* (Paul VI)
1965 - *Gaudium et Spes* (Vatican II)
1965 - *Dignitatis Humanae* (Vatican II)
1967 - *Populorum Progressio* (Paul VI)
1971 - *Octogesima Adveniens* (Paul VI)
1975 - *Evangelii Nuntiandi* (Paul VI)
1980 - *Dives in Misericordia* (John Paul II)
1981 - *Laborem Exercens* (John Paul II)
1987 - *Sollicitudo Rei Socialis* (John Paul II)
1991 - *Centesimus Annus* (John Paul II)

Vergara Menses, Raúl, *et al.*,

1988   *Centroamérica: La Guerra de Baja Intensidad*. San José: DEI.
Verkuyl, J.
1982   *De Kernbegrippen van het Marxisme-Leninisme*. Kampen: Kok.
Verkuyl, J. & H.G.Schulte Nordholt
1970   *Verantwoorde Revolutie: Over middelen en doeleinden in de strijd om transformatie van samenlevingen*. Kampen: Kok.
Vidal, Marciano y Pedro R. Santidrian
1981   *Etica: Social y Política*. Madrid: Paulinas.
Vidales, Raúl y Luis Rivera Pagán, *eds.*,
1983   *Esperanza en el Presente de América Latina: "Discernimiento de Utopías"*. S.José: DEI.
Vijver, H.W.
1985   *Theolgie en Bevrijding*. Amsterdam: Vrije Universiteit.
Vogel, H.Ph.
1984   *Geschiedenis van Latijns-Amerika*. Utrecht: Aula.
Vogeler, Ingolf & Anthony R.de Souza
1980   *Dialectics of Third World Development*. New Jersey: Allanheld & Osmun.
Walker, Thomas W., *ed.*,
1987   *Reagan Versus the Sandinistas: The Undeclared War on Nicaragua*. London: Westview.
Wallerstein, Immanuel, *ed.*,
1975   *World Inequality*. Montreal: Blackrose.
Wertheim, W.F.
1974   *Evolution and Revolution: The Rising Waves of Emancipation*. New York: Penguin.
Wiarda, Howard J.
1981   *Corporatism and National Development in Latin America*. Boulder: Westview Press.
Wiarda, Howard J. & Harvey F.Kline
1990   *Latin American Politics and Development*. Boulder, Colorado: Westview Press.
Williams, Edward J.
1967   *Latin American Christian Democratic Parties*. Knoxville: University of Tenessee.
Wogaman, J.Philip
1977   *Christians and the Great Economic Debate*. London: SCM.
1985   *Economics and Ethics: A Christian Enquiry*. London: SCM.
1988   *Christian Perspectives on Politics*. London: SCM.
Wolf, Eric R. & Edward C.Hansen
1972   *The Human Condition in Latin America*. London: Oxford University Press.
Wolterstorff, Nicholas
1982   *Until Justice and Peace Embrace*. Grand Rapids: Eerdmans.
Womack, John, *ed.*,
1983   *Trouble in Our Backyard*. New York: Grove Press.
Woodward, Ralph Lee, *ed.*,
1988   *Central America: Historical Perspectives - Contemporary Crises*. N.York: Greenwood.
Wynia, Gary W.
1984   *The Politics of Latin American Development*. Cambridge University Press.
Zea, Leopoldo
1987   *Filosofía latinoamericana*. Mexico: Trillas.
Zeylstra, Willem Gustaaf
1975   *Aid or Development: The Relevance of Development Aid to Problems of Developing Countries*. Leyden: Slijthoff.

INDEX
selected